The Forever Crisis

This book is an introduction to complex systems thinking at the global governance level. It offers concepts, tools, and ways of thinking about how systems change that can be applied to the most wicked problems facing the world today.

More than an abstract argument for complexity theory, the book offers a targeted critique of today's highest-profile proposals for improving the governance of our environment, security, finance, health, and digital space. It suggests that we should spend less effort and resources on upgrading existing institutions, and more on understanding how they (and we) relate to each other.

The volume will be essential reading for public policymakers, NGOs and think tanks, foreign policy experts, government officials, and global decision-makers.

Adam Day is Head of UN University Centre for Policy Research in Geneva. He co-led the Secretariat of the UN High-Level Advisory Board on Effective Multilateralism and supported the Secretary-General's *Our Common Agenda* report. He previously served as Senior Political Advisor to the UN peace operation in the Democratic Republic of the Congo, and in UN operations in Sudan, South Sudan, and the Middle East. A former human rights lawyer, Adam worked for Human Rights Watch, the International Criminal Tribunal for the former Yugoslavia, and Open Society Justice Initiative in Cambodia. Amongst many publications on complexity, Adam's previous book, *States of Disorder*, applies complexity thinking to UN state-building.

The Forever Crisis

Adaptive Global Governance for an Era of
Accelerating Complexity

Adam Day

Routledge
Taylor & Francis Group

LONDON AND NEW YORK

Designed cover image: Courtesy of Nuri Keli
First published 2025

by Routledge
4 Park Square, Milton Park, Abingdon, Oxon OX14 4RN

and by Routledge
605 Third Avenue, New York, NY 10158

Routledge is an imprint of the Taylor & Francis Group, an informa business

© 2025 Adam Day

British Library Cataloguing-in-Publication Data
A catalogue record for this book is available from the British Library

ISBN: 978-1-032-69949-3 (hbk)
ISBN: 978-1-032-82808-4 (pbk)
ISBN: 978-1-003-50638-6 (ebk)

DOI: 10.4324/9781003506386

Typeset in Sabon
by Deanta Global Publishing Services, Chennai, India

For Kaia and Satya,
My future generations

Contents

Acknowledgments

Books are like complex systems, emerging in non-linear ways from the inter-actions of many actors. *The Forever Crisis* is no different. It evolved over several years of discussions with experts in a wide array of topics, many of which I knew very little about going in. The result is heavy on footnotes and equally laden with gratitude.

To Michèle Griffin and Volker Turk, who gave me the opportunity to work with the Secretary-General's office on the big ideas, thanks for letting me be the "red" in "red team."

To Anne-Marie Slaughter, whose enthusiasm for complexity is only out-done by a love of birdwatching, thank you for inspiring my thinking on networks, spiderwebs, and chessboards.

To Rachel Kleinfeld, who was the reason I started thinking about com-plexity many years ago (yes, at times I blame you), you remain the best exam-ple of how to think and write clearly about these issues.

To Charlie Hunt, we all exist in symbiosis, and I fear I have developed more of an amensal dependency on you than offering much mutualism. Thank you for being the first reader of everything.

To Cedric de Coning, whose work on adaptive peacebuilding is the most important in the field, thank you for your generosity and constantly con-structive ideas.

To Kim-Fredrik Schneider and my Mum, who have been trying to get me to tell a compelling story for 30 years. I hope I'm getting closer.

For the crash course in all things AI, I owe a debt to Tshilidzi Marwala, Jason Hausenloy, Max Stauffer, Konrad Seifert, Eleonore Fournier-Tombs, Eleonore Pauwels, Eduardo Albrecht, and Claire Dennis. Referring to you as my "foundation models" clearly shows I have more to learn.

To Inger Andersen, Ligia Noronha, Radhika Ochalik, Nicolas Bertrand, Lizzie Sellwood, and Rafael Peralta at UNEP, thank you for the chance to discuss environmental governance in a real-world setting. And thanks to Arunabha Ghosh, Maja Goff, David Obura, Jens Orback, Ilona Szabo, Tom Hale, Janos Pasztor, Anja Olin-Pape, and Arthur Dahl for the serious ideas on planetary governance.

To David Passarelli, for letting me do this project, and for being the driv-ing force for UN University's work on global governance.

To the two Richards (Ponzio and Gowan) for the disappointing realization that most of my "new" ideas on peace and security had already been thought of by one of you.

Complexity thinkers are an idiosyncratic bunch, but they share one thing in common: all seem open to sharing ideas with complete strangers. To Rakhyun Kim, Amandine Orsini, Ignasi Torrent, Didier Wernli, Rumtin Sepasspour, and David Krakauer, thank you for transforming a cold call into a warm conversation.

To Nudhara Yusuf, for calling me out when my ideas became too stale, pale, and male. I have a long way to go.

To Nuri Keli, whose wonderful cover artwork is by far the best thing about my books.

A special thanks to Fabiana Coccia, without whose help I would still be sitting on a runway somewhere.

This book was written in (and beyond) the margins of a full family life. Thank you to Wendy, Kaia, and Satya for putting up with me. And to our cat Reina, who kept me company in the predawn writing hours: you are missed.

Introduction

The forever crisis

In Joe Haldeman's famous science fiction novel, *The Forever War*, humanity confronts an alien force bent on conquering Earth. Over centuries of battle, we stay just ahead of alien advancements in technology, eventually shaping human society around an endless conflict against a constantly evolving enemy. We survive. But the costs of building a society as a form of crisis-driven war making are enormous, and stable peace is always beyond our grasp.[1]

Today we run a similar risk of being locked in perpetual battle against a combination of risks that are always one step ahead of us. Whether the accelerating impacts of climate change, the next deadly virus, lethal autonomous weapons, or artificial general intelligence, we lag behind the threats invading our lives. We may survive. But if we stay on our current trajectory, our survival will be defined by continual crisis management, like a child locked in a never-ending whack-a-mole game, or a weary Sisyphus pushing stones to the peak of infinitely high mountains.[2]

Worse, we are now in what is being called a "polycrisis" where risks converge and multiply. Artificial intelligence may generate pathogens that dramatically outstrip the lethality of the COVID-19 pandemic, or it could trigger a nuclear confrontation if left in charge of our military arsenals.[3] Our global financial system has deep path dependencies pushing pollution, biodiversity loss, and climate change over irreversible cliffs. And our deeply fractured geopolitics means that we are very unlikely to suddenly put aside our differences and collaborate to eradicate nuclear weapons, or develop a mutually beneficial approach to new technologies, or end our reliance on fossil fuels. Even in the case of an asteroid bearing down on Earth, our competitive and self-absorbed politics makes it very likely we won't look up until it is too late.[4]

Our crisis-driven world is already costing us. Global inequality skyrocketed during our panicked response to the COVID-19 pandemic and is set to worsen as we grapple with the effects of climate change and new technologies. The response to Russia's invasion of Ukraine was a dramatic increase in military spending, ironically increasing the likelihood of a nuclear confrontation

DOI: 10.4324/9781003506386-1

that could end humanity. The band-aids we put on the financial system during the 2008 crisis appear to have deepened our reliance on unsustainable economic practices, consolidating control amongst a small number of fossil fuel-reliant actors. Our reactions to global risks mirror a youth soccer game, where children cluster around the ball and kick furiously but ignore the broader playing field.

The word "crisis" comes from the Greek for "decision," referring to a turning point in a disease where the patient will either recover or decline irreversibly towards death. Like many Greek words, crisis holds a paradox: how can we take a meaningful decision when we have reached a point of irreversibility? We are now essentially beyond the 1.5-degree threshold scientists long warned was the limit for a sustainable, safe planet, meaning our climate crisis has only fully emerged as a global policy priority when it is too late. We know that ending our reliance on fossil fuels is the answer to reducing global warming, but how can we transition to renewables while still meeting people's growing energy needs, and what can be done to work against the powerful influences of big industry?

I have spent the last several years trying to generate answers to these questions. I supported the Secretary-General's team in developing his *Our Common Agenda* report, a vision for some of the big changes that need to happen at the global level. I worked with the High-Level Advisory Board on Effective Global Governance to produce some of the most far-reaching proposals for improving our response to planetary threats. As I write this book, I'm supporting the UN's 2024 Summit of the Future, where many of the most ambitious ideas for improving global governance are meant to be presented. I'll frequently circle back to discussions I've had with hundreds of experts who fed their best proposals into these processes. But I also want to push us further. Over and over, the conversations I've had with well-known experts have come back to the same challenge: we know what the problem is, and we know what a solution might look like, but we just can't see a way through. We know the "what" but not the "how". We know we should move off fossil fuels, but how can we generate that transition? We know that we need safety guardrails on artificial intelligence, but when it comes to influencing big tech companies, what can be done? Just like a doctor presented with a terminal patient, it often seems like we come to the crisis point too late, or without a clear sense of how to take meaningful action.

We struggle to know what to do because we are fundamentally ignorant in three related areas. First, we don't really know *why* things happen. What caused the 2008 economic collapse, or the spread of Ebola, or the ongoing death of the world's coral reefs, or the Arab Spring?[5] We have theories about triggers for these events – for example, we can point to Mouhamed Bouazizi lighting himself on fire in Tunis on 17 December 2010 as the trigger of the Arab Spring – but our understanding of the full range of causes of any global event is very limited. In fact, drawing bright lines between cause and effect is often difficult in so-called "wicked problems."[6]

We also don't know *who or what* makes things happen. Did the financial crisis really originate in Bear Stearns or were there other locations in the global financial system that drove it? How much was the war in Syria dictated by President Assad versus other actors within or outside Syria, or maybe it was the drought that hit the country just before the uprising? We still don't really know where COVID-19 came from, though we are able to map its spread and make some guesses about how it might have originated. Who is responsible for the global trend towards authoritarianism, or the series of coups in Africa over the past three years, or the recent increases in military spending? We have ideas and theories and evidence, but deep down we have an "inadequate knowledge of the social dynamics involved" in most global issues.[7]

Finally, we don't know *when* things happen, even in the near future. How much biodiversity loss will cause a total collapse of our environment? When will we reach an irreversible tipping point in global warming? When is it too late to stop artificial intelligence (AI) from taking control of our lives? Are we possibly already past all these thresholds? We can make very educated guesses at these moments, and sometimes we can identify events that accelerate change, but our immediate future feels very uncertain.[8] Predicting further into the future may be a useful exercise, but we are fooling ourselves if we think we will be right.

Why are we so fundamentally ignorant about our world? Surely in the 21st century, with all the data we generate, we should have a better understanding of how change happens. Especially when confronted with massive risks, we need to be able to take bold, innovative action based on solid facts. But uncertainty tends to paralyze us or make us keep doing what we know because it is familiar, or we overreact when a problem reaches a crisis point.[9] In an era of unprecedented quantities of data, we are becoming less and less certain of what to do.[10] We seem to be living in Yeats' *Second Coming*, where "the best lack all conviction."

In fact, our worst tendencies seem filled with passionate intensity. When a crisis occurs, vested powers tend to drive us back towards the status quo rather than enabling a positive transformation. The 2008 financial crisis is a clear example: the staggering bailouts offered to exactly those entities responsible for the financial collapse allowed us to stabilize the financial system. But was that the best outcome? The past 15 years of steadily growing global inequality and a concentration of wealth in even fewer hands suggests that the resilience of our system came at a huge societal cost.

This brings us to one of the thorniest problems of today: declining transparency. As our world has become more complex, we have built increasingly specialized institutions and professions to manage different fields. Niche areas of expertise have flourished, each more eager than the last to protect their distinct turf. Endless reform processes always seem to add layers and greater specialization, with fewer and fewer people understanding how the system works as a whole. Combined with short-term incentives for profit and power, we live in a world where a small number of deeply vested financial "experts" can decide the banking system needs a massive bailout in 2008, even when it's bad for most people in the long run. But because we can't see into the inner workings of a realm jealously guarded by those same experts, it is difficult to gainsay them. The same dynamic is taking place in AI today, where a tiny number of AI "godfathers" have dictated what most of us must take for granted as the necessary regulations for the most important technology in our lifetimes.

Loss of transparency leads to inefficient and dangerous trends in our social and political systems. It pushes us towards what complexity scientists call "self-organized criticality," where our systems reach irreversible tipping points. In some cases, like climate change, our growing awareness does not arrive in time, or with enough new incentives to generate the transformations needed to pull us back from the brink. Declining transparency adds to one of the most difficult and recurrent problems identified throughout this book: how to make decisions in conditions of uncertainty.

It is easy to say we need collective action to meet these challenges. But it is equally easy to say that collective action is impossible in today's world. Are we seriously expecting major powers to put aside their ideological and practical differences and suddenly agree to solve climate change, or AI risks, or nuclear weapons? Do we really believe that grassroots protests against fossil fuels are enough to curb the influence of big oil on politics? Do we trust the wealthiest people and countries to support a shift to more equitable finance for the developing world? If we are expecting the messiah of collective action and global cooperation, we should be ready for a long and painful wait. It is not surprising that two-thirds of young people are anxious and depressed about the future.[11]

But one thing does seem clear: unless we make some big, systemic changes, and fast, humanity will be defined by a forever crisis.

The promise of complexity thinking

The Forever Crisis proposes that *the concepts and tools of complexity thinking can help us manage the biggest risks facing humanity today.* We know today's global challenges are inherently complex, emerging from our increasingly interconnected world. Unfortunately, our global governance architecture has failed to keep pace with this shift to complexity, remaining stuck in complicated, siloed, and fundamentally inefficient institutions. Built in the aftermath of World War II, at the zenith of a linear, reductionist paradigm in the West, today's multilateral system is an unrealistic and ineffective response to today's problems.[12] Even where our governance approaches have adapted to complexity or become complex over time, it is generally the result of an unconscious and largely uncontrolled evolution rather than conscious design. This leads to a problem of fit between planetary-level risks and our ability to manage them. Worse, there is growing evidence that many of our efforts to respond to global crises have become part of the problem, producing conditions for collective failure and driving massive inequalities globally.[13] *To meet the challenge of today and tomorrow, we must intentionally reimagine and redesign global governance as a complex response to a complex problem.*

What is complexity and how can it help? We will explore the details and definitions in Chapter 1, but here it is useful to think of the example of our bodies' immune system.[14] An immune system is not controlled from outside but has its own patterns and rules of behavior guiding how it responds to new stimuli. An individual cell has no intelligence per se, but together the cells exhibit a capacity to self-organize and evolve in ways that go beyond the accumulated capacities of each cell. They have a form of collective intelligence that cannot be reduced to their separate forms.

The non-linear way an immune system responds to new stimuli is called its *emergent* quality. Only a few years ago, the scientific community struggled to anticipate how our bodies would react to new strains of COVID. But over time, and with the help of vaccines, we are now able to generate a much safer and more predictable response from our immune systems. Every day, our immune systems react to a barrage of dangerous bacteria, viruses, and poisons, most of the time fighting them off successfully. If you introduce a toxin, like nicotine or alcohol, your immune system may fail. But over hundreds of years of scientific advancements, we have learned to leverage our immune systems in predictable ways that help us survive.

The central characteristic of a complex system is that its response is *more and different* than the sum of its parts. If you merely add up all the actions of the cells of an immune system, you won't capture the collective intelligence of the system as a whole. A colony of bees produces a collective set of behaviors that is more and different than the sum of each bee's intelligence (though bees are pretty smart individually, too). In contrast, a merely complicated system – like a car engine – may have many intricate pieces, but a car engine produces an output that is the sum of its inputs. If you want to fix a car engine, you find the faulty piece and replace it. If you want to "fix" an immune system or understand what is causing a coral reef to die off, you can't just replace a part, you need to influence how the underlying system evolves.

Our social, political, and economic world is made up of overlapping and interdependent complex systems that evolve in surprisingly similar ways to immune systems, bee colonies, and galaxies. Our environment is the clearest and most familiar example of a complex global system, where we can see planetary-level adaptations all the time. Increases in greenhouse gases have generated a range of emergent behavior across the planet: coral reefs die off, rainfall patterns shift, deserts swell and migrate. But the environment is just one of several open systems that co-exist and interact with each other. Our global economy, the web of networks connecting our digital lives, and the social interactions that allow for the spread of communicable diseases, all co-exist as open, interdependent complex systems. When COVID-19 broke out, the health crisis did not stay in a silo but had massive ripple effects across our economy, our digital world, and our societies.

Our attempts to manage these risks are part of this complexity. The norms, institutions, and processes we have developed to manage international issues – what we call "global governance" – have now reached a level of interdependence and density that they evolve as complex systems. A growing body of scholarship has recognized complexity in our legal architecture, trade, finance, health, environmental regulations, and international relations practices.[15] This means global governance as a whole "should be described and analyzed through the lens of complexity."[16] This is an important point and is worth stressing: at a certain moment, the combination of people, institutions, processes, and activities that make up what we call "global governance" crossed a threshold and evolved into a complex system. Mostly this happened organically as a result of globalization, without us consciously designing with complexity in mind. Rather than think of global governance as something we do to the world, or a machine that can be fixed, it is better to think of governance as a process in which we participate, as nodes in a network, or as cells in an organism.

If this makes you uncomfortable, it should. We are humans and we like to think of ourselves as free agents capable of shaping our own destiny. We like to tackle challenges as architects and problem solvers and mechanics. We like to fix things that are broken. We like to identify gaps and fill them. If an institution is not working well, we want to reform it or build something better. We have "a certain longing for streamlined order" that leads us to desire well-oiled global governance machines running the show.[17] But the core idea of this book is that we cannot "fix" our way out of the polycrisis because our global system (and us as actors within it) is complex, not just complicated.[18]

Nor can we just let the market take care of global governance – in fact, complexity thinking suggests that a laissez-faire liberal order approach to the crises we face today is likely to produce a range of catastrophic outcomes.[19] Instead, we must design a global governance architecture that can co-evolve alongside the challenges around us. In the end, complexity thinking may be the best way for us to regain a sense of agency and creativity in a world that feels too big and fast for us to manage.

Using complexity in global governance

The Forever Crisis is an introduction to complex systems thinking at the global governance level. It offers concepts, tools, and ways of thinking about how systems change that can be applied to the most wicked problems facing the world today. But I am offering more than just a generic argument for complexity or a past-tense case study. I am presenting a *forward-looking application* of complexity to some of the most well-known proposals for improving global governance on the table today.[20] Over the past several years I have been involved in some of the highest-profile discussions in and around the UN, contributing directly to proposals being discussed by world leaders, and listening to globally renowned experts offer their best ideas.[21] I have brought together experts in the areas of environment, technology, finance, security, health, and more, trying to understand and build consensus on the best ideas and proposals out there. I have met some extraordinary thinkers, from the astrobiologist modeling energy consumption on thousands of theoretical worlds, to an organizer of local communities disrupting deforestation, to a high school student building a new architecture for AI.

Many of these experts intuitively think in systemic ways, with a sort of gut-level, experience-driven understanding of how their actions will cause ripple effects more broadly. Some of them explicitly speak in complexity terms and describe feedback loops and tipping points in our global governance architecture. But when it comes to moving from complex problems to proposing and implementing solutions, we all tend to become paralyzed by a linear logic and command-and-control mentality that is totally out of place in today's world.[22] This outdated mindset shows up in three recurrent tendencies I see across global governance decision-making today.

The first is to try to *upgrade a piece or plug a gap* in our governance architecture. This "crisis and fix" mentality is one of the most popular, and it is very intuitive.[23] If we look at the international laws of war, none of them explicitly mentions cyberwarfare, so let's generate a new treaty on cyberwar, or amend an existing one. We don't have an international body governing AI risks, so let's create one. The Security Council is broken, so let's either upgrade it with new members, or create a new body that can deal with the many non-military risks facing humanity today. The idea here is that we are stuck with rusty, 20th-century-era machines of governance, but the best we can do is patch them up a bit and get them back on the road.

The second tendency is the *IPCC panacea*. The Intergovernmental Panel on Climate Change is an extraordinary body of scientists dedicated to providing consolidated information to policymakers to address the climate crisis. For decades, thousands of scientists in the IPCC have been generating sophisticated, actionable evidence demonstrating both the human causes of climate change and what needs to be done to stay below 1.5 degrees of global warming. It has helped us grip the complexity and interdependence behind our climate crisis and for that reason is often held up as the model for other issue areas. Over the past three years, I have heard, "We need an IPCC for AI … we need an IPCC for nuclear threats … we need an IPCC for data … we need an IPCC for the whole planet." There may be merit to some of these proposals, and I discuss them later in the book. But they all tend to suffer from the same problem of lag that characterizes the IPCC. If we wait for full scientific consensus, our decisions will always come too late. Like coal mining 60 years ago, or the effects of repeated concussions in American football today, we may all know something is unhealthy, but the forces that prevent change tend to create a big gap between knowledge and action.[24] Just knowing about a problem is often insufficient to get us out of the deeply rooted patterns and path dependencies that keep a system operating the same way.

The third tendency is the *Leviathan mirage*, where we try to create a governance umbrella the size of the Earth. This is a form of top-down governance that becomes very appealing when we see smaller, fragmented efforts failing. "We need a global environmental council to adjudicate all environmental harms ... we need a single authority to govern AI risks globally ... we need a global pandemic council to prevent the next COVID-1... we need a global fund to solve inequality." The Leviathan approach is also intuitive, matching a big problem with a big solution, appearing to break down silos in a highly fractured system, and possibly giving some coercive power to a system that tends to lack teeth.[25] But, as I will explore in later chapters, the promise of a hegemonic global authority to address the crises facing us today is largely an empty one, often more likely to cause further gridlock than to generate the kind of systemic change needed today and tomorrow.[26]

Together, these three tendencies have left us with an astonishingly poor capacity to respond to global threats and a very high failure rate in generating collective action.[27] Worse, our failures may have become part of the system itself, something we not only accept but expect.[28] I think of the rare word "atychifilia" – the love of failure – when my UN colleagues shrug at the poor results of the 25-year-old peacekeeping intervention in the Democratic Republic of the Congo, or the ridiculous ways the fossil fuel industry has circumvented the carbon-pricing system, or the hypocrisy of the G8 making decisions for 8 billion people. "What can we do?" my colleagues ask. "There is no political will for change."

But if failure is both the starting and the end point of global governance, if we accept (and even perversely begin to relish) that we can't really do much in a world that feels out of our control, then our ideas will necessarily come up short.[29] Instead of thinking creatively, we are constrained by a nostalgia for an imaginary past era where the world was "rules-based," easy to comprehend, and controllable. Such an era never existed and is therefore impossible to regain. In complexity terms, our sense of failure becomes a feedback loop that limits us, causes us to self-censor, and prevents transformational change.

My goal with *The Forever Crisis* is to offer a dynamic and impactful approach to global governance, based on a set of relatively simple design and policy options to drive systemic change and open doors to new forms of action. The starting point is the need to evolve alongside and within our social, political, economic, and environmental systems, rather than attempting to master or control them. Complexity thinking may not provide all the answers, but I find that it puts us in a different headspace and allows for more creative solutions.

This is not the first effort to tackle complexity and aspects of global governance; in fact, it was 20 years ago that scholars noted a "complexity shift" in the social sciences.[30] Environmental governance is well advanced in complexity-driven thinking, and the ideas are beginning to permeate other fields like technology, security, health, and finance. But the overwhelming bulk of scholarship today is either retrospective (focusing exclusively on past case studies), exploring the promise of complexity in the abstract, or narrowing in on one tool from complexity thinking (e.g. network approaches). And almost all of it is very academic, using complex language to describe complex systems.

This book draws heavily from the insights generated in that growing body of scholarship.[31] But I also try to take my mother's somewhat sarcastic advice when she read my previous book on complexity: "Next time, write something that *even a grandma* can read."[32] Nuanced scholarly arguments not only make readers glaze over, they may also inhibit good theory and practice.[33] Today's policymakers, with their packed schedules and Twitter-length attention spans, do not have time to wade through the "ontopolitics of the Anthropocene" (sorry, David Chandler).[34] They want what one government official described to me as "a red phone with solutions at the other end." Of course, there is no red phone, but there is the reality that high-level decision-makers often feel like firefighters, trying to put out the most immediate blaze without enough time to look up and consider the smoke on the horizon.[35]

The Forever Crisis offers the concepts of complexity in straightforward terms, and then applies them directly to some of the most important proposals on the table today. Whether in the fields of environment, security, cyberthreats, health, or AI, I argue that today's big ideas can be connected and networked more effectively with each other using the concepts and design tools of complexity thinking. This does not mean all of the solutions are simple – there are no panaceas or shortcuts for collective challenges like our environment, nuclear weapons, or how to deal with the future generations.[36] But rather than try to impose train tracks on the turbulent waters of today's world, this book offers a sextant for us to navigate, largely by starlight.[37] And it is meant to be something fundamentally exciting, dynamic, and maybe even fun in a world that often feels dominated by doom, gloom, gridlock, and paralysis.

Overview of the book

Chapter 1 is a simple guide to complexity thinking, offering the basics of what constitutes complex systems, how they organize themselves, and how change takes place over time. Whether an ant colony, a galaxy, a financial market, or the network of actors involved in managing climate change, complex systems display a similar set of characteristics that can help us anticipate and respond to dynamic changes. Non-linear change means we must rethink what it means to try to control and govern, moving away from top-down models towards more networked, multilevel ones. We will also need to think differently about how time works, and how systems evolve in surprising, but not entirely unpredictable ways over long periods of time.

Chapter 2 starts with the uncontroversial point that global challenges like climate change, poverty, and artificial intelligence are complex. But it goes further, arguing that the governance processes to manage global challenges also constitute complex systems and should be addressed with the tools of complexity thinking. This is a transformative idea, offering us a paradigm where the actors, institutions, and processes for managing global issues are considered part of the system itself. Rather than attempt to control the world, complexity thinking demands that we aim to co-evolve our governance design alongside and within it. The concept of "adaptive governance" has extraordinary potential to generate dynamic, effective responses to global crises. The chapter concludes with a framework for designing adaptive global governance systems, applied throughout the remainder of the book.

Chapter 3 delves into environmental governance and our attempts to reach a balance between human and planetary wellbeing. It explores some of the most ambitious ideas for transforming our modes of production away from carbon-based industry, shifting green technology around the world, and overhauling our environmental, financial, and trade institutions. Should we have a Global Environmental Council, as some have suggested? Could all our environmental obligations be contained within a single treaty, with a world court overseeing our planet? Complexity thinking points us in a new direction, offering a model of environmental governance that looks more like the fungal structures that connect tree roots and move resources where they are most needed. Here, I argue we should invest more in the processes and networks that can improve our planetary early-warning system, triggering quick responses and cascading change across social, economic, and political levels.

In his 2021 *Our Common Agenda* report, the UN Secretary-General referred to peace as a "global public good." This idea of peace as a collective benefit for all of humanity sounds appealing, but it quickly runs into the realpolitik of a world characterized by deep divisions amongst great powers, a highly competitive battle for geopolitical influence, and growing risks of violent conflict across much of the planet. *Chapter 4* takes on this question of preventing and managing large-scale violent conflict. It analyzes our current global security framework and some of the major proposals to improve governance of security risks. Here, we seem caught in a vicious cycle, where increases in insecurity drive greater militarization and result in even higher risks. Violence also appears to act more like a pathogen in today's world, spreading and metastasizing in ways that are difficult to contain with traditional approaches. Employing concepts of negative feedback loops and correctives in systems, this chapter will offer designs to escape these cycles and move into positive, self-reinforcing peace.

What can we do when our system becomes infected, when a bug is introduced that rapidly produces a much bigger disruption? *Chapter 5* explores this kind of problem via one of the most pernicious forms of infection: cyberattacks. Here, traditional governance approaches that rely on large, top-down institutions and global legal frameworks are likely to be frustrated by fast-moving, hard-to-detect emerging risks. Attempts to prevent cyberthreats by erecting virtual walls around our national boundaries seem destined to fail. Instead, complexity thinking offers us a governance model more akin to an immune system, featuring early warning and response capacities that can identify risks, swarm around them, and decouple parts of our systems when they become infected.

Chapter 6 explores the rapid rise of artificial intelligence, seen as a panacea by some and a Pandora's box by others. Efforts to manage the risks of AI while still benefiting from its enormous potential have resulted in regional regulatory systems (e.g. the EU) and new proposals for a global governance body. Many of these regulatory and institutional proposals seem likely to fail for the simple reason that AI is part of a broader system of economic incentives, where unfettered advancements in technology are rewarded far more than the risks they produce (for now). Institutionalizing our response to AI will result in a slow, cumbersome response when we need a fast, agile one. Here, complexity offers concepts of fit, function, and feedback that can help us build a nimble, decentralized network to manage AI. The idea of a global observatory for AI – put forward by two leading thinkers – could be a viable starting point for building such an architecture.

The existential risks posed by AI lead us to the broader question taken up in *Chapter 7*: How should we think about the future of this planet (or even beyond it)? How can we make decisions today that account for the wellbeing of the billions of people who have not yet been born? How should we respond to the kind of events that could put future generations' entire existence at risk? Can we balance the immediate prerogatives to feed, clothe, educate, and protect today's billions with the possibility of the end of humanity, or a dystopian life for the trillions of people who may be born in the future? We humans have an astonishingly poor ability to think about the future. We suffer from a range of biases and myopias that allow us to ignore catastrophic risk, even when it is unacceptably high. We have a strong tendency to prefer short-term solutions, even when it is abundantly clear that we are baking in longer-term risks for huge numbers of people.

Here, complexity thinking demands that we break down the artificial distinction between short and long term, paying close attention to how the decisions we take today can create systemic path dependencies or close off possibilities for decades to come. Rather than focus our resources and attention exclusively on resilience to immediate shocks, we need to build a transformative global governance architecture, capable of reorienting our political, social, and economic systems towards a collective future. This is not naïve thinking – one of my central arguments is that global cooperation is extremely unlikely in today's world. But, just as ants display a form of collective intelligence beyond their individual actions, we can build a governance architecture to generate a collective survival. We can "human-proof" global governance.

I conclude with a radical idea that has only come to light with the growing possibilities of artificial general intelligence. Could we build a "planetary immune system," drawing on the massive amounts of data produced around the world, and developing an early warning/response to planetary threats? This would constitute a shift from complexity *thinking* (using the concepts of complex systems to improve our approaches) to complexity *science* (applying computational modeling). As I have spent the last several years speaking with experts in a variety of fields, I have noticed a recurrent pull towards this idea of collective intelligence, whether it is building a single science-policy framework for the environment, a centralized anticyberattack system, or an AI to govern AI. My sense is the Overton window of political feasibility for such an approach is gradually being inched open as the technology reaches maturity. Sooner than we think, complexity science may offer us one of the most important ways to understand and act for the future.

A final point before we jump in: the role of the global financial system. Scholarship on financial and economic complexity is both abundant and sophisticated, with a range of important contributions to the broader field of complexity.[38] And financial shocks are some of the most important crises for global governance. Our financial architecture is so fundamental to all areas of global governance, I have attempted to weave it through all the chapters. This does not mean we should avoid a direct discussion about governing the financial system; the arguments in every chapter suggest that financial leaders have comprehensively failed to appreciate the tightly coupled nature of risks in today's world. If anything, the increasingly complex web of financial systems has contributed the kind of uncertainties that make bad decisions more likely.[39] Even when costs are well identified, the deeply ingrained path dependencies of our financial system – not least the rewards given to leaders who expose us to risks with relative impunity – have pushed us into a planetary crisis that markets are very unlikely to fix on their own. The findings across these chapters point to the need for a transformation of our international financial system, positioning it to better appreciate interconnected risks, and to generate resources in a more adaptable and fairer manner.[40]

Ultimately, *The Forever Crisis* offers a set of concepts and approaches for policymakers to employ complexity thinking in both day-to-day decision-making and the design of global governance. It lays out a theory of action in a world that feels too big and unwieldy for us to exert any control.[41] It helps us answer questions like, how can we trigger small changes in relationships that will have a cascading effect across the system? Which kind of actors need to be involved to create a tipping point in our modes of production, our relationships in digital space, and/or our balance with the environment? What does "cooperation" look like in a highly competitive, polarized world? *The Forever Crisis* charts a pathway to co-evolve our global governance architecture within a system that is itself constantly evolving.

Notes

1 J. Haldemann, *The Forever War* (St. Martin's Griffin, reprint, 2009).
2 N.B.: The Collins Dictionary 2022 Word of the Year was "permacrisis."
3 E. Pauwels, "The new geopolitics of converging risks: the UN and prevention in the era of AI," Centre for Policy Research, UN University, 2 May 2019.
4 See, S. Barrett, *Why Cooperate: The Incentive to Supply Global Public Goods* (Oxford: Oxford University Press, 2010).
5 V. Galaz, ed., *Global Challenges, Governance, and Complexity Applications and Frontiers* (Edward Elgar, 2019). See also, T. Tenbensel, "Complexity and health policy," in R. Geyer & P. Cairney, eds, *Handbook of Complexity and Public Policy* (Cheltenham: Edward Elgar, 2015). See also, D. Sornette, *Why Stock Markets Crash: Critical Events in Complex Financial Systems* (Princeton, NJ: Princeton University Press, 2003).
6 C. de Coning, Cédric, "Adaptive Peacebuilding," *International Affairs* 94(2) (2018): 301–317.
7 V. Galaz, *Global Challenges, Governance, and Complexity Applications and Frontiers* (Edward Elgar, 2019), 191.
8 For example, one of the best systemic risk reports was the 2013 Global Risk Report by the World Economic Forum. Many of its broad predictions of risk were born out. Available at: https://www3.weforum.org/docs/WEF_GlobalRisks_Report_2013.pdf.
9 For a description of this policy whiplash, see, M. Stauffer et al., "Setting expectations for global catastrophic risk mitigation through policy change," Simon Institute for Longterm Governance, 21 July 2021.
10 A similar point is made about the growing "epistemic uncertainty" in the world today. See E. Seger, "Should Epistemic Security Be a Priority GCR Cause Area?" Proceedings of the Stanford Existential Risks Conference 2023, 18–37.
11 R. Harrabin, "Climate Change: Young People Very Worried – Survey," BBC World News, 14 September 2021.
12 For this point the origins of today's linear global governance, see, R. Geyer, "Beyond the Third Way: The Science of Complexity and the Politics of Choice," *British Journal of Politics and International Relations* 5(2) (2003): 237–257, 241.
13 See, J. Kreienkramp & T. Pegram, "Governing Complexity: Design Principles for the Governance of Complex Global Catastrophic Risks," *International Studies Review* 23 (2021): 779–806, 786.
14 See, J. Holland, *Hidden Order: How Adaptation Builds Complexity* (New York: Helix Books, 1995).
15 See, J. Ruhl & D. Katz, "Harnessing the complexity of legal systems for governing global challenges," *Global Challenges, Governance, and Complexity Applications and Frontiers* (Edward Elgar, 2019). See also, A. Orsini & P. le Prestre, "Complex Systems and International Governance," *International Studies Review* (2019).
16 A. Orsini & P. le Prestre, "Complex Systems and International Governance," *International Studies Review* (2019). For an excellent overview of how various public policy disciplines have taken up complexity, see, M. Stauffer et al., "A Computational Turn in Policy Process Studies: Coevolving Network Dynamics of Policy Change," *Complexity* (2022): 1–17.
17 C. Seyle & R. Spivak, "Complexity Theory and Global Governance: Is More Different?" *Global Governance* 24 (2018): 491–495.
18 Though many of today's problems are "both hideously complicated and bewilderingly complex." G. Mulga & C. Leadbeater, *Systems Innovation* (London: Nesta, 2013), 43.
19 See, B. Ramalingam, "Exploring the Science of Complexity Ideas and Implications for Development and Humanitarian Efforts," Working Paper 285. London:

Overseas Development Institute, 2008, 78 (arguing that complexity can be a cloak for a neo-liberal agenda). Cf. A. Day & C. Hunt, "A Perturbed Peace: Applying Complexity Theory to UN Peacekeeping," *International Peacekeeping* 30(1) (2023): 1–23, 6.

20 For some of the most interesting case study applications of complexity in the field of international politics and relations, see, N. Harrison, ed., *Complexity in World Politics* (Albany: State University of New York Press: 2006).

21 I was part of a small drafting team supporting the Executive Office of the Secretary General in the production of the Our Common Agenda report and was the co-lead in supporting the High-Level Advisory Board on Effective Multilateralism. See, hig hleveladvisoryboard.org/.

22 See, J. Kreienkramp & T. Pegram, "Governing Complexity: Design Principles for the Governance of Complex Global Catastrophic Risks," *International Studies Review* 23 (2021): 779–806, 782.

23 B. Chaffin, H. Gosnell, and B. Cosens, "A decade of adaptive governance scholarship: synthesis and future directions," *Ecology and Society* 19(3) (2014): 56.

24 M. Gladwell, *The Tipping Point: How Little Things Can Make a Big Difference* (Back Bay Books, 2002).

25 M. Mazower, *Governing the World: The History of an Idea* (New York: Penguin, 2012).

26 T. Hale, D. Held, and K. Young, *Gridlock: Why Global Cooperation is Failing when We Need It Most* (London: Polity, 2013).

27 E. Ostrom, M. Janssen, and J. Anderies, "Going Beyond Panaceas," *Proceedings of the National Academy of Sciences* (25 September 2007), 104.

28 D. Chandler, "How the World Learned to Stop Worrying and Love Failure: Big Data, Resilience and Emergent Causality." *Millennium: Journal of International Studies* 44(3): 391–410.

29 P. Bargués-Pedreny, *Deferring Peace in International Statebuilding: Difference, Resilience and Critique* (Oxon, UK: Routledge, 2018), 8–17.

30 R. Geyer, "Beyond the Third Way: The Science of Complexity and the Politics of Choice," *The British Journal of Politics and International Relations*, 5(2) (2003): 237–257.

31 R. Zelli et al., "Complexity, Governance & Networks," *Special Issue: Global Governance in Complex Times: Exploring New Concepts and Theories on Institutional Complexity* 6(1) (2020): 1–13; O. Young, *Grand Challenges of Planetary Governance: Global Order in Turbulent Times* (Northampton, MA: Edward Elgar Publishing, 2021); A. Thiel, W. Blomquist, and D. Garrick, *Governing complexity: analyzing and applying polycentricity* (Cambridge: Cambridge University Press, 2019); J. Kreienkramp & T. Pegram, "Governing Complexity: Design Principles for the Governance of Complex Global Catastrophic Risks," *International Studies Review* 23 (2021): 779–806.

32 A. Day, *States of Disorder, Ecosystems of Governance: Complexity Theory Applied to UN Statebuilding in the DRC and South Sudan* (Oxford: Oxford University Press, 2021).

33 K. Healy, "Fuck Nuance," *Sociological Theory* 35:2 (2017): 118–127.

34 D. Chandler, *The Ontopolitics of the Anthropocene: An Introduction to Mapping, Sensing, and Hacking* (Routledge: 2018).

35 See, M. Maas, "How Viable Is International Arms Control for Military Artificial Intelligence? Three Lessons from Nuclear Weapons," *Contemporary Security Policy* 40(3) (2019).

36 For the point on panaceas, see, E. Ostrom, *Understanding Institutional Diversity* (Princeton, NJ: Princeton University Press, 2005). See also, C. Folke et al., "Adaptive governance of social ecological systems," *Annual Review of Environment and*

Resources 30 (1) (2005): 441–473; T. Sterner et al., "Quick fixes for the environment: Part of the solution or part of the problem?" *Environment: Science and Policy for Sustainable Development* 48 (10) (2006): 20–27.

37 R. Kleinfeld, "Improving Development Aid Design and Implementation: Plan for Sailboats Not Traintracks," Carnegie Endowment for International Peace, 2015; V. Galaz, *Global Challenges, Governance, and Complexity Applications and Frontiers* (Northampton, MA: Edward Elgar, 2019), 193 (noting the need for governance to be "isomorphic with the complexity").

38 See, e.g., S. Battiston et al., "Complexity Theory and Financial Regulation," 351 *Science* 6275 (2016): 818; J. Farmer et al., "A Complex Systems Approach to Constructing Better Models for Managing Financial Markets and the Economy," 214 *European Physical Journal of Special Topics* (2012): 295; P. Gai, *Systemic Risk: The Dynamics of Modern Financial Systems* (Oxford: Oxford University Press, 2013); D. Helbing & A. Kirman, "Rethinking Economics Using Complexity Theory," 64 *Real World Economic Review* 1 (2013); N. Johnson & T. Lux, "Financial Systems: Ecology and Economics," 469 *Nature* 302 (2011); R. May, "Networks and Webs in Ecosystems and Financial Systems," 371 *Philosophical Transactions of the Royal Society* (2013); S. Schwarcz, "Regulating Complexity in Financial Markets," 87(2) *Washington University Law Review* (2009): 211; R. Zeidan & K. Richardson, "Complexity Theory and the Financial Crisis: A Critical Review," 14(6) *Corporate Finance Review* (2010): 10; L. Baxter, "Internationalization of Law – the Complex Case of Bank Regulation," in *The Internationalization of Law*, M. Hiscock & W. van Caenegem, eds (Northampton, MA: Edward Elgar, 2010).

39 I. Anabtawi & S. Schwarcz, "Regulating Systemic Risk: Towards an Analytical Framework," 86 *Notre Dame Law Review* (2011): 1349. See also, S. Schwarcz, "Disclosure's Failure in the Subprime Mortgage Crisis," 3 *Utah Law Review* (2008): 1114–1115.

40 For argument that financial actors underappreciate interconnected risks, see, I. Anabtawi & S. Schwarcz, "Regulating Systemic Risk: Towards an Analytical Framework," *Notre Dame Law Review* 86 (2011): 1349.

41 See, K. Rogers et al., "Fostering complexity thinking in action research for change in social–ecological systems," *Ecology and Society* 18(2) (2013): 31.

1 A simple guide to complexity

We have been conditioned by centuries of linear thinking. If you hit a billiard ball, it will travel on a knowable trajectory; an airplane will lift off the ground when it reaches a known speed; a position on a chessboard can be calculated into the best series of moves. These phenomena, we have learned, can be broken up into smaller sets of knowable causes and effects. A billiards game is just clusters of atoms striking each other in deterministic ways; a plane's takeoff can be understood as a combination of acceleration, wind resistance, and gravity. Great thinkers from Aristotle to Descartes to Newton all thought the world could be understood if we reduce things to their isolated form, analyze them, and put them back together.[1] Even today, we still tend to think in this mechanical way. Very difficult processes are knowable: we can break them into pieces, figure out how they work, and reverse engineer a way back to a better solution.[2] We can build a winning baseball team player by player. We can find the missing piece of the Israeli-Palestinian conflict. We can fix a failed state by assembling the right institutions.[3]

But Aristotle, Descartes, and Newton were (at least partially) wrong. Some things cannot be understood by breaking them into smaller pieces and analyzing them in isolation.[4] Émile Durkheim's famous study of suicide rates in Paris is a good example.[5] Durkheim found that it was impossible to predict whether any individual would commit suicide, because there is an infinite variety of reasons a specific person might decide to kill themselves. But, at the level of the city of Paris, there is a very predictable number of suicides per year. How can we know so little about individuals, but so much about large groups of those same people? What happens between the person in isolation and all of them living together in Paris?

Scientists across disciplines are familiar with this problem. Economists know that markets behave in ways that cannot be reduced to the behaviors of individual investors. Biologists know that beehives and ant colonies display a collective intelligence that far outstrips each bee or ant. Physicists know that solid objects behave in predictable ways, even if we don't know whether each atom within them is acting as a wave or a particle (or whether Schrödinger's cat is alive or dead). Statisticians have "no dependence on the predictability of individual events" but still they can make very accurate claims about large groups of actors.[6] Karl Popper captured this nicely: "The world is no longer

DOI: 10.4324/9781003506386-2

a causal machine. It now can be seen as a world of propensities, as an unfolding process of realizing possibilities and of unfolding new possibilities."[7]

This is the beginning of complex systems thinking. It changes everything, including change itself.[8]

What is a complex adaptive system?

An ant colony is an extraordinary thing to observe. Long streams of ants pour in and out of the colony, touching antennae to exchange pheromones as they pass by. Some dig tunnels, others bring in food or guard the queen. Over time, they construct an enormous network below ground, living according to a strict hierarchical order, each ant performing a crucial and separate role. New ants are born and immediately join the workforce. The dead are buried in mass graveyards. Aphids are enslaved as livestock. Wasps are driven away by phalanxes of soldiers. A sudden storm will generate a scurry of activity against the water flows and debris. A nearby picnic may direct a new column of explorers. A war against a nearby colony may result in glorious victory or existential defeat.[9] This extraordinary capacity for collective intelligence is how ants have survived for millions of years, adapting to massive changes in the environment, the growth of human cities, and countless daily shocks to their colonies.

An ant can be taken out of the colony and analyzed individually, but the accumulated knowledge of each ant will be less than how they act when together. Something happens between the individual and the collective. An ant colony displays the characteristics of a complex adaptive system:

1. *Many actors/agents.* While there is no specific threshold, complex systems require many actors. Two or three ants will wander in circles and eventually disperse, looking for a larger group. But several hundred may begin to display collective behavior. In fact, one of the key objectives when ants begin a colony is to rapidly increase their population to begin generating that collective behavior. In other complex systems, the agents involved may be neurons in a brain, buyers in a market, signals in a computer, or stars in a galaxy. We don't know exactly how many actors are needed for a given system to shift into complexity, but we know it usually requires a lot.
2. *Open.* An ant colony interacts with other systems around it. The colony must respond to changing weather, new food sources, or the malignant magnifying glass of a genocidal child. Sometimes one complex system will be part of a larger one – a network of mushrooms may support a cluster of trees, which is part of a larger rainforest.[10] In contrast, a closed system will have clear boundaries that prevent outside influence. A car battery is (more or less) a closed system.
3. *Self-Organizing.* While ant colonies have a queen, she does not directly dictate how each ant behaves. Instead, the ants behave according to their

own set of patterns, and they do so *stochastically* – rather than following fixed rules, they react according to probabilities. A patroller ant, for example, will decide to patrol when the morning temperature rises. The higher the temperature, the more likely for a patroller ant to leave, though it will make its own decision.[11] The way in which the ants interact with each other around these probabilistic patterns allows the colony to adjust and survive new conditions: if there is a shortage of food, the colony will dedicate greater resources to exploration; if the population gets too big, they will adjust their reproduction rates, or seek a new location. None of this is decided ahead of time or by a single authority, and no single ant really knows what is going on across the colony. Systemic behavior evolves through the relationships and information exchange amongst individual ants. This self-organization through local relationships is common to all complex adaptive systems.[12] Neurons relate to each other via synapses; schools of fish swim in harmony by following a few simple distance and angle rules amongst them; galaxies of billions of stars self-organize by the simple gravitational pulls, spins, and trajectories caused by their individual interactions.

4. *Emergent.* The collective actions of the ant colony evolve over time as it responds to new circumstances.[13] This system-level change is called its "emergent behavior." Emergence means that the activities of a system are *more and different* than the sum of individual actions at the local level.[14] Unlike a car engine, where you can easily predict what will happen when a piston fires, an ant colony's behavior is impossible to predict with certainty. The colony's behavior is non-linear; it cannot be described as cause-and-effect and is better understood as a patterned response over time.[15] It is DEEEP: Difficult to Explain, Evolve, Engineer, or Predict.[16] It presents a "causal thicket" that can't be broken down into discrete pieces.[17]

These are the four essential elements of complex adaptive systems. They can be used to decide whether a system has crossed from complicated to complex, or whether a complex system may have collapsed. A sudden flood might kill off most of an ant colony's population, leaving the individual members wandering aimlessly, having lost the critical mass required for them to behave with collective intelligence. As with most aspects of complexity, these elements don't create bright lines between one type of system and another, but they offer a starting point for knowing whether the concepts and tools of complexity will be helpful.

How do complex adaptive systems work?

Ants live in relationship with each other. When one ant touches the antennae of another and receives the scent of food or an enemy, it will react in a specific way, scuttling off to tell the others what it has discovered. These interactions build into a collective response by the system, causing the colony to send forth armies against enemies, or develop long chains to bring food back home. *Relationships between local agents* are the foundation of self-organization.[18] We see this in all complex systems, whether it is neurons firing across synapses, stars exerting gravitational pulls on each other, fish shifting position based on those around them, or people making decisions based on their surroundings. Some relationships are fleeting, like the momentary readjustment of a fish based on the position of its neighbors in the school. Others are much longer, like the symbiotic connection between a fungus and the root structure of a tree, or the orbits of galaxies that evolve over billions of years. But the starting point for all complex adaptive systems is that relationships matter.

Complex adaptive systems organize themselves through *feedback loops*, passing information back into the system to regulate it. We can see this in the way ants pass information back into the colony, creating system-wide effects over time. In fact, we are all familiar with feedback loops because we are using one right now to regulate our body temperature. If we begin to get too cold, our bodies will start to shiver, the movement creating warmth to bring our temperature up. If we get too hot, we sweat to cool our bodies. These are negative feedback loops that operate to prevent too much change in a system and maintain equilibrium. We see examples of negative feedback across complex systems: plant photosynthesis speeds up in response to increases in carbon dioxide levels and allows them to continue to grow at steady rates. An increase in a sheep population might lead to an increase in the number of wolves, reducing the sheep back to a state of predator/prey equilibrium. Negative feedback dampens change, driving systems back towards a steady state.[19]

In contrast, positive feedback amplifies and accelerates change. The most well-known example of this is climate change. As greenhouse gases build up, they cause the Earth's atmospheric temperature to rise, leading to an increase in atmospheric water vapor, which contributes to a further rise in atmospheric temperature, and the cycle continues. Other factors can accelerate or inhibit this change. For example, as global temperatures rise, the melting of the polar ice caps eliminates a reflective surface on the Earth, allowing the planet to absorb more heat and accelerating global warming.[20] The movie *The Day After Tomorrow* describes a rapidly accelerating positive feedback loop that (literally) snowballs Earth into an ice age in a matter of hours. Some of the thinking around solar radiation management discussed in the next chapter proposes the creation of a new reflective surface on the clouds or the oceans, a negative feedback loop that could potentially offset loss of reflective ice sheets and curtail global warming (or potentially end life on this Earth, according to some scientists).[21]

Driven by feedback loops, *self-organization in complex systems is nonlinear*: change does not happen in a smooth, predictable, input-output fashion. Instead, complex systems display what is called "threshold behavior," "tipping points," or (in everyday language) "surprise." A system may go through a period of apparent stability, punctuated by sudden change, or other periods of unstable equilibriums where it has not settled on a longer-term state but seems to swing between two or more states. Biologists have observed this in the evolution of animal species, where populations exist for long periods without much change and then suddenly undergo a significant adaptation, appearing to "jump" in their evolution.[22] Sociologists have observed a similar pattern in human urbanization trends, where populations will spend long periods of time in dispersed agricultural livelihoods and then appear to suddenly cluster into cities.[23] Such change in complex adaptive systems may feel uncertain and difficult to anticipate, but it is not random or chaotic.

Complex adaptive systems tend to *operate in cycles*, whether through external stimuli like seasons, or internal factors like the lifespan of the actors within them. Forests are a well-known example, where seasonal cycles of growth, death, decay, and reproduction create stable equilibria across the system over time. The height of the trees, the connections of the fungi in the earth below, the populations of animals living within the forest, all eventually reach a stable state resulting from many (sometimes millions) of cyclical iterations – seasons, the life and death of animals, and the lifespan of the trees themselves. That stability can be disrupted by a new event: a drought reduces nutrient production, or El Niño creates a new distribution of seeds, or a logging company arrives.[24]

Complex adaptive systems work across *scales of space and time*. They tend to evolve into "nested" structures, one system inside another. The term "panarchy" – meaning across hierarchies – describes how these nested systems influence each other, exchanging information and generating changes from below or from above. The system of fungi beneath a forest is within and below the larger complex system of trees, which is in turn part of the bigger ecosystem of this planet.[25] A disease in the mushroom structure can cause the death of the entire forest (bottom up); or increased global temperatures and drought can kill off the same forest (top down). In some cases, the entire system will experience a transformation (systemic change), while in others there may only be major disturbance at one level in a system (regime change).[26] Especially in "dense" or tightly coupled systems, change will not stay within its level but may "cascade" across scales.[27] When Mouhamed Bouazizi lit himself on fire in protest in Tunisia in December 2010, social change did not stay contained within his community or even his country. It spread across the region and became the so-called Arab Spring.

While change in complex adaptive systems is non-linear and difficult to predict, most systems settle into some form of steady state. A wolf-sheep population will eventually reach a stable ratio; the foliage of a cluster of trees will spread until it reaches the leaves of its neighbors; the stars and planets in a newly formed galaxy will eventually fall into stable orbits. Each of these systems displays what complexity scientists call *"attractors,"* or *"basins of attraction*," a set of states towards which the system tends to evolve and then stay. The basins can be literal, such as a ball bearing eventually settling at the bottom of a bowl, or rain collecting at the lowest point in a valley.[28] Attractors explain the strong tendency for mammals to develop four legs as the most efficient form of survival, the pull of our bodies to return to around 98.6 degrees Fahrenheit, or even the strong likelihood for the Israeli and Palestinian organizations to fight with each other.[29] In some systems, attractors may appear as rules or patterns that emerge over time, though the term "rule" may be a bit misleading. If you have trouble imagining an attractor, go to a child's birthday party, observe the apparent chaos of dozens of children running around, and then see what happens when a ball or a trampoline is introduced.[30] Toys are strong attractors.

While complex adaptive systems tend to seek out stability in the long term, they can also experience *recurrent volatility*, or even *self-organized criticality and collapse*. The 2008 financial crisis offers a good example, where the market crash was caused in large part by a willingness of investors to take greater and greater risks, fueled by an overvaluation of derivatives and the need to finance a housing market that was racing ahead of wages. Another factor was the ability for investors to profit off a collectively bad outcome: short selling is a bet on a future loss, a way to gain from falling stock prices. Over time, the financial market responded to the reality that many investors profit from volatility, not necessarily just growth, creating a positive feedback loop that accelerated instability. Our response in 2008 was deeply troubling: by pumping new money into the same system and only marginally increasing the safety net, we have all but guaranteed another financial collapse in the future, and in the meantime must deal with the effects of a system organized around volatility. As Dirk Helbing and his colleagues elegantly wrote, "Capital injections fertilize a system that already has lost its stability."[31]

It can be easy to lose hope when thinking about complex adaptive systems. It can feel like there is no scope for agency, for individual actors to generate change. After all, if we are like drops of water falling into a ravine, what chance do we have of ever escaping? People living in communities affected by cycles of violence or seasonal disasters often describe the feeling of helplessness as another cycle appears to descend upon them. Maybe there is nothing we can do; maybe, every time we try to generate change, "the system pushes back."[32]

A reassuring answer comes from Ilya Prigogine in his Nobel Prize-winning thermodynamics research, when he demonstrated that *change in complex systems is the result of the interaction between the form of a system and specific events or actions*.[33] In social systems, this means there is always room for agency and individual action, but that action always occurs within a landscape that shapes decisions and their impacts. Jane Boulton captured this beautifully as a complex system's "dance between detail and structure, between science and history, between form and individualism."[34] In social systems, attractors are not always the most visible feature of the terrain;

latent attractors like stereotypes and objectification can exert a strong gravitational pull within a system while remaining largely below the surface. These "trajectories of accumulation" invisibly shape societies, even while individuals make decisions within them.[35] I may decide that I want to stop climate change, but my day-to-day surroundings (my car, the electricity in my house, my plastic food wrappers, etc.) all make it very difficult to change the broader system. I still have agency, but it is not completely unfettered, and I will need to think about collective behavior change if I want to have a systemic impact.

These characteristics mean complex adaptive systems do not have an infinite set of options in how they change. Instead, they present what complexity scientists call *"phase space."*[36] Drawn from physics and mathematics, the concept of phase space refers to all possible states within a system at a given moment. In some systems, the possibilities can easily be plotted out in a three-dimensional diagram. For example, how planets orbit a sun may involve millions of possible pathways, all limited by the gravitational pull of the sun. In other, more open systems, such as financial markets or communities of people, plotting the contours of possibility may become more difficult or even impossible. The idea of an Overton window is similar, describing the range of political possibilities at a given moment (though I discuss later how the notion of political will tends to obscure some of the more innovative pathways in some systems).

The key takeaway is that the possibilities are not endless; complex systems evolve patterns and contours that shape our actions within them. This does not mean we do not have agency or are without decision-making powers in complex systems. And it doesn't mean we are unable to change a phase space by transforming the system over time. But some decisions may face greater resistance than others. Peter Coleman vividly describes strong attractors as "a valley in the psychological landscape into which the psychological elements – thoughts, feelings and actions – begin to slide."[37] It may be possible to escape the valley, but often it demands the kind of persistent energy that few of us possess, and it may require a collective effort that is difficult to organize. How to generate that collective effort in a contested, fractured world is the core question behind this book.

Can we control complex adaptive systems? (Not really)

A mechanic can control a car engine by assembling its pieces in the right way, or changing its inputs (adding higher-performing gas, or fixing a broken piece, for example). We cannot control or fix complex adaptive systems because they display emergent, non-linear change. In some cases, like our immune system, we have a good idea of how to generate a specific response. A chicken pox vaccine predictably produces a resistance to chicken pox. But when we ourselves are actors within a system, speaking of "control" is the wrong starting point. Social scientists have long understood that it is essentially impossible to isolate variables and make empirically strong arguments about cause and effect in social systems.[38] Instead, it is better to think of exerting influence, or affecting the underlying patterns a given system.

Complexity theorists have developed a wide range of concepts for exerting influence in social and political systems, including fun terms like "harnessing," "steering," "taming," "bridging," "embracing," "clustering," "linking," and "orchestration."[39] While each of these has unique properties (and are explored throughout this book), they all share a common set of starting assumptions. First, that *top-down efforts to control on their own are not sufficient to generate predictable outcomes.* While there are often important roles for powerful players, change tends to involve engagement at different levels and the involvement of many actors. Climate change is a good example, where a combination of state-level structures (e.g. The Intergovernmental Panel on Climate Change), cities, private sector, and civil society groups are seen as necessary to generating meaningful change.[40] Multi-scalar interventions that move across hierarchies and levels are almost always needed in complex systems, recognizing that in some cases relatively small impacts at one level can have broader systemic effects.[41]

Second, *relationships drive change* in complex systems. In nature, the range of symbiotic relationships amongst plants and animals drives change. Pick up almost any academic piece on complexity, and you will see a diagram of a network, showing how different actors relate to each other.[42] In fact, it is probably most helpful to think of complex systems as a set of relationships, rather than a fixed arrangement of actors or institutions.[43] Exerting influence in complex systems is more about how relationships evolve and change, and how those relationships can have a broader impact on the entire network. In my previous book on UN state-building, for example, I explore how changing the relationships between the police and local communities could have a broader cascading impact on stability in eastern Congo.[44]

Third, *change must "fit" by working across different scales.*[45] Think of a forest floor, filled with decomposing vegetation. As the plant matter is consumed by fungi, it produces a small amount of carbon dioxide released into the atmosphere. There is a relationship between the microscopic scale of the work of the fungi, the forest as an ecosystem, and the atmosphere at the global level. If you're trying to reduce global warming, you will need to think of how to exert change across these levels, perhaps designing different interventions at the level of forests than at the level of the atmosphere. Scaling can be vertical (from very local to the level of the system) or horizontal (bringing in a broader range of actors relevant to a problem).[46] Where the intervention is poorly matched to the scale of a system, or where it fails to address the level where change is needed, we speak of a "fit" problem.[47] As discussed later, getting the fit right often requires a shift from "monocentric" governance (based on a single steering authority) to multilevel or even adaptive governance (addressing change at different, constantly changing levels).[48]

Here it is worth highlighting a counterintuitive finding from complexity thinking: *the limits of networks*. Today's world is defined by the term "network." We think of networks as the best way to harness divergent actors and processes. Rather than build new institutions, we prefer to network existing efforts. Anne-Marie Slaughter's brilliant book *The Chessboard and the Web* is subtitled *Strategies of Connection in a Networked World*. While I wholeheartedly agree with her arguments, I add a note of caution. Connectivity and interdependence in complex systems can create risks as well. The 2008 financial collapse spread across the globe in part because of our high levels of financial interdependence. Cyberattacks travel through our tightly coupled digital systems. COVID-19 cascaded around a world where physical connectivity is the norm. While networks are a key adaptive response to today's complexity, throughout this book I will also explore how complex systems can shut down, compartmentalize, and decouple when necessary for our survival.

Fourth, *change happens over time, but not smoothly*. Punctuated equilibrium theory is based on a simple observation: political systems are generally stable, changing incrementally over time, but occasionally display sudden and massive departures.[49] The Arab Spring is a clear example of decades of authoritarian rule upended by a seemingly small act of defiance that snowballed into system-wide change. This tendency is true of most complex systems, which seek out one or more states of equilibrium and remain in them for long periods of time. The attractors of systems drive them back into that state of equilibrium, helping them to remain stable and survive. Every day, our bodies are bombarded by viruses, temperature changes, and potentially lethal bacteria, but most of the time our immune system fends off these disruptions and keeps us alive. If a positive feedback loop is introduced, or a tipping point is reached, systems can suddenly experience massive and unexpected change, possibly even system collapse. The COVID pandemic was an example of system shifts at both the human level (our immune systems were not able to handle the new virus) and the global level (our health systems were initially unable to cope with the influx of infected people).

Orchestrating change in complex systems is often about generating tipping points, accelerating snowball effects, and triggering cascades that can move from localized to systemic change. But it is also about understanding that in some cases time is not on our side and systems are likely to remain locked into certain pathways until specific windows of opportunity open.[50] One of the most striking examples of this is the 1972 *The Limits of Growth* report, produced by MIT on the basis of what today looks like very rudimentary modeling of the future.[51] *The Limits of Growth* predicted that our collective consumption and energy habits would lead to ecological overshoot in the first half of the 21st Century, leading to many of the scenarios we see playing out today. Though a bestseller, the book was largely ignored by policymakers, and our path dependency on fossil fuels became locked in. We should be worried about how accurate that report has been so far, particularly given that that one of the most likely scenarios identified in that report was "global environmental collapse" right around now.[52]

Fifth, *the system "pushes back."* Complex adaptive systems tend to resist change to their underlying rules and patterns. In fact, the concept of "resilience" at the heart of much of complexity thinking refers to the ability of a system to return to a state of equilibrium after a serious shock.[53] Resilience can be a good thing, such as a community's ability to maintain healthy social relationships in the face of a food shortage or a natural disaster. But resilience also speaks to the ability of authoritarian regimes to resist democratization attempts, or even the strong dependence of our global capitalist system on fossil fuels. "Turbulence" in political systems may appear unpredictable and chaotic from one moment to the next, but still allow for powerful leaders to stay in power for decades.[54] If resilience refers to the ability of a system to retain function in the face of disturbance, we should recognize that some of those functions (for example dictatorships or unsustainable capitalism) may be undesirable.

In fact, the harder we push for transformational change, the harder the system pushes back. Moments of crisis and upheaval are also when the system is exerting its strongest pulls back to its prior equilibrium. Our tendency to try to generate change during moments of crisis could in fact be the *least* likely to result in the changes we want. It is well known that you shouldn't take vaccines when you're sick. Maybe the latest coup in Africa is not the best moment to try to put in place a democratic regime. Maybe a financial crisis is not the best moment to try to generate new governance rules for our global financial system. We tend to think of our social and political systems as thixotropic substances: like honey or cement, they are easier to mold when they are in motion.[55] But this might be at least partially wrong. Complexity thinking suggests that shocks to systems activate the strongest attractors, trying to drive the system back to a state of equilibrium. Unless we are sure we can achieve systemic-level change, our attempts to govern by continual opportunistic crisis management will produce some serious unintended consequences.[56]

Thinking about change in complex systems can feel daunting. I have noticed even the most ambitious decision-makers tend to throw up their hands in the face of today's challenges and resign themselves to failure.[57] How can we bring an end to the fossil fuel era when our daily lives depend so heavily on carbon-based energy? How can we transform our financial system to be more equitable when powerful countries have a stranglehold on our international financial institutions? How are we meant to de-nuclearize when decades of foreign policy are built on the deterrence of nuclear weapons? Speaking of empowering local actors, or generating collective action, can feel good, but it seems to run into the reality that our world is divided, fractured, and seemingly locked into self-destructive, unfair pathways. If poorly applied, complexity thinking might contribute to this overwhelming feeling of powerlessness, offering "managerial snake oil" and empty jargon instead of real-world solutions, or deferring action in the face of uncertainty.[58] But, as the next chapter explores, the tools of complexity can also be employed to help us break us out of our malaise, to energize our response, and to give us hope for the kinds of systemic change needed to save ourselves and our planet.

Notes

1 R. Descartes, "Rules for the direction of the mind," in E. Anscombe & P. Geach, *Descartes: Philosophical Writings* (Bobbs-Merrill Educational Publishing, 1954).

2 K. Rogers et al., "Fostering complexity thinking in action research for change in social–ecological systems," *Ecology and Society* 18(2) (2013): 31. See also, J. Boulton et al., eds., *Embracing Complexity: Strategic Perspectives for an Age of Turbulence* (Oxford: Oxford University Press, 2015).

3 A. Ghani & C. Lockhardt, *Fixing Failed States* (Oxford: Oxford University Press, 2009).

4 S. Lansing, "Complex Adaptive Systems," *Annual Review of Anthropology* 32 (2003): 183–204, 185.

5 E. Durkheim, *Suicide: A Study in Sociology*, Trans. J.A. Spaulding, G. Simpson (New York: Free Press, 1979).

6 T. Porter, *The Rise of Statistical Thinking* (Princeton, NJ: Princeton Univ. Press, 1986), 114.

7 K. Popper, *A World of Propensities* (Bristol, UK: Thoemmes, 1990), 18–19.

8 For some of the foundational pieces on the science of complexity, see W. Weaver, "Science and Complexity," *American Scientist* 36(4) (1948); S. Kaufman, *The Origins of Order: Self-Organization and Selection in Evolution* (New York: Oxford University Press, 1993); P. Bak, *How Nature Works* (New York: Copernicus, 1996); C. Holling, "Two Cultures of Ecology," *Conservation Ecology* 2(2) (1998); S. Levin, Fragile Dominion: Complexity and the Commons (New York: Basic Books, 2000); J. Holland, *Complexity: A Very Short Introduction* (New York: Oxford University Press, 2014); and W. Arthur, *Complexity and the Economy* (New York: Oxford University Press, 2015).

9 See, e.g., Swiss National Science Foundation, "The Complex Organisation of an Ant Colony," 18 June 2021, available at: https://www.snf.ch/en/zpKlA4Jda-Je0EaCg/news/the-complex-organisation-of-an-ant-colony.

10 C. Allen et al., "Panarchy: Theory and Application," *Ecosystems* 17 (2014): 578–589.

11 For an excellent description of ant colonies as complex systems, see J. Ladyman & K. Wiesner, *What is a complex system?* (New Haven and London: Yale University Press, 2020), 38.

12 Melanie Mitchell, *Complexity: A Guided Tour* (Oxford: Oxford University Press, 2009).

13 D. Gordon, "Collective Wisdom of Ants," *Scientific American* (2016).

14 A. Orsini & P. le Prestre, "Complex Systems and International Governance," *International Studies Review* (2019). See also, J. Holland, *Emergence: From Chaos to Order* (Cambridge, MA: Perseus Books, 1998).

15 See, J. Pearl & D. Mackenzie, *The Book of Why: The New Science of Cause and Effect* (New York: Basic Books, 2018).

16 S. Page, "What Sociologists Should Know About Complexity," *Annual Review of Sociology* 41 (2015): 21–41.

17 W. Wimsatt, "The ontology of complex systems: levels of organization, perspectives, and causal thickets," *Canadian Journal of Philosophy* 20 (1994): 207–274.

18 A. Duit & V. Galaz, "Governance and Complexity – Emerging Issues for Governance Theory," *Governance* 21 (2008): 311–335. V. Grimm et al., "Pattern-Oriented Modeling of Agent-Based Complex Systems: Lessons from Ecology," *Science* (2005): 987–991.
19 B. Flores, "Feedback in tropical forests in the Anthropocene," *Global Change Biology* (2022).
20 K. Kastens et al., "How Geoscientists Think and Learn," *Eos* 90 (31) (2009): 265–266.
21 B. Berwyn, "60 Scientists Call for Accelerated Research into Solar Radiation Management That Could Temporarily Mask Global Warming," Inside Climate News, 27 February 2023, available at: https://insideclimatenews.org/news/27022023/solar-radiation-management-global-warming/.
22 N. Eldridge & S. Gould, "Punctuated Equilibrium: An Alternative to Phyletic Gradualism," in *Models in Paleobiology* ed. by T. Schopf, pp. 82–115 (San Francisco: Freeman Cooper, 1973); P. Bak, *How Nature Works* (New York: Copernicus, 1996).
23 T. Harper, "Punctuated Equilibrium, a Pattern Common to Big History that also Characterizes the Pattern of Urbanization," *Social Evolution & History* 16(1) (2016): 86–127; A. Korotayev, "The World System Urbanization Dynamics: A Quantitative Analysis," *History and Mathematics. Historical Dynamics and Development of Complex Societies*, ed. by P. Turchin et al., 44–62 (Moscow: KomKniga/URSS, 2006).
24 L. Curran, "Impact of El Niño and logging on canopy tree recruitment in Borneo," *Science* 286 (1999): 2184–2188.
25 For a deeper description, see C. Holling, "Resilience of ecosystems: local surprise and global change," in W. Clark ed., *Sustainable Development of the Biosphere* (Cambridge: Cambridge University Press, 1986), 292–317.
26 C. Allen et al., "Panarchy: Theory and Application," *Ecosystems* 17 (2014): 578–589.
27 A. Duit & V. Galaz, "Governance and Complexity – Emerging Issues for Governance Theory," *Governance* 21 (2008): 311–335.
28 C. Lucas, "Attractors Everywhere: Order from Chaos," available at: http://www.calresco.org/attract.htm.
29 P. Coleman, "Navigating the Landscape of Conflict: Applications of Dynamical Systems Theory to Addressing Protracted Conflict," in *The Non-Linearity of Peace Processes: Theory and Practice of Systemic Conflict Transformation*, ed. by Tobias Debiel et al. (Opladen: Verlag Barbara Budrich, 2011).
30 *How to Organize a Children's Birthday Party*, Youtube video, available at: https://www.youtube.com/watch?v=Miwb92eZaJg.
31 D. Helbing, *Thinking Ahead: Essays on Big Data, Digital Revolution, and Participatory Market Society* (Cham, Switzerland: Springer Press, 2015), 37.
32 P. Senge, *The Fifth Discipline: The Art & Practice of The Learning Organization* (New York: Currency Doubleday, 1990).
33 I. Prigogine et al., "Long term trends and the evolution of complexity," in *Goals in a Global Community, vol. 1: Studies on the Conceptual Foundations*, E. Lazlo & J. Bierman, eds (New York: Pergamon Press, 1977); I. Prigogine, "Time, structure and fluctuations," *Science*, vol. 201, no. 4358 (1978): 777–785.
34 J. Boulton et al., eds, *Embracing Complexity: Strategic Perspectives for an Age of Turbulence* (Oxford: Oxford University Press, 2015).
35 C. Cramer, "Trajectories of accumulation through war and peace," in *The Dilemmas of Statebuilding: Confronting the Contradictions of Postwar Peace Operations*, Roland Paris and Timothy Sisk, eds (New York: Routledge, 2009), 130.

36 See, D. Nolte, "The Tangled Tale of Phase Space," *Oxford Scholarship Online* (2010); see also, J. Gleick, *Chaos: Making a New Science* (New York: Viking, 1987) (referring to "phase space" as one of the most important inventions of all time).

37 Peter Coleman, "Navigating the Landscape of Conflict: Applications of Dynamical Systems Theory to Addressing Protracted Conflict," in *The Non-Linearity of Peace Processes: Theory and Practice of Systemic Conflict Transformation*, T. Debiel et al., eds (Opladen: Verlag Barbara Budrich, 2011).

38 E. Bienenstock, "Operationalizing Social Science for National Security," in *Adaptive Engagement for Undergoverned Spaces: Concepts, Challenges, and Prospects for New Approaches*, A. Frank & E. Bartels, eds, (RAND, 2022); see also, J. Bryant, "On Sources and Narratives in Historical Social Science: A Realist Critique of Positivist and Postmodernist Epistemologies," *British Journal of Sociology* 51(3) (2000).

39 See, e.g., J. Ruhl & D. Katz, "Harnessing the complexity of legal systems for governing global challenges," *Global Challenges, Governance, and Complexity Applications and Frontiers* (Edward Elgar, 2019); X. Insausti, "Distributed Clustering Algorithm for Adaptive Pandemic Control," in *IEEE Access*, vol. 9 (2021): 160688–160696; X. Cao et al., "Linking Adaptive Governance, Strategic Flexibility and Responsible Innovation: Evidence from China," *International Journal of Innovation and Technology Management* (2023).

40 T. Hahn et al., "Trust-building, knowledge generation and organizational innovations: the role of a bridging organization for adaptive comanagement of a wetland landscape around Kristianstad, Sweden," *Human Ecology* 34 (2006): 573–592.

41 H. Pattee, ed., *Hierarchy Theory: The Challenge of Complex Systems* (New York: George Braziller, Inc., 1973); R. O'Neill, *A Hierarchical Concept of Ecosystems* (Princeton N.J.: Princeton University Press, 1986); V. Ahl & T. Allen, *Hierarchy Theory* (New York: Columbia University Press, 1996); P. Agre, "Hierarchy and History in Simon's 'Architecture of Complexity,'" *Journal of the Learning Sciences*, vol. 12, no. 3 (July 2003): 183–216.

42 R. Kim, "Is Global Governance Fragmented, Polycentric, or Complex? The State of the Art of the Network Approach," *International Studies Review* 22(4) (2020): 903–931.

43 For a good description of relationality in systems, see, M. Brigg, "Relational peacebuilding: promise beyond crisis," *Peacebuilding in Crisis: Rethinking paradigms and practices of transnational cooperation*, Tobias Debiel et al., eds (Oxford: Routledge, 2016), 58.

44 A. Day, *States of Disorder, Ecosystems of Governance: Complexity Theory Applied to UN Statebuilding in the DRC and South Sudan* (Oxford: Oxford University Press, 2021).

45 E. Brondizio, E. Ostrom, and O. Young, "Connectivity and the governance of multilevel social-ecological systems: the role of social capital," *Annual Review of Environment and Resources* 34 (2009): 253–278; D. Cash et al., "Scale and cross-scale dynamics: governance and information in a multilevel world," *Ecology and Society* 11(2) (2006): 8.

46 L. Andonova & R. Mitchell, "The Rescaling of Global Environmental Politics," *Annual Review of Environment and Resources* 35:1 (2010): 255–282.

47 G. Cumming, D. Cumming, and C. Redman, "Scale mismatches in social- ecological systems: causes, consequences, and solutions," *Ecology and Society* 11(1) (2006):14; C. Folke et al., "The problem of fit between ecosystems and institutions: ten years later," *Ecology and Society* 12(1) (2007): 30.

48 C. Termeer et al., "Disentangling Scale Approaches in Governance Research: Comparing Monocentric, Multilevel, and Adaptive Governance.," *Ecology and Society*, vol. 15, no. 4 (2010).

49 J. True et al., "Punctuated-Equilibrium Theory Explaining Stability and Change in Public Policymaking," in *Theories of Policy Processes*, ed. P. Sabatier (Westview Press, 2007), 155; J. Gupta, "Global change: analyzing scale and scaling in environmental governance," in O. Young, L. King, and H. Schroeder, eds, *Institutions and environmental change: principal findings, applications, and research frontiers* (Cambridge, MA: MIT Press, Cambridge, 2007), 225–258.

50 See, P. Olsson et al., "Shooting the rapids: navigating transitions to adaptive governance of social-ecological systems. *Ecology and Society* 11(1) (2006): 18.

51 D. Meadows, J. Randers, D. Meadows, *Limits to Growth: The 30-Year Update* (Vermont: Chelsea Green Publishing, 2013).

52 See, G. Turner, "Is Global Collapse Imminent?" MSSI Research Paper No. 4, Melbourne Sustainable Society Institute, 2014. The University of Melbourne. See also, G. Herrington, "Update to limits to growth: Comparing the world3 model with empirical data," *Journal of Indigenous Ecology* 25 (2021): 614–626.

53 See, A. Duit et al., "Governance, complexity, and resilience," *Global Environmental Change* 20 (3) (2010): 363–368.

54 A. de Waal, *The Real Politics of the Horn of Africa: Money, War and the Business of Power* (London: Polity Press, 2016), 17.

55 I owe the concept of thixotropic substances and their application to social systems to a conversation with Stephen Jackson. I have not seen it published elsewhere.

56 See, e.g., A. Day & C. Hunt, "Distractions, Distortions and Dilemmas: The Externalities of Protecting Civilians in United Nations Peacekeeping," *Civil Wars* 24:1 (2022): 97–116.

57 In fact, failure may have become baked in to some of our international engagements. See, e.g., P. Bargués-Pedreny, *Deferring Peace in International Statebuilding: Difference, Resilience and Critique* (Oxon, UK: Routledge, 2018), 8–17.

58 O. Sorenson, "Book review of 'Emergence," Chaos, Complexity and Sociology 1, no. 2 (1999): 149–151. See also, C. Pollitt, "Complexity theory and evolutionary public administration: a sceptical afterword," in *Managing Complex Governance Systems* (Routledge, 2009), 229 (critiquing complexity as a hodgepodge of other disciplines).

2 Applying complexity to global governance

Global challenges like climate change, poverty, and war are undoubtedly complex. But the central contention of this book is that the *governance processes to manage global issues also constitute complex systems and should be addressed with the tools of complexity thinking.* In some areas, like environmental governance, the complexity of global governance arrangements is well recognized. In others, like the growing field of governing artificial intelligence, the lack of mature public institutions may obscure the complexity of social, political, and legal actors already involved. I hope that by the end of this book you see the utility of complexity approaches across all global governance domains, seeing both the challenge and the attempt to govern it as part of a unified complex system.

Systemic approaches to global governance are not new. We can go back at least as far as Robert Jervis's 1997 *System Effects* or even Bob Keohane and Joseph Nye's 1970s "complex interdependence" to find its early seeds.[1] David Byrne applied complexity to analyze the impacts of health, education, and urban governance policies in England two decades ago, while a range of other scholars have proposed complexity-driven approaches to public policy by national governments.[2] Michael Woolcock, Duncan Green, Rachel Kleinfeld, and Ben Ramalingam, among others, have drawn from complexity thinking to suggest innovative approaches to international development and humanitarian assistance.[3] Bousquet and Curtis have argued for a more concerted application of complexity thinking to international relations, a call that was taken up by Emilian Kavalski in his analysis of world politics, and most recently by Jack Donnelly in his excellent book *Systems, Relations, and the Structures of International Societies.*[4] Similar applications of complexity thinking have now been suggested for international policing efforts,[5] humanitarian delivery,[6] military operations, international law,[7] and peacebuilding.[8] Recent special editions of *Global Governance* and *International Studies Review* have been dedicated to the "vibrant field" of complexity and global governance.[9] There are of course critics and skeptics who argue that complexity offers little more than a fuzzy veneer, or a hodgepodge of concepts from other disciplines.[10] But the field is increasingly accepted as relevant to the kinds of questions we are exploring here.

DOI: 10.4324/9781003506386-3

The contribution of *The Forever Crisis* is to offer a complexity-informed framework for meeting the major global governance challenges of today, and then to apply that framework to some of the most promising ideas currently being proposed on the world stage. It is a forward-looking application of complexity thinking. I draw on some of the most innovative scholarship on fragmentation, polycentricity, and network theory, but I am not trying to carve out a specific methodological niche.[11] Instead, what I have found most useful about complexity is its flexibility, dynamism, and mind-opening capacities. You will notice that I use the term "complexity thinking" more than complexity theory or science. This is intentional: I am applying a way of thinking about planetary challenges and our global governance design in real time, offering viable options to those directly involved in shaping global governance.

Defining global governance

Global governance is both a ubiquitous and "notoriously slippery" term.[12] For some, it means an attempt to impose a "rules-based order" on a world that feels increasingly out of control. For others, it describes the different spheres of authority around the planet, from local mayors up to international treaties.[13] A quite common definition focuses on how institutions and processes facilitate collective action on global issues.[14] Following in Max Weber's footsteps, some of the more popular definitions see governance as a monopoly of the means of violence and coercion.[15] Another definition employs the analogy that global governance is doing internationally what governments do at home.[16] Oran Young's elegant definition calls global governance "a social function centered on steering societies away from collectively undesirable outcomes and toward collectively good ones."[17] For some it is just an easy stand-in for the United Nations, or multilateralism, or anything that feels somewhat "planetary." If defined in broad terms as any effort to influence beyond national boundaries, global governance could mean "almost anything."[18]

An exact definition of global governance is not especially important, but some key characteristics do matter.[19] First, it is *governance*, not government.[20] There is no single global authority that can decide for everyone, no planetary Leviathan that has universal control. As Hedley Bull famously noted, we live in an anarchical world without a world government.[21] Nation-states matter, of course, but states are actors within a system, not lords over it.[22] What matters more are the rules and constraints on behavior that shape how actors relate to each other.[23] Thinking of governance as "collective actions" to manage common resources is a helpful starting point, though we should not underestimate how much of global governance is a competitive, fractious process.[24] And we should be careful not to assume that what works within a state – for example national regulation – has a corollary at the international level.

Second, governance can include a range of formal or informal norms, activities, processes, and/or institutions. It has both an institutional and a functional aspect. For example, the global prohibition against torture involves a norm, a legally binding treaty amongst states, a set of international institutions, national laws in nearly every country, anti-torture civil society groups, and the behavior of everyday citizens. Some governance arenas appear to have very formal, state-centered structures, such as nuclear weapons (though even here the role of advocacy groups and norms should not be underestimated). Other areas may seem dominated by a relatively small number of big powers, such as the board of the World Bank, or the 15 members of the UN Security Council. Setting precise parameters to any governance regime is difficult and not necessarily helpful when employing complexity thinking. It may be more appropriate to think of governance as a verb rather than a noun.

Our definition of global governance includes the recognition that our world has become more interconnected and interdependent, largely because of globalization and our increasing digital existence. This is less of a definition and more of a characteristic or trend, but it is important because it points to our global governance systems as complex. If, for example, we think of climate governance as only the institution of the Intergovernmental Panel on Climate Change, we are missing the broader picture of cities, civil society, private sector, and other actors who play a key role in addressing the global impacts of climate change. If we only think of global security as the UN Security Council, we ignore the web of actors involved in driving violence, military spending, and peacebuilding. As the scholarship on "regime complexes" suggests, we live in a world of overlapping and interacting networks of actors and processes, where the relationships amongst entities are central to governance.[25] This interdependence of many actors means that we cannot rely on inter-state or inter-institutional arrangements alone.[26]

While recognizing the many actors involved in governance, we should be careful not to dismiss the state as the central player in most global arenas.[27] States remain the only actors consistently able to participate in multilateral organizations like the United Nations, enter into binding treaties, or make decisions about strategic assets like nuclear weapons.[28] A predominant portion of our global wealth is controlled by states (though this is shrinking proportionately as private actors accumulate more and more). And we tend to describe actors in terms of whether they are "state" or "non-state," reflecting a clear priority given to states in much of global governance. Better than thinking in binary terms of state and non-state – or the state and its competitors – systems thinking sees states as important nodes in networks of many different players.[29] The scholarship describing the shift to more "liquid" forms of state-led governance,[30] or the role of the state as "steering rather than rowing,"[31] or international relations as a "web, not a chessboard"[32] reflects this growing recognition of the state as part of a system rather than all of it.

Finally, as Tom Weiss concisely puts it, the "global" in global govern-ance refers to "everything happening worldwide."[33] Here, we can distinguish "global" from "international," the latter of which tends to concern rela-tionships amongst states. In contrast, "global" means our efforts to manage issues with a planetary impact. Critics could point to a problem here: if our planetary system is complex and interdependent, arguably everything has a planetary impact. The famous idea that a butterfly's wings could theo-retically cause a hurricane comes into play here.[34] But we can take a com-mon-sense approach and identify some key areas that are clearly relevant for global governance: the environment, finance, health, security, and technolo-gies. These are of course linked to other issues – for example, our relation-ship with our environment pervades every aspect of our daily lives – but the attempts to regulate and address the planetary impacts are what concern us most directly. And where our attempts fall short, we enter the world of undergoverned spaces.

Ungoverned and undergoverned spaces

Quite literally, there is no ungoverned space on Earth. Some areas may appear unregulated, such as the sheets of ice and snow on the Antarctic, or the mostly empty space in our high atmosphere, or the Mariana Trench seven miles below sea level. But there are treaties covering all of them. Similarly, when a government collapses, or loses control of its territory to rebels, there is a tendency to think of it as ungoverned, a "black hole" of governance where warlords and criminals roam free.[35] But even in the most chaotic conflict set-tings, even in areas where there appears no law and order whatsoever, there is governance.[36] Where there are people, there are systems of governance.

But "undergoverned" spaces do exist. These are areas where our govern-ance approaches are very unlikely to generate predictable or desirable out-comes, or where the rules that dictate our behavior are unsettled. While there is no bright-line definition of undergoverned spaces, they all tend to exhibit shortcomings in: (1) enforcement (agreements between actors are easily ignored), (2) attribution (it is difficult to know who is responsible for what), and (3) regulation (the rules do not necessarily apply to everyone).[37] A high-profile example of an undergoverned space is cyberwarfare today, where the traditional laws and rules of war may have a limited capacity to constrain behavior and/or achieve accountability.

Undergoverned spaces can also arise when well-established governance arrangements become disrupted or obsolete by new, competing sources of authority. For example, China's Belt and Road Initiative is often cited as an alternative trade and investment regime that could at least partially replace or disrupt existing global trade systems.[38] Similarly, a governance system may become obsolete due to changes in the positions of the parties or shifting contexts. The US withdrawal from the Iran nuclear deal in 2018 sent a shock through our global nuclear governance system and a scramble to shore up other security arrangements. Today, a combination of climate change and technological advances may point to the erosion of our global governance regime for the Arctic region, potentially requiring an upgrade to existing treaty obligations.[39] The proliferation of space-based technologies in recent years has strained the outdated governance arrangements put in place decades ago.[40] And the deeply unfair, opaque nature of our international financial system could point towards financial undergovernance as well.

Today's polycrisis can be summarized as a rapid growth of undergoverned spaces. We do not have sufficiently robust governance arrangements to generate predictable, desirable outcomes in today's world. Those who lament the decline of a "rules-based international order" are in essence demanding fixes to undergoverned spaces. Facing an increasingly uncertain future – and in a world where reaching new binding international agreements feels impossible – there is a strong tendency to try to patch up our current system, stretch it over emerging risks, and hope it holds. A proposal that we should simply expand existing laws of warfare to cover cyberwarfare is an example of this thinking (but not the only one).[41] Most of the proposals considered in the later chapters of this book, from Security Council reform to global environmental regulation, can be thought of as an attempt to patch up and expand regulations for undergoverned spaces.

Towards adaptive global governance

Undergovernance contributes to uncertainty. If we don't know the rules of the game, or if there are no rules in place, we don't know how others will behave. We risk being tripped up by what Donald Rumsfeld famously called "unknown unknowns." Or we spend our time building an increasingly sophisticated understanding of a problem, but never feel ready to act without a clearer picture of what might happen. Or we run around whacking moles in a state of constant crisis management. No surprise that one of the top priorities for AI research today is "reasoning under uncertainty."[42] But until we reach a *Minority Report* level of modeling the future, we are stuck with a partial understanding of what might happen, even in the near term. We must make do with decision-making in conditions of "deep uncertainty."[43]

Adaptive governance is one attempt to foster effective responses in uncertain conditions.[44] Its first application was in the field of environmental governance more than 30 years ago.[45] Early experts noted that the regulation of ecosystems like marshlands, forests, reefs, or open waters was especially difficult because it involved regulating the human-environment relationship. Static regulatory institutions did not match up well with the fluid, constantly evolving aspects of these relationships.[46] Rather than try to direct our environmental responses from above, adaptive environmental governance arose as a set of practices to encourage dialogue amongst resource users, build layered institutions and structures at different levels, develop a mixture of formal and informal institutions, encourage experimentation, and build constant learning loops.[47] In evolutionary terms, we need governance systems that evolve alongside ecosystems so they don't become extinct (irrelevant).[48]

Here, it is important to underline the relationship between adaptive governance and resilience. In general terms, resilience is an ability to respond to stresses and shocks while preserving system identity and its main functions.[49] When applied to the human-environment relationship, resilience means the ability of a community to thrive and change in a sustainable balance with a constantly changing environment.[50] Adaptive environmental governance arose as an attempt to build that kind of resilience by creating structures and processes that feed back into the system, working across its different scales and levels to respond to new dynamics.[51]

Not all resilient systems accomplish what we want: Mugabe's authoritarian rule over Zimbabwe was extraordinarily resilient but also very corrupt; our fossil fuel-based economy is proving very resilient to transformational change; structural racism is an insidious and resilient part of many communities. Throughout this book, I use resilience carefully, keeping this double-edged aspect in mind.

Adaptive environmental governance theory and practice has grown over the past decade and is now applied in a wide range of ecosystems management.[52] Adaptation has increasingly been considered in fields beyond the environment as well.[53] In the security realm, adaptive approaches to military campaigns are now well-established, adaptive management is frequently applied in development settings,[54] and newer concepts like adaptive peacebuilding appear to be taking hold.[55] In areas as diverse as financial regulation, pandemic response, and long-term decision-making, the concept of adaptive governance appears to be taking hold.[56] And as explored in Chapter 6, many of the discussions around governing AI are influenced by theories of adaptation as well.

While it may take many different forms, adaptive governance generally consists of four core elements: (1) mapping the dynamics and underlying patterns of complex systems; (2) designing organizations that can adapt to shifting circumstances; (3) encouraging multiple stakeholders in decision-making; and (4) feeding the experience back into future iterations of governance.[57] One of the most well-known models is the Act-Sense-Decide-Adapt cycle, which is based on a feedback loop of knowledge into decision-making.[58]

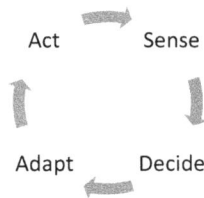

Act   Sense

Adapt   Decide

The insight to be taken from this diagram is that we need to be able to go around this cycle quickly, many times, evolving better responses each time.

Fighter jet pilots will recognize this as an "OODA loop" (Observe, Orient, Decide, Act), and they know that whoever can move through the loop the fastest will likely win the dogfight.[59] Forests must go through countless seasonal cycles to fall into a stable relationship with their environment. Ant colonies cycle through dozens of generations as their populations come into balance with their surroundings. Adaptive governance mirrors these cyclical processes. Like the ant colony, adaptive governance draws on the interactions of many actors and feeds information back into the system, recalibrating in response to constantly updated data. Like our forest ecosystem, adaptive governance is cyclical, developing new responses at the end of each cycle.

At the far end of adaptation is the recognition that some changes will need to be transformational of the system itself. Transformation can be thought of as the most extreme form of adaptation.[60] It refers to a deeper systemic change, a more radical shift in the underlying rules and attractor basins in a system.[61] I would argue that our planetary crisis is triggering a transformation in our relationship with energy, though the strong attractors of the fossil fuel industry are preventing it from being fully realized. In general, the scholarship on transformations is good at identifying when a transformation has happened (ex post facto) but less adept at shaping a transition that is underway or about to occur (ex ante).[62] This book suggests we need to become better at designing transformative governance for emerging risks.

While adaptive approaches to governance have demonstrated an extraordinarily strong ability to address complex social-environmental settings, we should be clear on some of the challenges. These can be described as three uncertainties around (i) objectives, (ii) context, and (iii) effectiveness.[63] Uncertainty over objectives points to the difficulty in setting clear goals in complex social settings. Many environmental governance regimes, for example, set goals of "sustainability" and "balance" as their main objectives. But it can be very difficult to pin these concepts down, and people may have wildly different interpretations of what constitutes success.[64] Objectives like "improving resilience" only punt the issue down the road: resilience to accomplish what? How do we know we have been effective and achieved an objective in a system that is constantly in flux? When we get to transformational governance – radical shifts to systems' underlying rules and patterns – the challenges become even more acute, and the gap between the present system and an imagined future becomes greater. What would a world populated by AI-enhanced humans look like and how should it be governed? What does successful governance of international threats to peace and security look like? We simply don't know.

There are also challenges related to the kind of participatory, inclusive processes called for by adaptive governance. One of the most important questions is how to decide which stakeholders should be involved. For example, we may agree that cities are crucial to environmental governance – given that much of the decision-making on resource usage is made at the city level – but who decides which cities should be included in a global process? We may agree that more actors need to be involved in our global financial architecture, but on what basis should new members be brought into the boards of the World Bank and the International Monetary Fund? One of the most challenging areas explored in Chapter 7 concerns the inclusion of future generations in global governance: who best represents the rights and needs of people who haven't yet been born?

Once we do involve many more stakeholders, we also must be careful of the biases that creep in when we try to make collective decisions.[65] Humans are especially bad at estimating and responding to risks in highly uncertain settings.[66] We are very susceptible to confirmation bias and tend to base our assessment of risks on our own experiences instead of reality.[67] In undergoverned settings, where there is often little reliable information generated by the governance structures themselves, these biases and uncertainties drive us to bad governance responses. We need a framework that helps us anticipate and deal with the shortcomings of humanity.

A framework for adaptive global governance design

How should leaders act when faced with complex global problems? What information should they consider? How can they grapple with highly ambiguous contexts? What decisions can be taken when the outcome of the decisions feels very uncertain? What are the right objectives to set for today's governance responses? Lack of clarity around these questions of context, purpose, and outcomes means busy leaders often defer decisions, or pursue ineffective policies just because they are already in place, or tinker around the edges of big problems because the risks appear lower.[68]

Drawing on the emerging practices of adaptation, I here offer a framework for designing governance in today's increasingly complex environment. The framework is intentionally quite general, offering a flexible set of steps and questions that can help decision-makers understand how a given system works, what objectives make sense, and whether a proposed course of action is likely to achieve objectives. Parts of it will be used in the later chapters to interrogate some of the big proposals being considered today, demonstrating the real-world utility of complexity thinking to global governance.

Step 1: Map the system

Strategists tend to start with objectives, setting organizational goals from the outset. But when dealing with complex systems, it is important to understand and map out the system before setting goals. This aids in understanding the "phase space" – the range of possible outcomes – in each moment. And crucially, it helps us understand both the challenge and the governance structures together, as part of a single system. There is no "right" way to undertake such a mapping, though most approaches involve some combination of the following steps:

a) Mapping how actors relate to each other, often displayed in a network showing relationships, scales, and hierarchies.[69]
b) Defining the key characteristics of a system, such as whether it displays very dense, tight-knit relationships, whether it has highly fragmented actors, or whether it is quite centralized.[70] A threshold question for some governance arenas is whether there is sufficient density and interconnectedness to constitute a complex system at all.[71]
c) Describing how change happens within a system. This builds off the mapping, but gets into questions of influence, how change may cascade across levels, and what past catalysts for change can be identified.[72] Often it requires us to describe how change has taken place in the past, building a sense of what cluster of variables tends to cause big shifts in systems.
d) Together, this helps us in identifying a system's "phase space," the range of potential outcomes at a given moment.

To be clear, mapping a system will not provide a complete, fully accurate, or fixed understanding of a complex system. As Cedric de Coning points out, "uncertainty is an intrinsic quality of complex systems," and we must become comfortable with incomplete knowledge.[73] But mapping can help to develop a sense of which actors are involved, how they relate to each other, and where the most important relationships lie in a system.

Step 2: Orient towards goals, adapt goals continuously

How can we set objectives in complex systems? On the one hand, complex systems display non-linear change, so overly restrictive goals that demand a specific link between input and outcome are not realistic. But a shortcoming of some adaptive governance approaches is an overriding focus on open, participatory processes involving many actors, which may fail to identify what these processes are meant to achieve. Including many stakeholders is necessary to develop an adaptive approach and set meaningful objectives, but it is not necessarily an end in itself. In highly competitive arenas, the involvement of conflicting stakeholders can make it more difficult to set common objectives. Take the UN General Assembly debates on matters of global security – disagreement at all levels is the norm. We need something between the overly rigid results-based budget input/output that we often see in multilateral processes, and the tendency of some adaptive approaches to be mired in participatory processes for their own sake.

Should resilience be the main goal? In the environmental arena, the end state is usually some form of sustainability, and systemic resilience is both the means and the end. Whether that is sustainable resource management, or "the capacity of complex and dynamic ecosystems to generate services for human well-being,"[74] the role of adaptive governance is often described in terms of sustainable, resilient systems.[75] Here, effective governance means helping ecosystems respond to shocks without breaking down.[76] Resilience makes sense when we speak of environmental issues: we must constantly adjust the human-environment relationship so that shocks do not overwhelm the system. And we can measure success by how well governance systems respond to new events and trends. For example, our response to climate change is clearly failing to prevent us from crossing planetary tipping points that in turn will disrupt human wellbeing.[77] The widespread death of coral reefs, melting of the Antarctic ice shelves, and massive loss of biodiversity all point to our current governance failure.

But it is more difficult to apply the concept of resilience to other fields of global governance, where the goals are less clear. What does "resilient" governance of AI look like? How can we speak of resilience in the context of global security, where states and peoples have highly competitive goals? Does it make sense to think of a resilient financial system when the current financial architecture is deeply unfair to most of the world? There is a risk that resilience – without something else – could lead to unintended outcomes, including the perpetuation of unequal systems.

Here, we can supplement resilience with goal-setting. While we tend to think of governance as regulation and rules, goal-setting can orient a global system in a specific direction. The Millennium Development and Sustainable Development Goals are examples of what some scholars call "problem-oriented governance."[78] This is policy design that takes a specific set of challenges as a starting point and then asks what approaches are most likely to resolve those challenges.[79] China's experiments with goal-oriented urbanization are another example.[80]

As explored in Chapter 3, one goal of environmental governance could be, "avoiding dangerous anthropogenic interference with the climate system." For AI (Chapter 6), it might be "mitigate the risks associated with AI development while maximizing its benefits to humanity." Or for longer-term risks (Chapter 7), it might be "develop plans for today that also meaningfully take into account the needs of unborn generations." Common across problem- or goal-oriented governance is the establishment of a broad objective, identifying relevant targets to show progress, and prioritizing the use of resources towards the targets.[81] Goal-setting can include rule-making: for example, the SDGs resulted in a wide range of national legislation designed to achieve the targets. The goal of replenishing whale populations was achieved by regulating whaling. We have an ozone layer in large part due to the prohibition of certain aerosols.

It may seem intuitive to say, "we need to identify our objectives," but it is surprisingly elusive in real-world practice. I once asked a senior leader in the UN what the peace and security goals for the organization were. After a long pause, she said, "we need to do prevention better." When I pressed her how we know we are doing prevention better, or what that might look like, she drew a blank and ended up speaking about needing more resources to do more prevention. This is a great (if depressing) example of linear thinking: if we can do X amount of conflict prevention with our current resources, then if we add Y amount of additional resources, we will achieve X + Y amount of prevention. This kind of thinking leads to cookie-cutter approaches and a lack of innovative thinking within a stagnant bureaucracy.

The important lesson here is to be demand-driven and flexible, asking what specific problem within a system needs to be addressed and being open to a non-linear progress towards that goal. There is a risk that being too goal oriented will lock us back into gradualism and a sense that systems will proceed incrementally. With issues like climate change, it can be extraordinarily difficult to know when "dangerous anthropogenic interference in the climate system" has been avoided. Some combination of goal-setting and rule-making may be needed, and we may need to consider a range of subordinate goals that help us understand when we need to shift course. Most importantly, we will need an approach to goals that changes over time, revisiting objectives based on constantly updated information.

Step 3: Design a "fit" response

One of Darwin's most important and enduring concepts was that of fitness. The descendants of an organism will have traits that vary slightly from those of their parents. Those traits make them either slightly more or slightly less able to survive in their environment. Beneficial traits have a greater tendency to be passed along by species that survive longer, so over time an organism will develop a better "fitness" to its environment.[82]

Goal-oriented governance mimics that fitness process through design. We set a goal and then evaluate which approaches are most effective at achieving that goal, replicating and resourcing approaches that demonstrate the best fit. Over time – and over many cycles of testing – we can evolve a fit response. Adaptive governance suggests that we must continually test, validate, and modify hypotheses, feeding information back into the design of future interventions. In some settings, it may be necessary to try many approaches at the same time, allowing the system to provide feedback on which ones work best.[83] Just as natural selection shows how unfit organisms are weeded out, adaptive governance will discard ineffective approaches through testing.[84]

One promising technique is to develop a theory of change linked to the problem statement. For example, a theory of change in environmental governance could be "if sufficient financial incentives are provided for public and private investment in renewable energy, it will accelerate decarbonization and keep us below 2 degrees of global warming." There are many devils in details – such as what it would take to generate such financial flows, or how existing path dependencies in our energy system might resist such change – but at least we start with a link between the proposed actions and a desired end state. If there has been a good mapping of the networks of actors involved in environmental governance, we can start to see how and where these incentives might begin to generate systemic change.

Finding the right "fit" is the main goal.[85] In general terms, fitness refers to the match between the problem and the solution.[86] It can be assessed in several ways:

- *Spatial*: Does the governance approach cover the geographic reach of the problem? For example, national regulations of water usage might run into the reality that a river crosses national boundaries. This would be a poor spatial fit. Equally, a global treaty regulating pandemic responses between countries could be a poor match for local interactions amongst doctors and hospitals. The concept of polycentric governance, consisting of many independent units operating in ways that account for each other, can help address the problem of spatial fit and produce more adaptable systems.[87]
- *Temporal*: Does the governance approach match up with the timespan of change within a system? Invasive species may destroy ecosystems much faster than the cumbersome legislative processes meant to limit their distribution. The UN Security Council's need to determine a threat to international peace and security before acting means that most of the tipping points around violent conflict are already passed by the time it passes a resolution. UNAIDS was created during the height of the AIDS epidemic and still maintains a large bureaucracy focused on a problem that no longer has the same global impact. One of the most important challenges across the global governance arenas is the fact that action needs to happen now, but many of the effects may be decades into the future.
- *Flexible*: Is the governance approach able to address new, unforeseen changes in the system? For example, facing a food shortage, many governments have historically invested in monocultures that increased yield and efficiencies. But this response also exposed the agricultural sector to greater vulnerability to single crop failure, in some cases leading to massive food shortages. In arenas like AI and biological weapons, our governance regimes similarly may allow for crucial tipping points and cascade effects to occur before the response kicks in, essentially acting after the horse has bolted from the barn. Or we may overreact and over-regulate in the short term, baking in longer-term, systemic risks.

Here I have noticed a tendency to try to match problems immediately with institutions. In Chapter 3, we see how the planetary challenges of climate change have generated a range of proposals to establish global bodies tasked with planetary oversight. Will a "global environmental court" be able to adjudicate the problem of environmental change? Does it make sense to try to cobble together all our environmental treaties into a single hegemonic planetary one? Maybe. But complexity thinking suggests that scaling and fitting governance responses can be less about fixed institutions and more about activation, linking, and orchestration across levels.[88] Creating a governance structure the size of the planet may sound good, but it can also result in other fit problems, including the difficulty of adapting such a big structure to new systemic shocks. In some cases, building networks of actors that can connect local, regional, national, and international actors can be more powerful than creating a top-down governance body.[89] In fact, guiding the self-organization processes of some systems may mean that a small number of "first movers" triggers a snowball effect and brings others with it.[90]

An important lesson is not to assume that more input equals more output in complex systems. Even those who understand the way complex systems work intuitively expect linear relationships between cause and effect.[91] For example, if a small amount of foreign aid slightly increases economic growth, we tend to expect that more aid should produce greater growth. But as a recent study demonstrated, foreign investment can often have the undesired effect of increasing conflict risks,[92] or in some cases can unintentionally bolster authoritarian tendencies.[93] Similarly, "more governance" in the form of bigger, stronger institutions will not necessarily lead to better fit. Tom Hale has pointed out that more governance processes and institutions have unintentionally contributed to greater gridlock around crucial global issues.[94] It may take several iterations and failures to find the right fit that delivers the outcomes we need. But if we have already poured the concrete on an institution, we will miss an opportunity to adapt.

Step 4: Test robustness and resilience

How do we know if an approach is working? Particularly in the realm of global governance, there is seldom a "mission accomplished" moment. The world carries on, the challenges shift, we are never finished. And if we only measure success around an abstract notion of resilience, or the circular concepts of "good governance," we may end up with systems that don't deliver the outcomes we want but still manage to carry on for long periods of time. Our global financial system is extraordinarily resilient, but few people would suggest it is succeeding in addressing issues of inequality or underdevelopment very effectively.

But resilience paired with robustness could offer us a way to know whether our approach is working towards our desired set of objectives. If resilience is about the system absorbing shocks, robustness is a related term that focuses more on designing systems that can deliver in conditions of uncertainty.[95] As Steven Popper wrote, "A plan as robust if it is one that performs well, compared with the alternatives, over a wide variety of plausible futures."[96] For example, we could ask, "Is our current global health infrastructure robust?" Part of the answer would be based on how it has done so far in terms of protecting against major diseases. But we also could imagine a range of future health crises – a more dangerous version of COVID-19, a biological weapon created by a malicious actor, an acceleration of immune-resistant infections – and then test them against our current system. The extent to which the system was able to survive and deliver agreed-upon outcomes would be its measure of resilience and robustness.

Measuring robustness and resilience should be both a forward- and a backward-looking exercise. It should be backward-looking because we must evaluate how a system has done over time. For example, there is ample evidence to indicate that our governance of the ozone layer has been extraordinarily effective, based on several decades of information following the Montreal Protocol showing a retreating hole in the ozone. But we also must be forward-looking, imagining plausible scenarios in the future and identifying how our governance system might address them.[97] Success may look more like some form of anticipatory governance, measured by "the ability of global networks to anticipate and reorganize in the face of new information and changing circumstances."[98]

Step 5: Rinse, repeat, ... transform?

Every complex system evolves via feedback loops, passing information back into the system and adapting based on the changed circumstances. Returning to our ant colony, as the ants touch antennae, crucial information about the changing world around them is cycled back into the colony. This is the basis for the colony to make collective decisions whether to flee an oncoming attack, go out to gather more food, or prepare for a cold winter. Our global governance systems also need to feed information back in, constantly adjusting our responses to a changing world. The coming chapters will focus on how to create fast, action-oriented information flows that can help us respond to imminent threshold breaches and tipping points. Like a fighter pilot involved in a dogfight, we will aim to cycle through the observe-orient-decide-act process as quickly as possible.

The key distinction between the ant colony and our global governance systems is that we can design our own feedback loops. Yes, a certain amount of feedback happens via our collective everyday behaviors (e.g. we all drive cars, keeping the demand for gas high and contributing to how the system responds to environmental regulation). But our global policies are also a form of feedback loop; they create rules that respond to new stimuli and they constantly produce new information.[99] Facing a growing hole in the ozone, we agreed a treaty regulating aerosol sprays that changed how all of us behave today. All our global rules, from the prohibition against torture, to the laws of international trade, to the limits placed on whaling are a form of feedback into our governance systems.

This does not mean all forms of feedback are the same. Some global governance structures do not efficiently feed information back into the system, or they distort the information as it passes into the system's response. The Universal Periodic Review (UPR) of human rights is a good example. While there are tens of thousands of actors involved in promoting and protecting human rights worldwide, the UPR only allows national governments to report on the human rights situation in their respective countries. That means the global human rights system only has partial information feedback, leading to serious limitations on how quickly the system can adapt to emerging human rights issues.

In some cases, the feedback process can incrementally adjust a system to evolving settings on the ground.[100] But what happens when a system is unable to perform the functions we need? In many arenas, we may find ourselves trapped in an undesirable attractor basin where the path dependency of the system is too difficult to change without a more fundamental transformation. Those who have pushed for an end to capitalism as the dominant form of global finance often point to the exploitative, unfair, and unsustainable outcomes of a system based on infinite growth of capital.[101] They claim that the entire capitalist system must change if we are to meet the needs of humans and the planet at the same time. Such a drastic change may be needed, but so far global leaders have offered no pathway to get from the capitalist system that dominates the world today to anything else.

In these cases, it can become necessary to consider more radical transformative changes to the system, generating new rules and policies that will break us out of our existing attractor basins.[102] This notion of transformation refers to the capacity to create a fundamentally new system "defining and creating new stability landscapes by introducing new components and ways of making a living, thereby changing the state variables, and often the scale, that define the system."[103] Such transformative moments include the Industrial Revolution, the end of the Cold War, and perhaps the emerging reality of AI.[104] President Biden's 2022 Inflation Reduction Act could be considered at least a partially transformative approach, aiming to shift enough of our incentives around renewal and fossil fuel energy so that a new set of relationships will emerge and accelerate a transition off carbon.

From a global governance perspective, a tension may arise between the need to maintain resilience in an existing system (upon which billions of people depend for their day-to-day livelihoods) and building towards a moment of transformation. These tensions are very real. During the 2008 financial crisis, many pundits suggested it was a good time to transform the global financial system, ending the ways capitalism tends to drive inequalities. But such a transformation could have been enormously disruptive, potentially causing a much bigger downturn that could have cost trillions of dollars.[105] The decision was taken (by those most likely to benefit from it) to patch up the existing system through bailouts.

Ultimately, a key lesson is that we need to be aware of what feedback is telling us: are we able to adjust existing systems to achieve the goals we want, or is something more radical needed to change the "phase space" (and if so, what are the potential upsides and downsides of pursuing that more radical pathway)?

Putting it all together

Evolution is composed of three steps: (1) trait variation, (2) selection, and (3) inheritance. Those organisms able to adapt to their surroundings survive and propagate; those that cannot, die off. Adaptive governance mimics evolution by adopting three similar steps: (1) experimentation, (2) selection/adoption, and (3) inheritance (moving forward with a selected approach).[106] The advantage we have as conscious beings is that we can help to shape all three stages, choosing to adopt traits that help us accelerate towards a collective goal. The disadvantage is that we are creatures of habit and path dependency, often pursuing existing models because they are familiar, or because they are where we have a job, or because it just feels like too big a task to reform an entire system. Our ideology also gets in the way, telling us that certain approaches are "good" even when their outcomes are clearly against our interests.

These human limitations mean we often fail to generate what nature has done for billions of years: diversity. We tend to circle back to the same approaches, unwilling to experiment, afraid to test innovative ideas because they might fail, or we are worried they might be too disruptive. Adaptation only works in conditions of diversity, where iterations try and fail, and where decision-making in the face of uncertainty is the norm. This does not mean we end up with an infinite number of governance models. In nature, organisms display an extraordinarily strong tendency to transform into crabs, a process called carcinization.[107] This is probably because a crab-like organism has important benefits over other evolutionary options. It may be that some governance models are equally crab-like, versatile and effective across a wide range of tasks and arenas. But we will only find out if we enable adaptation. We need to think of global governance as an evolutionary life cycle, where our ability to generate a wide variety of testable options could mean the difference between life and death.[108] Adaptive governance demands that we not only think out of the box, but that we govern out of it.[109]

Notes

1 R. Jervis, *System Effects: Complexity in Political and Social Life* (Princeton, NJ: Princeton University Press, 1997), 243–245; R. Keohane & J Nye, "Power and interdependence," *Survival* 15(4) (1973): 158–165.
2 D. Byrne, *Complexity Theory and the Social Sciences, An Introduction* (New York: Routledge Press, 1998); R. Geyer & S. Rihani, *Complexity and Public Policy: A New Approach to 21st Century Politics, Policy and Society* (New York: Routledge, 2010); G. Room, *Complexity, Institutions and Public Policy: Agile Decision-making in a Turbulent World* (Cheltenham, UK: Edward Elgar, 2010); G. Morçöl, *A Complexity Theory for Public Policy* (New York: Routledge, 2012); M. Rhodes et al., *Public Management and Complexity Theory: Richer Decision-making in Public Services* (New York: Routledge, 2011); W. Kickert, E. Klijn, and J. Koppenjan, *Managing complex networks: strategies for the public sector* (London: Sage, 1997).
3 M. Woolcock, "Towards a plurality of methods in project evaluation: a contextualised approach to understanding impact trajectories and efficacy," *Journal of*

Development Effectiveness 1(1) (2009): 1–14; D. Green, *From Poverty to Power*, Oxfam e-books: available at: https://oxfamblogs.org/fp2p/; B. Ramalingam, *Aid on the Edge of Chaos: Rethinking International Cooperation in a Complex World* (Oxford: Oxford University Press, 2013); R. Kleinfeld, "Improving Development Aid Design and Implementation: Plan for Sailboats Not Traintracks," Carnegie Endowment for International Peace (2015).

4 E. Kavalski, *World Politics at the Edge of Chaos: Reflections on Complexity and Global Life* (Albany: State University of New York, 2015). J. Donnelly, *Systems, Relations, and the Structures of International Societies* (Cambridge University Press, 2023). See also, A. Bousquet & S. Curtis, "Beyond models and metaphors: complexity theory, systems thinking and international relations," *Cambridge Review of International Affairs*, 24:01 (2011): 43–62.

5 C. Hunt, *UN Peace Operations and International Policing: Negotiating Complexity, Assessing Impact and Learning to Learn* (London: Routledge, 2015).

6 B. Ramalingham & H. Jones, "Exploring the Science of Complexity: Ideas and Implications for Development and Humanitarian Efforts," Overseas Development Institute, Working Paper 285 (2008).

7 J. Murray, T. Webb, S. Wheatley, eds, *Complexity Theory and Law: Mapping an Emergent Jurisprudence* (New York: Routledge, 2018).

8 K. Richardson, G. Mathieso, and P. Cilliers, "Complexity Thinking and Military Operational Analysis," in *Knots, Lace and Tartan: Making Sense of Complex Human Systems in Military Operations Research*, Kurt Richardson, ed. (Litchfield Park, AZ: ISE Publishing); L. Moe & M. Müller, *Reconfiguring Intervention: Complexity, Resilience and the 'Local Turn' in Counterinsurgent Warfare* (London: Palgrave MacMillan, 2017). E. Brusset, C. de Coning, and B. Hughes, *Complexity Thinking for Peacebuilding Practice and Evaluation* (London: Palgrave Macmillan, 2017).

9 V. Galaz, ed., *Global Challenges, Governance, and Complexity Applications and Frontiers* (Edward Elgar, 2019); A. Orsini, & P. Le Prestre, "Complex Systems and International Governance" *International Studies Review* (2019).

10 See, C. Pollitt, "Complexity theory and evolutionary public administration: a sceptical afterword," in *Managing Complex Governance Systems* (Routledge, 2009), 229 (critiquing complexity as a hodgepodge of other disciplines).

11 R. Kim, "Is Global Governance Fragmented, Polycentric, or Complex? The State of the Art of the Network Approach," *International Studies Review* 22(4) (2020): 903–933; D. Kenett, M. Perc, and S. Boccaletti, "Networks of Networks: An Introduction," *Chaos, Solitons and Fractals* 80 (2015): 1–6.

12 T. Weiss & R. Wilkinson, "Rethinking Global Governance? Complexity, Authority, Power, Change," *International Studies Quarterly* 58 (2014): 207–215.

13 See, James N. Rosenau, "Governance in the Twenty-first Century," Global Governance 1, no. 1 (winter 1995): 15.

14 See, F. Fukuyama, "What Is Governance?" *Governance* 26(3) (2013).

15 S. Krasner & T. Risse, "External Actors, State-Building, and Service Provision in Areas of Limited Statehood: Introduction," *Governance* 27(4) (2014): 549.

16 L. Finkelstein, "What Is Global Governance?" *Global Governance* 1 (1995): 367–372.

17 O. Young, *Grand Challenges for Planetary Governance: Global Order in Turbulent Times* (Cheltenham: Edward Elgar, 2021), 36.

18 L. Finkelstein, "What Is Global Governance?" *Global Governance* 1 (1995): 367–372.

19 For an excellent overview of global governance, see, T. Weiss, *Global Governance: Why? What? Whither?* (New York: Polity Press, 2016).

20 See, J. Kooiman, *Governing as governance* (London: Sage, 2003).
21 H. Bull, *The Anarchical Society: A Study of Order in World Politics*, 2nd edition (New York: Columbia University Press, 1977), 57. See also, B. Buzan, C. Jones, and R. Little, *The Logic of Anarchy: Neorealism to Structural Realism* (New York: Columbia University Press, 1993).
22 See, e.g., C. Hill & L. Lynn, "Is hierarchical governance in decline? Evidence from empirical research," *Journal of Public Administration Research and Theory* 15 (2004): 173–195; A. Jordan, "The European Union: an evolving system of multilevel governance...or government?" *Policy & Politics* 29 (2001): 193–208.
23 See, J. Padgett, "Evolvability of Organizations and Institutions," in D. Wilson & A. Kirman, eds, *Complexity and Evolution: Toward a New Synthesis for Economics* (Cambridge, MA: MIT Press, 2016).
24 See R. Väyrynen, "Norms, Compliance and Enforcement of Global Governance," in R. Väyrynen, ed., *A Pioneer in International Relations, Scholarship and Policy-Making. Pioneers in Arts, Humanities, Science, Engineering, Practice* (Springer, 2023).
25 K. Alter & K. Raustiala, "The Rise of International Regime Complexity," *Annual Review of Law and Social Science* 14 (2018): 329–349; A. Orsini, J. Morin, and O. Young, "Regime Complexes: A Buzz, a Boom, or a Boost for Global Governance?" *Global Governance: A Review of Multilateralism and International Organizations* 19 (1) (2013): 27–39.
26 See, e.g., T. Porter "Global governance as configurations of state/non-state activity," in *Advances in Global Governance*, J. Whitman, ed. (Basingstoke: Palgrave Macmillan, 2009), 87–104.
27 See, M. Lee, G. Drop, and J. Wiesel, "Taking the State (Back) Out? Statehood and the Delivery of Collective Goods," *Governance* 27(4) (2014).
28 For more on the role of the state, see, J. Migdal, *State in Society: Studying How States and Societies Transform and Constitute One Another* (New York: Cambridge University Press, 2001); E. Grande & L. Pauly, eds, *Complex Sovereignty* (Toronto, Canada: University of Toronto Press, 2007); C. Pierson, *The Modern State* (New York: Routledge, 2012).
29 H. Spruyt, *The Sovereign State and Its Competitors* (Princeton, N.J.: Princeton University Press, 1994).
30 N. Krisch, "Liquid Authority in Global Governance," *International Theory* 9(2) (2017): 237–260.
31 D. Osborne & T. Gaebler, *Reinventing Government: How the Entrepreneurial Spirit Is Transforming the Public Sector* (New York, N.Y: Plume, 1992).
32 A.M. Slaughter, *The Chessboard and the Web: Strategies of Connection in a Networked World* (New Haven: Yale University Press, 2018).
33 T. Weiss, *Global Governance: Why? What? Whither?* (New York: Polity Press, 2016).
34 K. Dooley, "The Butterfly Effect of the Butterfly Effect," *Nonlinear Dynamics, Psychology, and Life Sciences*, vol. 13, no. 3 (2009).
35 See, e.g., R. Rotberg, *When States Fail: Causes and Consequences* (Princeton: Princeton University Press, 2004).
36 T. Risse, *Governance Without a State: Policies and Politics in Areas of Limited Statehood* (New York: Columbia University Press, 2013); Z. Mampilly, *Rebel Rulers: Insurgent Governance and Civilian Life during War* (Ithaca: Cornell University Press, 2011); J. Rosenau & E. Czempiel, *Governance without Government: Order and Change in World Politics* (Cambridge: Cambridge University Press, 2010); P. Jackson, "Warlords as Alternative Forms of Governance," *Small Wars and Insurgencies* 14 (2003): 131–150; R. Hall & T. Bierstecker, eds, *The Emergence of Private Authority in Global Governance*

(Cambridge: Cambridge University Press, 2009); C. Cheng, *Extralegal Groups in Post-Conflict Liberia: How Trade Makes the State* (Oxford: Oxford University Press, 2018).

37 A. Frank & E. Bartels, eds, *Adaptive Engagement for Undergoverned Spaces: Concepts, Challenges, and Prospects for New Approaches* (RAND, 2002), available at: www.rand.org/t/RRA1275-1.

38 See, A. Chatzky and J. McBride, "China's Massive Belt and Road Initiative," Council on Foreign Relations, 28 January 2020; C. Mott, "Don't Fear China's Belt and Road Initiative," *Survival* 62(4) (2020); G. Wang, "Towards a Rule-Based Belt and Road Initiative – Necessity and Directions," *Journal of International and Comparative Law* 6(1) (2019).

39 S. Borgerson, "The Coming Arctic Boom: As the Ice Melts, the Region Heats Up," Foreign Affairs, vol. 92, no. 4, 2013; E. Rowe, *Arctic Governance: Power in Cross-Border Cooperation* (Manchester: Manchester University Press, 2018).

40 S. Flanagan & B. McClintock, "How Joe Biden Can Galvanize Space Diplomacy," Politico, 15 January 2021; B. McClintock et al., "Responsible Space Behavior for the New Space Era: Preserving the Province of Humanity" (Santa Monica, Calif.: RAND Corporation, 2021).

41 New Zealand Ministry of Foreign Affairs and Trade, "The Application of International Law to State Activity in Cyberspace," 1 December 2020.

42 For a foundational discussion of this issue, see S. Russell and P. Norvig, *Artificial Intelligence: A Modern Approach, 2nd ed.* (Upper Saddle River, N.J.: Pearson Education, Inc., 2005).

43 A. Vincent et al., eds, *Decision Making Under Deep Uncertainty: From Theory to Practice* (Cham, Switzerland: Springer, 2019).

44 The first instance I could find of the term was in T. Dietz, E. Ostrom, and P. Stern, "The struggle to govern the commons," *Science* 302 (2003): 1907–1912.

45 C. Folke, "Social-ecological systems and adaptive governance of the commons," *Ecological Research* 22 (2007): 14–15. See also, B. Chaffin et al., "A Decade of Adaptive Governance Scholarship: Synthesis and Future Directions." *Ecology and Society*, 19(3) (2014); L. Hasselman, "Adaptive management; adaptive co-management; adaptive governance: what's the difference?" *Australasian Journal of Environmental Management*, 24:1 (2007): 31-46; R. Brunner et al., *Adaptive governance: integrating science, policy, and decision making* (New York: Columbia University Press, 2005).

46 T. Dietz, E. Ostrom, and P. Stern, "The struggle to govern the commons," *Science* 302 (2003): 1907–1912.

47 For a literature review on adaptive governance, see L. Sharma-Wallace, S. Velarde, A. Wreford, "Adaptive governance good practice: Show me the evidence!" *Journal of Environmental Management* 222 (2018): 174–184. See also, B. Walker et al., "Resilience, adaptability and transformability in social-ecological systems," *Ecology and Society* 9(2) (2004): 5.

48 D. Lake, "The organizational ecology of global governance," *European journal of international relations* 27 (2) (2021): 345–368. See also, R. Djalante, "Adaptive governance and resilience: the role of multi-stakeholder platforms in disaster risk reduction," *Natural Hazards & Earth System Sciences* 12 (2012): 2933–2945; R. Djalante, C. Holley, and F. Thomalla, "Adaptive governance and managing resilience to natural hazards," *International Journal of Disaster Risk Sciences* 2:1 (2011): 14.

49 F. Berkes & H. Ross, "Panarchy and community resilience: Sustainability science and policy implications," *Environmental Science & Policy* 61 (2016): 185–193.

50 See, B. Chaffin & L. Gunderson, "Emergence, institutionalization and renewal: Rhythms of adaptive governance in complex social-ecological systems," *Journal*

of Environmental Management 165 (2016) 81–87; C. Folke et al., "Adaptive governance of social ecological systems," *Annual Review of Environment and Resources,* 30 (1) (2005): 441–473.

51 See, e.g., C. Folke, "Resilience: the emergence of a perspective for social-ecological systems analyses," *Global Environmental Change* 16 (2006): 253–267; R. Nelson, M. Howden, and M. Smith, "Using adaptive governance to rethink the way science supports Australian drought policy," *Environmental Science & Policy* 11 (2008): 588–601; C. Pahl-Wostl, "A conceptual framework for analysing adaptive capacity and multi-level learning processes in resource governance regimes," *Global Environmental Change* 19 (2009): 354–365; R. Biggs et al., "Toward principles for enhancing the resilience of ecosystem services," *Annual Review of Environment and Resources* 37(1) (2012).

52 See, D. Armitage & R. Plummer, *Adaptive Capacity and Environmental Governance* (Berlin: Springer-Verlag, 2010); B. Chaffin et al., "A Decade of Adaptive Governance Scholarship: Synthesis and Future Directions," *Ecology and Society,* 19(3) (2014).

53 See, e.g., C. Walch, "Adaptive governance in the developing world: disaster risk reduction in the State of Odisha, India," *Climate and Development* 11:3 (2019): 238–252; B. Cosens et al., "The role of law in adaptive governance," *Ecological Society* 22(1) (2017): 1–30. X. Cao et al., "Linking Adaptive Governance, Strategic Flexibility and Responsible Innovation: Evidence from China," *International Journal of Innovation and Technology Management* (2023).

54 G. Wilson, "What is adaptive management?", USAID Learning Lab, 11 November 2016, available at: https://usaidlearninglab.org/lab-notes/what-adaptive-management.

55 C. de Coning, "Adaptive peacebuilding," *International Affairs* 94 (2) (2018): 301–317.

56 See, e.g., L. Baxter, "Adaptive Financial Regulation and RegTech: A Concept Article on Realistic Protection for Victims of Bank Failures," *Duke Law Journal* 66, no. 3 (December 2016): 567–604; S. Li, "Algorithmic Financial Regulation: Limits of Computing Complex Adaptive Systems," *American University Business Law Review* 13(2) (2023); X. Insausti, "Distributed Clustering Algorithm for Adaptive Pandemic Control," in *IEEE Access,* vol. 9 (2021): 160688–160696; W. Chang, S. Patil, and P. Tetlock, "Accountability and Adaptive Performance Under Uncertainty: A Long-Term View," *Judgement and Decision Making* 12(6) (2017): 610–626.

57 RAND. See also, I.N.S. Djenontin & A. Meadow, "The Art of Co-Production of Knowledge in Environmental Sciences and Management: Lessons from International Practice," *Environmental Management,* Vol. 61 (2018).

58 See, e.g., H. De Czege, "Systemic Operational Design: Learning and Adapting in Complex Missions – Complexity on the modern battlefield demands a new professional culture that embraces collaborative adaptation in operational art," *Military Review* 89(1) (2009): 2.

59 T. Hightower, "Boyd's OODA loop and how we use it," *Tactical Response* (2014).

60 S. Park et al., "Informing adaptation responses to climate change through theories of transformation," *Global Environmental Change* (2011).

61 B. Chaffin et al., "Transformative Environmental Governance," *Annual Review of Environment and Resources* 41 (2016): 399–423.

62 See, J. Patterson et al., "Transformations towards sustainability: Emerging approaches, critical reflections, and a research agenda," Earth System Governance Working Paper No. 33 (Lund and Amsterdam: Earth System Governance Project, 2015).

63 J. Rijke et al., "Fit-for-purpose governance: A framework to make adaptive governance operational," *Environmental Science & Policy* 22 (2012): 73–84.

64 See, S. Smith, "The politics of social–ecological resilience and sustainable socio-technical transitions. *Ecology and Society* 15 (2010): 11; W. Adger et al., "Governance for sustainability: towards a 'thick' analysis of environmental decision making," *Environment and Planning* 35 (2003): 1095–1110.

65 D. Kahneman, P. Slovic, and A. Tversky, eds, *Judgment Under Uncertainty: Heuristics and Biases* (Cambridge, United Kingdom: Cambridge University Press, 1982); S. Sherman & E. Corty, "Cognitive Heuristics," in R. Wyer & T. Srull, eds, *Handbook of Social Cognition, Vol. 1* (Mahwah, N.J.: Lawrence Erlbaum Associates, 1984).

66 G. Loewenstein et al., "Risk as Feelings," *Psychological Bulletin* 127(2) (2001); J. Lerner & L. Tiedens, "Portrait of the Angry Decision Maker: How Appraisal Tendencies Shape Anger Influence on Decision Making," *Journal of Behavioral Decision Making* 19(2) (2006).

67 J. Klayman, "Varieties of Confirmation Bias," *Psychology of Learning and Motivation* 32 (1995); R. Nickerson, "Confirmation Bias: A Ubiquitous Phenomenon in Many Guises," *Review of General Psychology* 2(2) (1998).

68 See, J. Rijke et al., "Fit-for-purpose governance: A framework to make adaptive governance operational," *Environmental Science & Policy* 22 (2012): 73–84.

69 See, A. Barabási, "Taming Complexity," *Nature Physics* 1 (2) (2005): 68–70; A. Barabási, "The Architecture of Complexity: From Network Structure to Human Dynamics," *IEEE Control Systems Magazine*, August 2007: 33–42; B. Campbell et al., "Latent Influence Networks in Global Environmental Politics," *PLOS One* 14 (3) (2019).

70 R. Kim, "Is Global Governance Fragmented, Polycentric, or Complex? The State of the Art of the Network Approach," *International Studies Review* 22(4) (2020): 903–933.

71 See, F. Zelli, L. Gerrits, and I. Möller, "Global Governance in Complex Times: Exploring New Concepts and Theories on Institutional Complexity," *Complexity, Governance & Networks* 6(1) (2020): 1–13.

72 P. Davis et al., "Understanding and Influencing Public Support for Insurgency and Terrorism," RAND Corporation, 2012, 113–209.

73 C. de Coning, "Adaptive peacebuilding," *International Affairs* 94 (2) (2018): 301–317. See also, B. Hughes, "Peace operations and the political: a pacific reminder of what really matters," *Journal of International Peace Operations* 16 (2012): 116.

74 P. Olsson et al., "Enhancing the fit through adaptive co-management: creating and maintaining bridging functions for matching scales in the Kristianstads Vattenrike Biosphere Reserve, Sweden," *Ecology and Society* 12(1) (2007): 28.

75 See, e.g., A. Lynch & R. Brunner, "Learning from climate variability: adaptive governance and the Pacific ENSO applications center," *Weather Climate and Society* 2 (2010): 311–319; P. Sanginga, R. Kamugisha, and A. Martin, "Strengthening social capital for adaptive governance of natural resources: a participatory learning and action research on bylaws reforms in Uganda," *Society & Natural Resources* 23 (2010): 695–710.

76 B. Walker & D. Salt, "A Resilient World," in *Resilience Practice* (Island Press, Washington, DC, 2012).

77 See, J. Rockström et al., "Planetary boundaries: Exploring the safe operating space for humanity," *Ecology and Society* (2009).

78 Q. Mayne, J. de Jong, and F. Fernandez-Monge, "State Capabilities for Problem-Oriented Governance," *Perspectives on Public Management and Governance* 3(1) (2019).

79 Another term that Oran Young and others use is "institutional diagnostics," which he defines as "diagnosing the essential features of specific problems and then devising institutional arrangements that are carefully crafted to address the key issues." O. Young, *Governing Complex Systems: Social Capital for the Anthropocene* (MIT Press Direct, 2017), 25–44.

80 See, J. Guo, & M. Liu, Experimental state rescaling, goal-oriented governance, and urban transformation in China: The case of Lanzhou," *Geoforum* 137 (2022): 72–82.

81 M. Mazzucato, "Mission-oriented innovation policies: challenges and opportunities," *Industrial and Corporate Change*, vol. 27(5) (2018): 803–815.

82 See, D. Roff, "Defining fitness in evolutionary models," *Journal of Genetics* 87 (2008): 339–348.

83 C. de Coning, "Adaptive peacebuilding," *International Affairs* 94 (2) (2018): 301–317.

84 J. Rijke et al., "Fit-for-purpose governance: A framework to make adaptive governance operational," *Environmental Science & Policy* 22 (2012): 73–84.

85 P. Olsson et al., "Enhancing the fit through adaptive co-management: creating and maintaining bridging functions for matching scales in the Kristianstads Vattenrike Biosphere Reserve, Sweden," *Ecology and Society* 12(1) (2007).

86 V. Galaz et al., "The Problem of Fit among Biophysical Systems, Environmental and Resource Regimes, and Broader Governance Systems: Insights and Emerging Challenges," in O. Young, L. King, and H. Schroeder, eds., *Institutions and Environmental Change: Principal Findings, Applications, and Research Frontiers* (Cambridge, MA, 2008; online ed., MIT Press Scholarship Online, 22 August 2013).

87 K. Carlisle & R. Gruby, "Polycentric Systems of Governance: A Theoretical Model for the Commons," *Policy Studies Journal* 47(4) (2019); E. Ostrom, "Polycentric Systems for Coping with Collective Action and Global Environmental Change," *Global Environmental Change* 20 (2010): 550–557.

88 G. Marks & L. Hooghe, "Contrasting visions of multi-level governance," in I. Bache & M. Flinders, eds, *Multi-level Governance* (Oxford: Oxford University Press, 2004), 15–30.

89 L. Gunderson, "Resilience, flexibility and adaptive management – antidotes for spurious certitude?" *Conservation Ecology* 3(1) (1999): 7.

90 P. Olsson, C. Folke, and F. Berkes, "Adaptive co-management for building social-ecological resilience," *Environmental Management* 34 (2004): 75–90.

91 R. Jervis, *System effects: complexity in political and social life* (Princeton: Princeton University Press, 1997), 6.

92 B. Ganson et al., "International Finance Corporation Projects and Increased Armed Conflict" (14 August 2023). Available at: SSRN: http://dx.doi.org/10.2139/ssrn.4540583.

93 A. Day et al., "Peacebuilding and Authoritarianism: The Unintended Consequences of UN Engagement in Post-Conflict Settings," UN University Centre for Policy Research, 2020.

94 T. Hale, D. Held, and K. Young, *Gridlock: Why Global Cooperation is Failing when We Need It Most* (London: Polity, 2013).

95 J. Anderies et al., "Aligning Key Concepts for Global Change Policy: Robustness, Resilience, and Sustainability," *Ecology and Society* 18(2) (2013).

96 S. Popper, "Designing a Robust Decision-Based National Security Policy Process: Strategic Choices for Uncertain Times," in *Adaptive Engagement for Undergoverned Spaces: Concepts, Challenges, and Prospects for New Approaches*, A. Frank & E. Bartels, eds, available at: www.rand.org/t/RRA1275-1.

97   In general terms, this aligns with Herbert Simon's approach of positioning outcomes between future opportunity and threat. H. Simon, "Rational Choice and
the Structure of the Environment," *Psychological Review* 63(2) (1956).

98   V. Galaz et al., "Global networks and global change-induced tipping points,"
International Environmental Agreements 16 (2016): 189–221.

99   J. Anderies et al., "Aligning Key Concepts for Global Change Policy: Robustness,
Resilience, and Sustainability," *Ecology and Society* 18(2) (2013).

100   P. Olsson et al., "Shooting the rapids: Navigating transitions to adaptive governance of social-ecological systems. *Ecology and Society* 11(1) (2006).

101   Jason Hickel, *Less is More: How Degrowth Will Save the World* (Penguin, 2021).

102   B. Walker et al., "Resilience, adaptability and transformability in social-ecological systems," *Ecology and Society* 9(2) (2004): 5.

103   B. Walker et al., "Resilience, adaptability and transformability in social-ecological systems," *Ecology and Society* 9(2) (2004): 5.

104   For more on transformations, see, L. Gunderson & C. Holling, eds, *Panarchy:
understanding transformations in human and natural systems* (Washington,
D.C., USA: Island Press, 2002).

105   For a historical example, Joseph Stiglitz has compared some of the "good" and
"bad" outcomes of the fall of the Soviet Union as the global system underwent
upheaval. J. Stiglitz, *Globalization and its Discontents* (New York: W. W. Norton
and Company, 2002).

106   A. Duit & V. Galaz, "Governance and Complexity – Emerging Issues for
Governance Theory," *Governance* 21 (2008): 311–335; D. Wilson, E. Ostrom,
and M. Cox, "Generalizing the core design principles for the efficacy of groups,"
Journal of Economic Behavior & Organization 90 (2013): 21–S32.

107   L. Hamers, "Why Do Animals Keep Evolving into Crabs?" *Scientific American*, 1
June 2023.

108   K. Kahler, "The Arc of Complex Global Governance: From Organization to
Coalition." APSA Preprints, 2020, available at: doi: 10.33774/apsa-2020-8dpq3.

109   T. Weiss & R. Wilkinson, "Rethinking Global Governance? Complexity,
Authority, Power, Change," *International Studies Quarterly* 58 (2014): 207–215.

3 Beyond the tipping point

Environmental governance in the Anthropocene

The problem: Humans

Roughly 12,000 years ago, the last ice age came to an end and Earth entered the Holocene era. In general, the conditions of the Holocene were good for humans: temperature variations were more or less comfortable, relatively stable levels of biodiversity allowed us to thrive, and the global supply of basic resources like clean water and air was sufficient.

The Holocene is over. Today, we live in the Anthropocene era, where human activity is the dominant cause of environmental change.[1] Things are not going well.

Environmental changes are happening at an unprecedented speed.[2] The combination of human-caused climate change, biodiversity loss, and pollution is causing the planet to cross irreversible thresholds, undermining our collective wellbeing.[3] Of the nine planetary boundaries identified as the "safe operating space for humanity," we have already gone beyond at least six.[4][5][6] And as eight billion people produce 530 kilograms of cement and 240 kilograms of steel per person each year, we are poised to rush across all planetary boundaries.[7] The sixth extinction has arrived, "climate breakdown" is here, and it could take us with it.[8]

Many of the deadliest impacts on our planet may have happened already, though we do not yet feel their full force. There are already enough greenhouse gases in our atmosphere to push global temperatures above the critical 1.5 degrees Celsius threshold identified by the Intergovernmental Panel on Climate Change (IPCC), even if we stopped all human production and consumption today.[9] Far from reducing our outputs, however, we appear to be accelerating them, driving us well above some of the worst scenarios identified by experts.[10]

We are already seeing the effects. Rising water temperatures and overfishing have already contributed to the death of more than half of the world's coral reefs, meaning we may have already crossed a tipping point for their irreversible decline and the extinction of an unknowable number of marine species.[11] It may be decades before we fully understand the impacts of our land, sea, and air use, and by then it will be far too late in many cases.

DOI: 10.4324/9781003506386-4

Despite these surprisingly fast transformations of our planet, we still tend to think of environmental change as gradual and linear. We imagine fish stocks being depleted over decades, glaciers gradually retreating, sea levels inching upwards, islands of plastic waste slowly expanding in the Pacific. This linear thinking affects how we respond to environmental challenges: we gradually ratchet up climate ambition over time; we try to replenish depleted resources as they get close to extinction; we regulate problems as they arise and reach what we think of as important thresholds.

But this is not how change happens. Socioecological systems are "discontinuous, abrupt, and surprising."[12] Change occurs under the surface, accumulating almost invisibly until a tipping point is reached and the system enters a new phase, often much more quickly than we might expect. This is what "punctuated equilibrium" looks like: long periods of apparent stability and then sudden, rapid change. By then, there is no going back. We cannot reverse engineer a complex system – we must get better at anticipating changes, evolving alongside them, and shaping the ongoing socioecological transition in real time.

This chapter takes as its starting point that we are already beyond (or rapidly crossing) enough of our planetary thresholds that we should be thinking in terms of the most extreme forms of adaptive governance: transformation.[13] Other forms of adaptation of course will be necessary to address the most acute secondary effects of our planetary crisis – food shocks, extreme weather, livelihood loss, mass migration, entire countries going under water.[14] We should not underestimate how important it will be to pre-position our resources for the coming floods of change.

But these will be insufficient in the face of the "catastrophic shift" underway.[15] We are already in a transformational moment for our socioecological system,[16] where new planetary thresholds are being identified and crossed all the time.[17] We have reached a state of evolutionary mismatch between ourselves and our planet,[18] where our activities have already overwhelmed our ecosystem in many areas.[19] Non-linear forms of change mean that we cannot put Pandora back in the box or incrementally trim back our current way of life – we need to think of a system of governance that transforms us alongside our planet.[20]

Helpfully, the scholarship on global environmental governance is extremely strong. The "regime complexes" of climate governance have been carefully mapped;[21] ideas of "polycentric" and "adaptive environmental governance" are well-established in the literature;[22] the insights of "Earth systems governance" are dynamic and quickly evolving.[23] Nearly all of the environmental experts I have spoken to over the past several years are well acquainted with the core concepts of complexity because they think in terms of interrelated ecosystems as their daily work.

But most of the environmental governance scholarship either identifies what has worked well in a specific local context or issue area (marine fishing, or carbon sequestration, for example) or speaks in structural terms about how some ecosystems and regime complexes have been organized. This can be valuable to understand how ecosystems of governance work in local settings or have worked in the past. But it does not necessarily help us evaluate what to do now. To paraphrase one group of experts, most scholarship is good for description, not prescription.[24]

Worse, there is a massive gap between the innovative ideas I hear from environmental experts and the relatively low-ambition policy proposals currently getting traction in international circles. Look at one compilation of 36 ideas to halve global emissions by 2030, offering tangible and economically-viable proposals could transform energy, industry, agriculture, and finance.[25] I have not seen any of these ideas mentioned in the member-state discussions on environmental governance at the UN Environmental Assembly. Similarly, a recent book entitled *Earth4All* offers a transformative approach to achieving planetary balance by focusing on inequalities and poverty.[26] These are great ideas, but tend to remain delinked from high-level policy processes, which gravitate towards technical fixes to our existing institutions and gradual expansion of our legal framework. As a member of the Earth Systems group told me, "We live in a constant state of suspended disbelief, filled with real insights about planetary governance but without a bridge to decision-makers."

This is partially because of the problem of expertise silos: people tend to be experts in trade, or green tech, or marine habitats, or global governance generally. These communities speak different languages, often don't speak much to each other, and rarely have access to policymaking circles. But it is also because we live in a world where science risks becoming an echo chamber of like-minded people, unable to connect to the decision-making processes or affect the underlying rules of the game.

Complexity thinking offers a bridge across different policy expertise areas and the decisions that policymakers must make today. It helps us understand how a wide range of very different ideas might coalesce and combine into a workable governance architecture. And crucially it may offer us a way to pull together the proposals that are currently being discussed by political leaders into an easy-to-understand, transformative package.

This chapter will examine several of the "big ideas" that are currently being considered by world leaders, the UN system, the various COP conferences, and in the lead-up to the 2024 Summit of the Future. While not an exhaustive list, the main proposals examined in this chapter aim to give a sense of the kind of initiatives and ideas that appear within the Overton window today, a sort of snapshot of where global environmental governance is right now. This snapshot will give a sense of some of the more ambitious ideas that have not been seriously considered by policymakers and world leaders (yet).

My main argument is that the proposals currently in play suffer from the kind of linear, gradualist thinking that characterizes much of global governance today. As I describe in Chapter 1, they tend to fall into one of four categories: (1) fixing a hole or plugging a gap in a dysfunctional machine; (2) the "IPCC panacea" that greater understanding will lead to sufficient action; (3) the "Leviathan mirage" where we try to create a governance umbrella the size of the Earth; and/or (4) stuffing Pandora back into the box, by reverse engineering climate change and biodiversity loss. This critique does not mean the proposals lack merit; in fact, many of them would have an incredibly important impact. But as I explore, some of the core concepts of complexity thinking can help link, "fit," strengthen, and ultimately coalesce the underlying ideas into an agenda for more transformative environmental governance.[27]

Four ideas for saving the planet

"We need to stop using fossil fuels today, set up a circular economy based on renewables, and establish a world environmental court." This was a verbatim proposal made during one of the expert sessions I convened on environmental governance. It sounds like a great future, but also totally impractical and divorced from the reality of today. How to get from today's world to that utopian future?

Over the past several years, I've observed some big ideas on the environment become global front-runners, like Prime Minister Mia Mottley's Bridgetown Initiative, which would generate massive new resources for climate adaptation. Others, like making "ecocide" an internationally punishable crime, do not seem to have much traction right now but could ripen soon. And still others fall into the "tear down capitalism" category of very unlikely to happen in the medium-term future (though not completely beyond the scope of possibility, as we shall see). Of the many proposals put forward in recent years, there are four main groupings that I think can be considered "on the table" of at least some world leaders today. This does not mean that others should be ignored, but it is worth starting with these as broad categories of ideas.

Big idea 1: A world body with teeth

"What we are missing is teeth," one of António Guterres' top advisors was fond of saying in our meetings. And it is true. Many of our commitments to the environment are voluntary, without clear systems of holding actors accountable. If we map out the hundreds of treaties on the environment, many of them rely on voluntary targets, or have goals of protecting certain areas without clear ways to enforce obligations.[28] Some, like the treaty on the ozone layer, or the treaty regulating whaling, have binding commitments, but in many of the most crucial arenas that regulate our impacts on climate, biodiversity, and pollution, we lack robust enforcement.

In response, a wide range of experts and leaders have proposed some form of a world body to oversee and adjudicate global environmental issues. Over the years, this proposal has taken the form of a "Global Environmental

Council," a "World Environmental Court," a "World Environmental Organization," or a "Global Resilience Council."[29] Many of the proposals include a global treaty consolidating all existing environmental obligations into a single set of legally binding international laws. Some proposals include new treaties, such as a recent initiative to ban all fossil fuel exploration and exploitation via a "fossil fuel non-proliferation treaty."[30] Others suggest that the International Court of Justice could have an expanded mandate to adjudicate environmental rights more directly.[31]

Common across these ideas is the demand for a coherent global legal framework enforced by a global judicial body. These bodies, it is argued, could handle disputes over environmental obligations, track progress, and hold actors accountable.

Big idea 2: An IPCC for the planet

The Intergovernmental Panel on Climate Change is the UN body composed of 195 member states and tasked with assessing the science related to climate change. A large group of government-selected scientists gathers on a regular basis, conducts extensive assessments of the current scientific understandings of climate change, and issues guidance for policymakers and experts. It is often held up as the best example of building scientific consensus around emerging climate-driven risks. And it is the gold standard for information related to climate change. The IPCC has been instrumental in shaping international efforts to address climate change, including the Paris Agreement, which aims to limit global warming to well below 1.5 degrees Celsius above pre-industrial levels.

But the IPCC only covers climate change. Other scientific bodies cover issues like biodiversity loss, but they operate largely in separate silos.[32] As a growing body of science is demonstrating, the risks to our planet are interconnected across a far broader range of human impacts, including our effects on biodiversity, pollution, and the use of critical natural resources. "What we need," one expert told me several years ago, is an IPCC for all of our planetary boundaries." There are many versions of this idea, but they all share the core concept of building up a science-policy interface to understand our impacts on the planet, how those impacts interact, and what policymakers can do to address them holistically.[33]

Big idea 3: Fix the global economy

There are dozens of proposals for increasing investment in climate adaptation and mitigation, most of which follow the broad idea that we must move from billions to trillions if we are to meet the planetary crisis of today.[34] The 2022 Finance for Climate Action report proposes a "recasting" of international and domestic finance to generate roughly $1 trillion per year to meet the Paris Treaty commitments on global warming.[35] The 2022 Bridgetown Initiative similarly proposes three steps to transform the global financial system by encouraging private sector environmental investment in developing countries. The Secretary-General's 2023 proposals on the international financial architecture are in part aimed at massively scaling up climate adaptation finance and de-risking private sector investment in developing regions.[36] The High-Level Advisory Board on Effective Multilateralism proposed that the World Bank be re-mandated towards treating the green energy transition as a "global public good."[37] The 2023 Summit for a New Global Finance Pact proposes an ambitious expansion of carbon markets to incentivize the transition off fossil fuels.[38] The 2023 Villars Framework proposes that the global trade system should be reoriented around sustainable environmental goals.[39]

These proposals have important contributions to the role of the international financial architecture in addressing the planetary crisis. They share a sense that the scale of investment must increase exponentially to meet the crisis and often offer innovative ideas for how to shift incentives away from fossil fuels and unsustainable industrial practices. As the following sections will explore, they offer important aspects of a transformation to a new economics of environmental governance.

Big idea 4: Stuff Pandora back into the box

Faced with the reality that we are headed well beyond many of our planetary boundaries, an increasing number of policymakers and scientists are turning to geoengineering as part of the solution.[40] In simple terms, geoengineering refers to interventions in the Earth's natural systems to mitigate the impacts of climate change or other environmental trends. One of the more prevalent practices is carbon dioxide removal (CDR), which aims to draw carbon dioxide from the atmosphere and reduce the greenhouse effect. This can include planting trees, direct air capture (think massive vacuums), and ocean-based fertilization to increase carbon capture. CDR has been recognized as a viable practice by the IPCC and is proceeding apace, with new discoveries and advances happening every few months.

Far more controversial techniques include solar radiation modification (SRM), which aims to reduce the amount of sunlight reaching the Earth's surface to counteract global warming. Some SRM involves injecting aerosols or other reflective particles into the stratosphere, deploying mirrors in space, or brightening marine clouds. Techniques like Albedo modification similarly would increase the reflectivity of the Earth's surface or the Arctic ice. A recent letter signed by hundreds of eminent scientists has raised alarm bells about techniques like these, given the unknown broader effects they could have on our planetary ecosystem.[41]

While geoengineering can take many forms,[42] the common element is an attempt to reverse engineer human effects on the environment. Most scientists do not consider such "techno fixes" as sufficient on their own, but many describe geoengineering as part of a package of tools that can help to address the increasingly unmanageable trends of the triple planetary crisis.

What can complexity offer to the big environmental proposals?

The proposals described above are important contributions to the current debates on global environmental governance. If implemented, they could make a serious difference in how we approach the triple planetary crisis. But they are also problematic, because they are essentially trying to fix part of a problem rather than address the planetary socioecological governance question as a whole. Without discarding these proposals, this section offers a sense of how complexity thinking can provide space for connecting, augmenting, and linking them, potentially into a viable environmental governance design.

A good question to begin with is, what is the "end state" we are looking for? While there may be different versions, I believe most environmental policymakers are looking for a stable human-environment relationship, where human wellbeing is achieved within an environment that evolves within sustainable boundaries, and where our responses to emerging environmental changes are flexible enough to maintain that balanced function.[43] In Kate Raworth's terminology, we need to live within the doughnut, where human wellbeing and a sustained planet coexist.[44] There are many ways we could achieve this (including theoretically by drastically reducing the human population or ending all electricity usage). But the most realistic scenarios are based on some basic assumptions, including continued population growth, continued (indeed increasing) energy needs, and likely an overall increase in demand for resources like cement, minerals, and water. This is the system we have today, and we will not change it overnight, but there may be a "middle ground" where our systems adapt and help to shape a transformation of our relationship with nature.[45]

How to achieve this end state? Complexity thinking demands that we begin with the strong attractors of the system, the centers of gravity around which the system tends to organize itself. In the socioecological context, the strongest attractor is our reliance on carbon-based energy to deliver human wellbeing. A second attractor is our unsustainable use of natural resources for industry and development, which is pushing us beyond many of our planetary boundaries. Our paradigms of progress, development, and human thriving are very much linked to these two attractor basins, and they create a powerful path dependency for all of us. Of course, they manifest very differently at local levels: think of the enormous difference between the person digging up the coltan in a mine in eastern Congo versus the person using coltan in their iPhone. Both are part of a broader system of extraction, pollution, emissions, but have very different roles and experiences within it.

This points to the need for a global governance system that has the right spatial and temporal fit, one that is able to shape the human-environment relationship towards new attractor basins while tailoring effects to very different communities and actors. As Elinor Ostrom frequently remarked, there are no panaceas: there is no single institution or approach that will deliver this transformation.[46] The more relevant and potentially impactful question concerns how to link the various ideas, processes, and institutions into a coherent system that can shape our relationship to the planet.[47] Some of the characteristics of that interlinked system could include the following insights from complexity thinking, which would also allow us to generate more from the four big ideas described above.

An octopus, not a Leviathan

Calls for a global treaty and judicial body on the environment reflect an attempt to manage from the top down. This "climate Leviathan" reflects the frustration of environmentalists who see big industry, big oil, and big states getting away with planetary murder.[48] Over and over, I have heard some version of, "We need a global ban on fossil fuels ... we need to criminalize harm to the planet ... we need to hold everyone accountable." In a highly fragmented global environmental system where major industries and big polluting states are largely given a free pass, a global treaty enforced by a world court offers an appealing and familiar coherence.[49] We all understand the concept of breaking the law and getting caught. A global treaty also speaks to the reality that many of the more local, citizen-driven approaches to the environment tend to lack clear lines of accountability and authority.[50]

A treaty approach could be powerful. A global ban on fossil fuel exploitation, for example, could add some much-needed teeth to the voluntary commitments underpinning the United Nations Framework Convention on Climate Change (UNFCCC).[51] And the plastics treaty being negotiated in late 2023 offers hope for more robust curbs on pollution. But it also seems very unlikely that we can achieve an overarching environmental treaty in the medium term, and several experts I spoke to suggested that even trying to bring it all together could undo decades of hard-won gains in fields like biodiversity, climate, and pollution. There are roughly 700 environmental treaties in existence today, each one reflecting a bespoke and often politically costly process of negotiation. As Oran Young notes, internationally binding instruments have an important role to play in planetary governance, but "there is no need to put all our eggs in this basket."[52]

Instead, complexity thinking suggests that we start with the system we have now, which is already characterized by high degrees of fragmentation, and then ask how the various pieces might work together to achieve widespread behavioral changes. Here, concepts of "collaborative environmental governance" would see the many different actors involved in environmental issues working closely together to address a set of common problems.[53] Short of open collaboration, the notion of "synergistic fragmentation" sees various governance actors operating in broad alignment without directly cooperating.[54] Or perhaps the most realistic would be some form of "orchestration," where the disparate governance regimes for climate, biodiversity, pollution, and others were only loosely kept in time by some sort of central actor.[55] Could, for example, the UN Environmental Programme (UNEP) play a greater "conductor" role in setting a common direction across environmental governance?[56]

While there are many different forms such orchestration (or steering) could take, complexity thinking suggests the governance structure should look more like an octopus than an umbrella, with much of the action taking place quite independently and far from the central nervous system.[57] An octopus possesses brain cells in each of its tentacles; the tentacles appear to be able to think and act with a relatively high degree of autonomy, but they relate back to the center. Similarly, there might need to be a central authority for environmental governance with a mandate that cut across all planetary boundaries, but it is unlikely that it would play a global regulatory role per se. Instead, in a system as fragmented as ours, such a structure would need to play the role of *enabling and conditioning* a deeper change in that human-environment relationship across our existing governance systems. This is not necessarily such a new idea: A wide array of issues are covered in the principles establishing the World Trade Organization, for example, but the WTO does not regulate them all per se.[58] We could envisage a similar set of overarching principles being set up around the planetary boundaries.

In fact, there are many tangible ways to move in the direction of orchestrated environmental governance, building on some of the proposals already on the table. Imagine if UNEP and the UNFCCC's current roles on the environment were bolstered with the following functions:

- *Upholding a set of agreed principles and commitments* on the planetary boundaries, with a baseline understanding that our goal is to stay within the safe operating space for humanity. These principles could act as connective tissue across existing legal frameworks (e.g. climate, biodiversity, pollution), but would not necessarily require a single treaty. They could be linked to a judicial body (such as a set of judges in the International Court of Justice), or they could be tracked within the domestic legislation of states.[59] One of the most important functions could be enabling and capacitating more national governments to enact ecological legislation, and to accelerate the incorporation of environmental issues into other bodies of law.[60]
- *An investigation/reporting* function where violations of environmental rights and commitments would be referred to relevant authorities.[61] Just as the UN Human Rights Council is able to form independent investigations into human rights violations, an effective environmental governance system would need greater capacities to respond to signals of environmental harm. Public reporting forums too could help build greater transparency and independent sources of information on environmental harms. This would create a more robust and independent feedback loop for our environmental governance system, moving beyond the current system in which national governments are often solely responsible for reporting on environmental issues.

- *Networking our institutions* by creating a common set of sustainability criteria across all the major multilateral bodies of today. This could be achieved by agreeing a common set of planetary system/thresholds that would need to be considered as core objectives of every multilateral body, including the World Trade Organization, World Bank, International Monetary Fund, International Labor Organization, and others. One of UNEP's roles could be to monitor, advise, and support these organizations in upholding these commitments, providing real-time responses and capacity support. An initiative that began in 2023 focused on greening the World Trade Organization shows the promise of such an approach in one of the most critical areas of global governance.[62] And complexity-driven studies have shown the enormous potential for small shifts in global trade to have a massive impact on environmental issues.[63]
- *Enabling a shift in our investments* by monitoring a set of agreed conditions for international financial institutions. For example, international investments might need to demonstrate net-zero carbon emissions and a nature-positive set of outcomes to keep us within planetary boundaries.[64] UNEP could sit on the boards of these bodies to ensure their decision-making processes reflected early consideration of these conditions, and the trajectory of international investments could form a more direct part of reporting on commitments.

Complexity points us away from static institutions or attempts to create a blanket approach, and instead towards these more networked, web-like functions for environmental governance. Imagine a cluster of agreed principles at the center of the web, with an agile spider that can move quickly along the strands to reinforce fraying strands or respond to vibrations in the peripheries. This will require a good early warning and response system, which is where we turn next.

Mushrooms, not echo chambers

Today, our environmental governance systems are designed to address incremental change in specific domains. We monitor and respond to declining fisheries populations as they reach critical thresholds; we ratchet up commitments to keep emissions below a certain limit; we list species as endangered when they reach a worrying point of decline. But our impacts on planetary boundaries do not operate this way – they intersect and cascade. This is what a group of experts call the "difference between trying to govern individual incremental environmental changes, versus rapid interacting change."[65] And it is extremely difficult: when complex systems reach critical thresholds, they don't necessarily advertise that change is coming.[66] In late 2023, scientists referred to the ice levels in the Antarctic as "mind-blowing," saying "we never thought extreme weather events could happen there."[67] The death of thousands of baby Emperor penguins only weeks earlier is a heartbreaking indicator that the Antarctic may be tipping into a new phase far quicker than expected.[68] In the Anthropocene, these mind-blowing ruptures are increasingly common.

If we are to build a better environmental governance regime, it will need a much faster feedback loop that acts as an early warning/action system for the planet. Like the mycelium fungi connecting tree roots, our early warning system will need to trigger resources and protective action to new stimuli in real time.[69] It will need to go beyond to what one expert told me was the "echo-chamber effect" of environmental science: "Scientists keep telling us we are headed towards disaster and after a while we seem to become numb to the repeated warnings of disaster." It's the story of the boy who cried wolf, but there has been a wolf massacring more and more sheep every time and we just stop caring about dead sheep after a while.

This is where the "IPCC for the planet" idea comes in.[70] Today, the IPCC gives us a comprehensive snapshot of our impacts on climate change, focused on the various ways we are causing global warming. An IPCC for the planet would expand that to include all major environmental impacts, including those related to biodiversity and pollution of our land, air, and water. Such a body theoretically would be able to capture the interlinkages between the planetary boundaries.[71] For example, it could help us trace the causal chain that runs from greenhouse gases to global warming to ocean acidification to coral bleaching to loss of marine biodiversity.[72] The idea of an IPCC for the planet is an attempt to create a holistic feedback loop based on our planetary boundaries.

This would be a massive step forward and very much aligned with complexity thinking. But what if we end up with "just" another IPCC experience, where decades of warnings about climate change have gone largely unheeded? Societies are notoriously slow in responding to signals of major transitions,[73] and this is especially the case when information is dispersed across a wide range of siloed institutions, or restricted to scientific reports.[74] As one comprehensive study on the failures of the past 30 years found, our deep path dependencies on fossil fuels and our addiction to endless economic growth means that even widespread knowledge of environmental damage has done little to curb our practices.[75] The politics of delay are dominant amongst decision-makers and world leaders.[76] Most of them have a four-year re-election horizon and demands to show short-term economic growth – not a good mindset for the kind of tough decisions needed today.

This means that any kind of IPCC for the planet needs to produce a much more immediate feedback loop of information that generates actions in response. We cannot afford another three decades of reasoned scientific consensus being largely ignored by policymakers. Complexity thinking would direct us towards a science-policy-*action*[77] approach with the following characteristics:

- *An early warning* function based on systemic thresholds and signals of change.[78] Across different complex systems there are common criteria that warn of impending tipping points,[79] including critical slowing, more erratic variations, flickering, and bifurcation.[80] We are living in an era of "global weirding," and that weirdness is often a signal of rapid change on the immediate horizon. An IPCC for the planet would need to have a constantly evolving and scientifically driven sense of these early warning signals, including how change in one arena might create change in another.[81] One of the most promising ideas in this arena is Dirk Helbing's "Planetary Nervous System," which would harness big data to map and respond to global risks.[82] I will return to this in the final chapter. Regardless of the exact model, an early warning system would need to be far more real-time than today's environmental monitoring, which tends to be done in annual or even biannual reports. This would not need to be built from scratch: initiatives like the Climate Action Tracker offer a good model and could be scaled and linked up.[83]

- *An accelerated learning/adaptation* function that enables rapid innovation and emerging technologies to respond to change in real time to risks.[84] We may not have long periods of time to try out new experimental solutions, and some experiments like solar radiation management could have a disastrous impact on our planet. At the same time, complexity suggests that it is possible for relatively modest changes to have an outsize effect on our socioecological system.[85] As natural selection has shown, a diversity of options is the best way to ensure the best evolutionary response to new challenges.[86] Iterative approaches to policies, treating them as experiments that can provide immediate feedback to the broader system, are an important way for the complex environmental regime to adapt more quickly in real time and manage risks.[87]

- *A co-production* function, where information about our planetary boundaries is not solely generated by elite scientists, but also by managers (heads of industry), resource users (fishers, farmers), and even private individuals (you and me). Research has shown that active involvement in knowledge generation by those involved in creating and implementing environmental policies produces more accurate and actionable results.[88] What is sometimes called a "multiple evidence base" approach that connects indigenous, local, and practitioner knowledge production with higher-level policymakers and scientists would help to address the spatial fit problems described above.[89] At the far end, one could imagine a sort of Wikipedia for the planet, where everyone was able to feed into a constantly updated picture of our impact on the Earth.

- *A conditioning role* with the major actors involved in energy and industry. Rather than producing standalone reports, an IPCC for the planet could report directly on the net-zero commitments by states and non-state actors.[90] Such a function could be more focused on our impacts in major sectors, building on the excellent analysis in products like the 2022 Emissions Gap Report produced by UNEP.[91] The process to agree a global plastics treaty (ongoing during the writing of this book) offers another entry point where big industry is directly involved and obligated. An IPCC for the planet could report directly on these obligations, linking also to that investigation/accountability function described above.

In his 2023 address to the General Assembly, Secretary-General Guterres spoke of the "great fracture" in global politics. Part of this fracture is that we increasingly tend to occupy echo chambers – social media groups that amplify our political opinions, political groupings that reinforce polarization, and global governance institutions that reflect only a small minority of member states.[92] It is one of the great ironies of today's world that our dramatically improved scientific understanding of planetary change gets caught up in these geopolitical and institutional fractures. The result is that crucial early warning information about planetary tipping points may not permeate into the decision-making circles that matter. Here, the metaphor of mushrooms and tree roots pushes us towards a model of information-generation that connects us beneath the surface, creating a network of responses in real time. It is worth remembering that mushrooms can break through even the hardest concrete over time.

A cascade, not a Band-Aid

We tend to think of environmental governance as a collective action problem. If we all just change our personal behaviors, recycle our bottles, buy electric cars, and "do our bit," our individual actions will accumulate into a livable planet. Similarly, we describe environmental governance as something that all states and major industries need to sign on to. It's "collective action or collective suicide," to use António Guterres' phrase.[93] It may be true that collective *behavior change* is needed, but the pathway to widespread change in a complex system is rarely a simultaneous decision by all actors within it. Even when we know what needs to be done and have a strong evidence base that it will work, our path dependencies work against the kind of widespread individual decisions needed.[94] Worse, in a deeply fractured geopolitical landscape, it is very unlikely we can speak of collective action in terms of cooperation amongst major powers/emitters.

Here, complex systems demand we look at how to shift the strong attractors, altering the underlying rules and creating a cascading effect across the system.[95] Collective behavior change results from an emergent property of the system, not necessarily a set of individual decisions within it. In the environmental arena, the attractor that needs to change is our very strong reliance on carbon-based, polluting, unsustainable forms of energy, industry, and consumption. This will require behavioral changes on multiple scales: at the level of states (which subsidize and encourage unsustainable practices), industry (which benefits from it), and consumers (which are used to a certain way of life).[96] If environmental changes cascade into and across our societies, our societies will need to cascade in response.[97]

In principle, much of this transition should be relatively easy, because the real costs of renewable energy are now less than fossil fuels.[98] If the market was functioning perfectly, we would gravitate naturally (and quickly) off fossil fuels. When paired with the overwhelming public support to end or reduce our reliance on fossil fuels, the green transition should feel inevitable.[99] Unfortunately, as Oran Young and others have pointed out, the market alone will not generate this transition.[100] This is because our current socio-ecological system has a set of negative feedback loops and path dependencies that prevent the kind of widespread behavioral changes needed for an accelerated transition to a green economy. Three of the most important inhibitors of change are (1) subsidies for fossil fuels, (2) barriers to the free distribution of green technology, and (3) path dependencies in how and where we produce energy and industry. A fourth, and often underestimated, inhibitor of change is (4) inequality, which has a combined effect of reducing some region's capacities to transition to green economies while also creating a greater demand for unsustainable forms of growth.

Unfortunately, many of the big proposals on the table today only aim to move resources around within the system, but do not focus on these inhibitors of more systemic change. Generating massive new flows of public and finance – especially for the Global South – is absolutely part of the solution, but without more systemic action risks becoming a green Band-Aid rather than a cascade. Complexity suggests that reform of the financial architecture should be geared around the following kinds of change:

- *Shifting financial incentives around carbon and pollution.* A wide range of environmental experts have pointed to subsidies as the most powerful obstacles to an accelerated green transition. Ending subsidies for fossil fuels and highly-polluting industries would be just one step of a broader financial package that could leverage the green market today. Two recent proposals (from the Bezos Foundation and the World Bank) suggest that large-scale investment in green energy, and conditioning public finance on positive environmental results, would potentially be sufficient to create a global tipping point in the costs of green energy.[101] A global system of carbon pricing that included an end to subsidies, a shift of resources to incentivize green energy, and greater transparency around the carbon market could drive us in the direction of a new "green attractor" in our system.[102] There is already good news on this front: the costs of renewable energies have plummeted in recent years, with solar energy now 90 percent cheaper than it was ten years ago.[103] Renewables now make up 80 percent of new electricity generation in the US, partially as a result of big steps like the Inflation Reduction Act.
- *Enabling the free, fast flow of green technology* around the world. While it is important to preserve technological "niches" that incentivize innovation in technology, global environmental finance should aim to spread that technology across the system as quickly as possible.[104] The

UNFCCC already plays a limited "clearinghouse" role for green technologies – this could be significantly scaled up. There is also a range of proposals in this vein, including a Green Technology Licensing Facility, a Distributed Renewable Energy Platform, and other nodes that could act as accelerants to the movement of technology. In addition, ideas around limiting intellectual property rights for certain green technologies and/or generating preferential trade regimes could help unlock the flow of technology.[105] An uninhibited flow of green technology would generate the kind of snowball effect that could tip our system away from fossil fuels much more quickly.

- *Moving beyond Gross Domestic Product.* Today, countries measure their progress overwhelmingly on the basis of economic activity, with GDP used as the gold standard for a country's status. Unfortunately, practices like deforestation, overfishing, fossil fuel consumption, and infrastructural industry are the main drivers of both GDP and the triple planetary crisis. This creates a destructive, but resilient, pattern within our socioecological system. Planetary destruction is not an externality of human consumption, it is the unintended consequence of a unified human/planetary system. Moving beyond GDP would make an important shift towards what Oran Young calls a "system of environmental ethics," where the strong attractor is activity that helps us achieve balance with the planet.[106] In my view, we are at a moment today where a global shift beyond GDP is within the phase space of our political system.

- *Poverty and inequality.* After decades of falling further behind, developing and middle-income countries are racing to catch up on the enormous dividends that are being enjoyed by the so-called Global North. This race is largely driven by carbon-based energy use and massively destructive urban development. The environmental justice movement – which started at a local level in the US – has now become a rallying cry of the developing world and an excuse to double down on carbon-based growth. The concepts of common-but-differentiated responsibilities are an important reflection of the reality that the world's biggest emitters and polluters are also those who have benefited most from development (with China managing to ride a sort of middle line here). And while justice is certainly a strong ethical reason to shift resources to the developing world, there are also persuasive practical reasons. In an exciting and empirically rigorous project, the Earth4All research group has demonstrated that addressing poverty and global inequality would do more to accelerate the green transition than almost any other set of actions.[107] Part of the "fit" of environmental governance must be a recognition that a significant shift of cheap, renewable resources to the developing world will allow for a transformation to a green economy for all of us.

Our present system based on fossil fuels

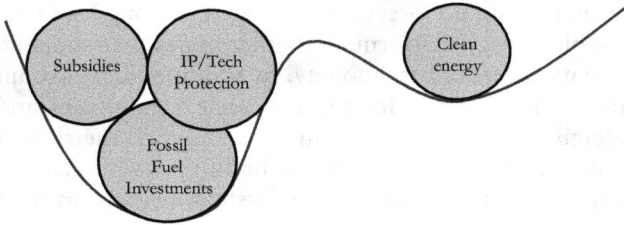

A tipping point for green energy

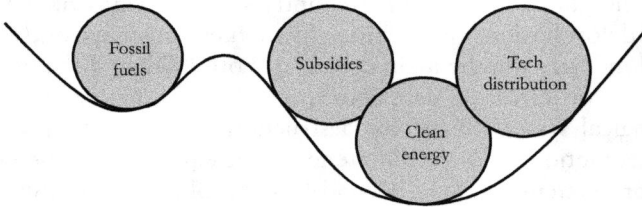

Potential future tipping points/attractors

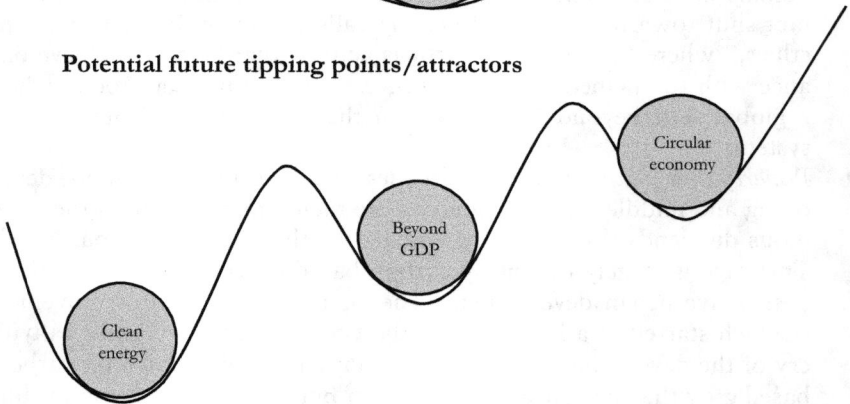

One way to think of transformation is as a failure of adaptation: a system breaks down, or a group of actors consciously decides that it is not meeting collective needs, so a new set of parameters/paradigms are put in place.[108] But not all actors have the same power to generate this kind of change in our socioecological system.[109] Because of their share of emissions and industrial strength, the US, China, India, and Europe have an outsized capacity to generate transformative change in our relationship with the environment.[110] Imagine a deal between "just" the US and China that involved a joint commitment to invest in green energy and remove trade barriers around green technology. That alone would likely cause a dramatic global shift towards the end of the fossil fuel era. Here, the concept of "plurilateralism," where a set of first-mover states enter into agreements that have a broader beneficial effect globally could accelerate change.[111]

But this is not the only theory of change in our socioecological system. If a critical mass of smaller states transitioned to green energy, it could also cascade across the system. We should remember that small island developing states were responsible for the momentum that led to the 2015 Paris Treaty. Rwanda and Peru were the principal drivers of the political momentum that led to the new global treaty on plastics. Barbados's Bridgetown Initiative is the single highest-profile initiative on climate adaptation in the world today. In an era where smaller states and marginalized communities are receiving proportionately less of global wealth, they may be less beholden to the strong attractors of the system, and more able to generate a sort of collective groundswell against prevailing norms. As middle powers grow in size and global impact, they will play maybe the most important role in driving systemic change.[112]

Not being sure where the tipping point may be, it may be best to pursue a "kitchen sink" approach, where we throw as many heavy things into the part of the attractor landscape as we can, and hope it creates enough gravitational pull to create a new pull towards sustainable energy and industry. This will likely involve harnessing the enormous power of bottom-up approaches, trying to connect them into a concerted counterweight against the strong path dependencies of our unsustainable current practices.

Lock in the transformation, not the institution

"Beware the self-licking ice cream cone," one of my first mentors in the UN system used to tell me. He was speaking of the strong tendency of any big bureaucracy to become self-referential, mired in its own processes and unable to adapt to new circumstances. This can lead to outdated institutions (does the UN system really need an entire organ dedicated to trusteeship for decolonizing countries today?) or slow to change to new circumstances (could a nimbler version of UNAIDS have been repurposed to address the COVID-19 pandemic?). The political costs of changes within governance regimes increase over time as they become more embedded. But the costs of not adapting are also significant: look at the UN Security Council today and its paralysis in the face of the wars in Ukraine and Gaza.

It would be a truly Pyrrhic victory if we managed to design an entirely new environmental governance regime only to find that it was unable to adapt to a new shock. Or worse, if the new system inherited all the negative attributes of the past one. Recall that the collapse of the Soviet Union created a new economic and political order but did not end the authoritarian tendencies within the Russian governance system. Having watched successive attempts at UN reform, I have noticed a similar tendency to just layer new arrangements over old ones, often adding bureaucratic processes and new requirements for coordination rather than creating synergies or casting off bad habits.

As I argue in Chapter 6 on artificial intelligence, the downsides of institutionalization may outweigh the benefits when it comes to emerging risks to the environment. The scholarship on polycentric and adaptive governance demonstrates that we can handle new risks by learning in an iterative fashion.[113] Of course, networks also can be captured by powerful players and get bogged down in endless coordination processes that inhibit many players from generating change.[114] And we will need to think how to respond quickly to the urgency of today's environmental crises while still building longer-term systemic responses.[115]

Here, the concept of "design" on its own may be unhelpful for environmental governance. Instead, we can draw inspiration from the idea of "institutional work," which shifts the focus away from institutions and towards the ongoing efforts to bring about change itself.[116] A transformation in a governance regime can quickly become overly focused on solidifying and building its own institutional strength.[117] New institutions tend to protect their own turf and pursue their own mandates.[118] Instead of spending too much time designing the web, complexity thinking pushes us to enable the spiders to move more quickly across it, tending to broken strands or expanding into new spaces where needed.[119]

Notes

1 S. Lewis & M. Maslin, "Defining the Anthropocene," *Nature* 519 (2015): 171–180.
2 W. Steffen et al., "The trajectory of the Anthropocene: The Great Acceleration," *The Anthropocene Review*, 2(1) (2015): 81–98.
3 Statement of UN Secretary-General António Guterres (21 April, 2022), available at: https://press.un.org/en/2022/sgsm21243.doc.html.
4 K. Richardson et al., "Earth beyond six of nine planetary boundaries," *Science Advances* (2023), available at: https://doi.org/10.1126/sciadv.adh2458.
5 J. Rockström et al., "Planetary boundaries: exploring the safe operating space for humanity," *Ecology and Society* 14(2) (2009): 32.
6 J. Rockström et al., "Planetary boundaries: exploring the safe operating space for humanity," *Ecology and Society* 14(2) (2009): 32.
7 W. Steffen et al., "Planetary boundaries: Guiding human development on a changing planet," *Science*, vol. 347 (2015).
8 A. Barnosky et al., "Has the Earth's sixth mass extinction already arrived?" *Nature* 471 (2011): 51–57; E. Kolbert, *The Sixth Extinction: An Unnatural History* (New York: MacMillan, 2014).
9 M. Dvorak et al., "Estimating the timing of geophysical commitment to 1.5 and 2.0 °C of global warming," *Nature Climate Change* 12 (2022): 547–552.
10 United Nations Framework Convention on Climate Change, "Updated NDC Synthesis Report" (25 October 2021), available at: https://unfccc.int/news/updated-ndc-synthesis-report-worrying-trends-confirmed.
11 J. Ashworth, "Over half of coral reef cover across the world has been lost since 1950," Natural History Museum, 26 September 2021. See also, A. Dietzel et al., "The population sizes and global extinction risk of reef-building coral species at biogeographic scales," *Nature Ecology & Evolution* 5(5) (2021): 663–669.

12 O. Young, *Governing Complex Systems: Social Capital for the Anthropocene* (MIT Press, 2017), 47.

13 B. Chaffin et al., "Transformative Environmental Governance," *Annual Review of Environmental Resources*, 41 (2016): 399–423.

14 W. de Vries et al., "Assessing planetary and regional nitrogen boundaries related to food security and adverse environmental impacts," *Current Opinion Environmental Sustainability* vol. 5 (2013): 392–402.

15 M. Scheffer et al., "Catastrophic Shifts in Ecosystems," *Nature* 413 (2001): 591–596.

16 R. Biggs, S.R. Carpenter, W.A. Brock, "Turning back from the brink: Detecting an impending regime shift in time to avert it," *Proceedings of the National Academy of Sciences,* 106 (2009): 826–831.

17 L. Persson et al., "Outside the Safe Operating Space of the Planetary Boundary for Novel Entities," *Environmental Science & Technology* 56 (3) (2022): 1510–1521. See also, S. Carpenter & E. Bennett, "Reconsideration of the planetary boundary for phosphorus," *Environmental Research Letters* 6 (2011); S.W. Running, "A measurable planetary boundary for the biosphere," *Science* 337 (2012): 1458–1459; D. Gerten et al., "Towards a revised planetary boundary for consumptive freshwater use: Role of environmental flow requirements," *Current Opinion Environmental Sustainability* 5 (2013): 551–558; G.M. Mace et al., "Approaches to defining a planetary boundary for biodiversity," *Global Environmental Change* 28 (2014): 289–297; M. MacLeod et al., "Identifying chemicals that are planetary boundary threats," *Environment Science and Technology* 48 (2014): 11057–11063; T.M. Lenton et al., "Tipping elements in the Earth's climate system," *Proceedings of the National Academy of Sciences* 105 (2008): 1786–1793 (2008); T. Lenton & H. Williams, "On the origin of planetary-scale tipping points," *Trends Ecological Evolution* 28 (2013): 380–382.

18 E. Lloyd, D. Wilson, and E. Sober, "Evolutionary Mismatch And What To Do About It: A Basic Tutorial," *Semantic Scholar* (2011).

19 W. Steffen, J. Crutzen, and J. McNeill, "The Anthropocene: Are humans now overwhelming the great forces of Nature?" *Ambio* 36 (2007): 614–621.

20 See, F. Biermann, "Planetary boundaries and earth system governance: Exploring the links," *Ecological Economics*, vol. 81 (2012): 4–9; K. O'Neill et al., "Methods and Global Environmental Governance," *Annual Review of Environment and Resources* 38:1 (2013): 441–471; R. Kim, "The emergent network structure of the multilateral environmental agreement system," *Global Environmental Change* Vol. 23(5) (2013): 980–991; B. Walker et al., "Looming global-scale failures and missing institutions," *Science* 80 (2009): 1345–1346.

21 D. Victor & R. Keohane, "The Regime Complex for Climate Change," *Perspective on Politics* (2010), 9.

22 See, e.g., H. Österblom & C. Folke, "Emergence of global adaptive governance for stewardship of regional marine resources," *Ecology and Society* 18(2) (2013): 4.

23 J. Patterson et al., "Transformations towards sustainability'. Emerging approaches, critical reflections, and a research agenda," *Earth System Governance Working Paper* No. 33 (2015).

24 A. Jordan et al., eds, *Governing Climate Change: Polycentricity in Action?* (Cambridge: Cambridge University Press, 2018), 357–383.

25 J. Falk et al., "Exponential Roadmap 1.5. Future Earth" (September 2019), available at: https://exponentialroadmap.org/wp-content/uploads/2019/09/ExponentialRoadmap_1.5_20190919_Single-Pages.pdf.

26 S. Dixson-Declève et al., *Earth4All: A Survival Guide for Humanity*, online version available at: https://earth4all.life/wp-content/uploads/2023/03/Earth4All _Exec_Summary_EN.pdf.

27 See, V. Galaz et al., "The Problem of Fit among Biophysical Systems, Environmental and Resource Regimes, and Broader Governance Systems: Insights and Emerging Challenges," in *Institutions and Environmental Change: Principal Findings, Applications, and Research Frontiers*, O. Young, L. King, and H. Schroeder, eds. (Cambridge, MA, MIT Press, 2008); A. Vatn, & P. Vedeld, "Fit, Interplay, and Scale: A Diagnosis." *Ecology and Society* 17, no. 4 (2012). See also, O. Young, A. Leslie, and H. Schroeder, eds, *Institutions and Environmental Change: Principal Findings, Applications, and Research Frontiers* (Cambridge, MA, MIT Press, 2008).

28 See, e.g., the United Nations Framework Convention on Climate Change (UNFCCC, 1992); the Kyoto Protocol (1997), the Paris Agreement (2015); the Montreal Protocol (1987); the Convention on Biological Diversity (1992); the Ramsar Convention on Wetlands (1971); the Basel Convention on the Control of Transboundary Movements of Hazardous Wastes and Their Disposal (1989); the Stockholm Convention on Persistent Organic Pollutants (2001); United Nations Convention on the Law of the Sea (UNCLOS) (1982).

29 See, e.g., F. Biermann & S. Bauer, *A World Environment Organization: Solution or Threat for Effective International Environmental Governance?* (Routledge: 2005); A. McMillan, "Time for a World Court for the Environment," International Bar Association (November 2019), available at: https://www.ibanet.org/article /71B817C7-8026-48DE-8744-50D227954E04.

30 See, Fossil Fuel Non-Proliferation Treaty Initiative, available at: https://fossilfuel-treaty.org/.

31 See, A. Lopez-Claros, A. Dahl, and M. Groff, *Global Governance and the Emergence of Global Institutions for the 21st Century* (Cambridge: Cambridge University Press, 2021); R. Killean, "From ecocide to eco-sensitivity: 'greening' reparations at the International Criminal Court," *International Journal of Human Rights*, 25:2 (2021): 323–347; S. Freeland, "Crimes Against the Environment: What Role for the International Criminal Court?" in E. Sobenes, S. Mead, and B. Samson, eds, *The Environment Through the Lens of International Courts and Tribunals* (The Hague, T.M.C. Asser Press, 2022).

32 See, e.g., the Intergovernmental Science-Policy Platform on Biodiversity and Ecosystem Services (IPBES).

33 See, e.g., *A Breakthrough for Planet and People, Report of the High-Level Advisory Board on Effective Multilateralism*, April 2022, available at: http://hig hleveladvisoryboard.org/breakthrough.

34 See, e.g., UN Secretary-General's SDG Stimulus to Deliver Agenda 2030, available at: https://www.un.org/sustainabledevelopment/wp-content/uploads/2023 /02/SDG-Stimulus-to-Deliver-Agenda-2030.pdf; https://press.un.org/en/2023/ sgsm21855.doc.htm.

35 V. Songwe, N. Stern, and A. Bhattacharya, "Finance for climate action Scaling up investment for climate and development Report of the Independent High-Level Expert Group on Climate Finance," (November 2022), available at: https://www .lse.ac.uk/granthaminstitute/wp-content/uploads/2022/11/IHLEG-Finance-for -Climate-Action-1.pdf.

36 Secretary-General's Policy Brief 6, "Reforms to the International Financial Architecture," May 2023, available at: https://indonesia.un.org/sites/default/files /2023-07/our-common-agenda-policy-brief-international-finance-architecture -en.pdf.

37 *A Breakthrough for Planet and People, Report of the High-Level Advisory Board on Effective Multilateralism*, April 2022, available at: https://highleveladvisoryboard.org/breakthrough/pdf/highleveladvisoryboard_breakthrough_fullreport.pdf.

38 *Call to Action for Paris Aligned Carbon Markets*, available at: https://nouveaupactefinancier.org/pdf/call-to-action-for-paris-aligned-carbon-markets.pdf

39 "Remaking Trade for a Sustainable Future", available at: https://remakingtradeproject.org/villars.

40 The term "geoengineering" has increasingly been replaced with more euphemistic terms like "climate altering technologies," but I prefer the more mechanistic term as I believe it captures the essence of the concept. See, e.g., https://www.c2g2.net/introduction/.

41 See "Open Letter" at https://www.solargeoeng.org/.

42 E. Kolbert, *Under a White Sky: The Nature of the Future* (New York: Crown Publishers, 2021).

43 K. Raworth, *Doughnut Economics: Seven Ways to Think Like a 21st-Century Economist* (London: Random House, 2017).

44 K. Raworth, *Doughnut Economics: Seven Ways to Think Like a 21st-Century Economist* (London: Random House, 2017).

45 See, R. Beunen & J. Patterson, "Analysing institutional change in environmental governance: exploring the concept of 'institutional work," *Journal of Environmental Planning and Management* 62:1 (2019): 12–29.

46 See, e.g., C. Pahl-Wostl et al., "From Applying Panaceas to Mastering Complexity: Toward Adaptive Water Governance in River Basins." *Environmental Science & Policy* 23 (2019): 24–34; S. Park et al., "Informing adaptation responses to climate change through theories of transformation," *Global Environmental Change* 22 (2019): 115–126.

47 H. Van Assel & F Zelli, "Connect the Dots: Managing the Fragmentation of Global Climate Governance," Earth Systems Governance Working Paper, 25 (2012).

48 J. Wainwright & G. Mann, *Climate Leviathan: A Political Theory of Our Planetary Future* (London: Verso, 2018).

49 On fragmentation, see, H. Van Assel & F. Zelli, "Connect the Dots: Managing the Fragmentation of Global Climate Governance," Earth Systems Governance Working Paper, 25 (2012).

50 L. Andonova & R. Mitchell, "The Rescaling of Global Environmental Politics," *Annual Review of Environment and Resources* 35:1 (2010): 255–282.

51 Fossil Fuel Non-Proliferation Treaty Initiative, available at: https://fossilfuel-treaty.org/.

52 O. Young, *Grand Challenges for Planetary Governance: Global Order in Turbulent Times* (Cheltenham: Edward Elgar, 2021), 11.

53 Ö. Bodin, "Collaborative environmental governance: Achieving collective action in social-ecological systems," *Science* (2017): 357.

54 H. Van Assel & F. Zelli, "Connect the Dots: Managing the Fragmentation of Global Climate Governance," Earth Systems Governance Working Paper, 25 (2012).

55 K. Abbott & D. Snidal, "International regulation without international government: improving IO performance through orchestration," *Review of International Organizations* 5 (2010): 315–344.

56 K. Abbott, "The transnational regime complex for climate change," *Environment and Planning, Government and Policy* 30 (4) (2010): 571–590.

57 In fact, this matches Ostrom's definition of polycentricity. See, E. Ostrom, "Polycentric systems for coping with collective action and global environmental change," in *Global Justice*, C. Barry, ed. (Routledge: 2016).

58 See, Marrakesh Agreement Establishing the World Trade Organization (1994) available at: https://www.wto.org/english/docs_e/legal_e/04-wto_e.htm. See also, V. Galaz et al., "Planetary boundaries' – exploring the challenges for global environmental governance," *Current Opinion in Environmental Stability*, 4 (2012): 80–87.

59 For an example of this kind of tracking, see, https://climate-laws.org/.

60 Excellent ideas on this front are found in C. Folke, T. Hahn, and J. Norberg, "Adaptive Governance of Social-Ecological Systems," *Annual Review of Environment and Resources* 30:1 (2005): 441–473; L. Kotzé & R. Kim, "Earth system law: The juridical dimensions of earth system governance," *Earth System Governance* 1 (2019); A. Garmestani et al., "The Integration of Social-Ecological Resilience and Law" in *Social-Ecological Resilience and Law*, A. Garmestani & C. Allen, eds (New York: Columbia University Press, 2014); J. Ruhl, "General Design Principles for Resilience and Adaptive Capacity in Legal Systems – with Applications in Climate Change Adaptation," 89 *North Carolina Law Review* (2011): 1373.

61 The human right to a clean, healthy and sustainable environment : resolution adopted by the General Assembly, 76th sess., Suppl. no. 49., A/RES/76/300, available at: https://digitallibrary.un.org/record/3983329.

62 *Remaking Trade for a Sustainable Future*, available at: https://remakingtradeproject.org/villars.

63 J. Morin et al., "The Trade Regime as a Complex Adaptive System: Exploration and Exploitation of Environmental Norms in Trade Agreements," *Journal of International Economic Law* 20 (2017): 365.

64 One proposal along this line would see conditions placed on the Green Climate Fund, see, H. Van Asselt & F. Zelli, "Connect the Dots: Managing the Fragmentation of Global Climate Governance," Earth Systems Governance Working Paper, 25 (2012).

65 V. Galaz et al., "Planetary boundaries – exploring the challenges for global environmental governance," *Current Opinion in Environmental Stability*, 4 (2012): 80–87.

66 M. James et al., "Anticipating critical transitions," *Science* 338 (2012): 344–348.

67 G. Rannard, B. Dale, and E. Rivault, "Antarctic sea-ice at 'mind-blowing' low alarms experts," BBC News, 18 September 2023, available at: https://www.bbc.com/news/science-environment-66724246.

68 J. Amos, "Thousands of penguins die in Antarctic ice break up," BBC News, 24 August 2023, available at: https://www.bbc.com/news/science-environment-66492767.

69 M. Sheldrake, *Entangled Life: How Fungi Make Our Worlds, Change Our Minds, and Shape Our Futures* (New York: Random House, 2020).

70 Though the idea has been circulating for some time, I was first introduced to it by Jens Orback at the Global Challenges Foundation.

71 Indeed, UNEP's Global Environmental Outlook attempts to do this today. See, https://www.unep.org/geo/. See also, V. Galaz et al., "Planetary boundaries – exploring the challenges for global environmental governance," *Current Opinion in Environmental Stability*, 4 (2012): 80–87.

72 C. Crabbe, "Climate change, global warming and coral reefs: Modelling the effects of temperature," *Computational Biology and Chemistry* 32(5) (2008): 311–314.

73 M. Scheffer, F. Westley, and W. Brock, "Slow response of societies to new problems: causes and costs," *Ecosystems* 6 (2003): 493–502.
74 V. Galaz et al., "Planetary boundaries – exploring the challenges for global environmental governance," *Current Opinion in Environmental Stability*, 4 (2012): 80–87.
75 I. Stoddard et al., "Three Decades of Climate Mitigation: Why Haven't We Bent the Global Emissions Curve?" *Annual Review of Environment and Resources* 46:1 (2021): 653–689.
76 W. Lamb et al., "Discourses of climate delay," *Global Sustainability* 3 (2021): 17.
77 For the phrase "science-policy-action network," see, *A Breakthrough for Planet and People, Report of the High-Level Advisory Board on Effective Multilateralism*, April 2022, available at: https://highleveladvisoryboard.org/breakthrough/pdf/highleveladvisoryboard_breakthrough_fullreport.pdf.
78 M. Scheffer et al., "Anticipating critical transitions," *Science* 338 (2012): 344–348.
79 M. Scheffer et al., "Early-warning signals for critical transitions," *Nature* 461 (2009): 53–59.
80 V. Dakos et al., "Slowing down as an early warning signal for abrupt climate change," *Proceedings of the National Academy of Sciences* 105 (2008): 14308–14312; S. Carpenter & W. Brock, "Rising variance: a leading indicator of ecological transition," *Ecological Letters* 9 (2006): 308–315; V. Guttal & C. Jayaprakash, "Changing skewness: an early warning signal of regime shifts in ecosystems," *Ecological Letters* 11 (2008): 450–460; V. Livina & T. Lenton, "A modified method for detecting incipient bifurcations in a dynamical system," *Geophysics Research Letters* 34 (2007).
81 This could be achieved via an expansion and strengthening of the Global Environmental Outlook. See, "The Global Environmental Outlook," UN Environment Programme, last accessed November 2023 at https://www.unep.org/geo/.
82 D. Helbing, "Creating ("Making") a Planetary Nervous System as Citizen Web," in *Thinking Ahead – Essays on Big Data, Digital Revolution, and Participatory Market Society* (Springer, Cham 2015).
83 See, e.g., Climate Tracker, available at: https://climateactiontracker.org/.
84 K. Simeonova, "Knowledge Sharing and Learning through a Global Climate Policy Clearinghouse: Options and Opportunities," Global Challenges Foundation.
85 O. Young, *Governing Complex Systems: Social Capital for the Anthropocene* (Cambridge: MIT Press, 2017).
86 M. Nilsson & A. Persson, "Can Earth system interactions be governed? Governance functions for linking climate change mitigation with land use, freshwater and biodiversity protection," *Ecological Economics* 81 (2012): 10–20.
87 C. Holling, "Understanding the complexity of economic, ecological, and social systems," *Ecosystems* 4 (2001): 390–405 (referring to policy as an experiment). See also, F. Westley et al., "Tipping Toward Sustainability: Emerging Pathways of Transformation," *AMBIO* 40 (2011): 762–780 (2011).
88 D. Armitage, R. de Loe, and R. Plummer, "Environmental governance and its implications for conservation practice," *Conservation Letters* 5 (2012): 245–255. See also, B. Forbes et al., "Reindeer management in northernmost Europe: linking practical and scientific knowledge in social-ecological systems," *Ecological studies* 184 (2006); C. Pohl et al., "Researcher's roles in knowledge co-production: experience from sustainability research in Kenya, Switzerland, Bolivia and Nepal," *Science and Public Policy* 37(4) (2010), 267–281.

89 M. Tengö et al., "Connecting Diverse Knowledge Systems for Enhanced Ecosystem Governance: The Multiple Evidence Base Approach," *Ambio* 43 (2014): 579–591.
90 Report of the UN High-Level Expert Group on the Net-Zero Emissions Commitments of Non-State Entities, available at: https://www.un.org/sites/un2.un.org/files/high-levelexpertgroupupdate7.pdf.
91 UNEP Emissions Gap Report, 2022, available at: https://www.unep.org/resources/emissions-gap-report-2022
92 But see, A. Arguedas et al., "Echo chambers, filter bubbles, and polarisation: A literature review," The Royal Society, 2022, available at: https://reutersinstitute.politics.ox.ac.uk/echo-chambers-filter-bubbles-and-polarisation-literature-review (suggesting that the effect of echo chambers may be overemphasized in the literature).
93 Secretary-General Press Release, 18 July 2022, available at: https://press.un.org/en/2022/sgsm21376.doc.htm.
94 E. Maibach et al., "Harnessing the Power of Communication and Behavior Science to Enhance Society's Response to Climate Change," *Annual Review of Earth and Planetary Sciences* 51:1 (2023): 53–77.
95 For an excellent description of fractals, see, A. Gowrisankar & S. Banerjee, "Frontiers of fractals for complex systems: recent advances and future challenges," *European Physical Journal Special Topics* 230 (2021): 3743–3745.
96 See, L. Andonova & R. Mitchell, "The Rescaling of Global Environmental Politics," *Annual Review of Environment and Resources* 35:1 (2010): 255–282.; Ö. Bodin, "Collaborative environmental governance: Achieving collective action in social-ecological systems," *Science* (2017): 357.
97 For an interesting framework based on cascading environmental change, see, T. Cernev, "Navigating cascading planetary boundaries: A framework to secure the future," Proceedings of the Stanford Existential Risks Conference 2023, 105–118.
98 M. Ives et al., "Empirically Grounded Forecasts and the Energy Transition," *Joule* (2022).
99 Global Solidarity Report 2023, available at: https://globalfundcommunityfoundations.org/wp-content/uploads/2023/09/Global-Solidarity-Report-2023.pdf.
100 O. Young, *Grand Challenges for Planetary Governance: Global Order in Turbulent Times* (Cheltenham: Edward Elgar, 2021), 11.
101 Bezos Earth Fund Press Release, Energy Transition Accelerator, 19 September 2023, https://www.bezosearthfund.org/news-and-insights/energy-transition-accelerator-world-bank-scale-up-clean-energy-finance; World Bank Scaling Climate Action by Lowering Emissions Program, available at: https://www.worldbank.org/en/programs/scale; The World Bank Group and Paris Alignment, available at: https://www.worldbank.org/en/publication/paris-alignment.
102 A Breakthrough for Planet and People, Report of the High-Level Advisory Board on Effective Multilateralism, April 2022, available at: https://highleveladvisoryboard.org/breakthrough/pdf/highleveladvisoryboard_breakthrough_fullreport.pdf.
103 K. Marvel, "I'm a climate scientist. I'm not screaming into the void anymore," New York Times, 18 November 2023, available at: https://www.nytimes.com/2023/11/18/opinion/climate-change-report-us.html.
104 For a description of these niches, see, F. Geels, "The Multi-Level Perspective on Sustainability Transitions: Responses to Seven Criticisms," *Environmental Innovation and Societal Transitions* (2011): 24–40.
105 A Breakthrough for Planet and People, Report of the High-Level Advisory Board on Effective Multilateralism, April 2022. https://highleveladvisoryboard.org/breakthrough/pdf/highleveladvisoryboard_breakthrough_fullreport.pdf.

106 O. Young, *Grand Challenges for Planetary Governance: Global Order in Turbulent Times* (Cheltenham: Edward Elgar, 2021), 15.

107 S. Dixson-Declève et al., *Earth4All: A Survival Guide for Humanity*, online version available at: https://earth4all.life/wp-content/uploads/2023/03/Earth4All_Exec_Summary_EN.pdf.

108 B. Chaffin et al, "Transformative Environmental Governance," *Annual Review of Environmental Resources*, 41 (2016): 399–423.

109 For a good description of power, see T. Morrison, "The black box of power in polycentric environmental governance," *Global Environmental Change*, vol. 57 (2019).

110 See, e.g., J. Klaus & M. Jänicke, *Environmental Governance in Global Perspective: New Approaches to Ecological and Political Modernisation* (Frei Universitat, 2006).

111 J. Bacchus, "The Future of the WTO: Plurilateral or Multilateral," Cato Institute, 2023, available at: https://www.cato.org/sites/cato.org/files/2023-05/bacchus-trade-pa.pdf.

112 H. Schmitz, "Who drives climate-relevant policies in the rising powers?" *New Political Economy* 22:5 (2017): 521–540.

113 R. Berardo & M. Lubell, "Understanding What Shapes a Polycentric Governance System," *Public Administration Review* (2016); R. Bixler, "From Community Forest Management to Polycentric Governance: Assessing Evidence from the Bottom Up," *Society & Natural Resources: An International Journal* 27 (2) (2014): 155–69. See also, A. da Silveira & K. Richards, "The Link Between Polycentrism and Adaptive Capacity in River Basin Governance Systems: Insights from the River Rhine and the Zhujiang (Pearl River) Basin," *Annals of the Association of American Geographers* 103 (2) (2013): 319–29; G. Marshall, "Polycentricity and Adaptive Governance," Working Paper presented at the 15th Biannual International Conference of the International Association for the Study of the Commons, Edmonton, Canada (2015); C. Pahl-Wostl et al., "From Applying Panaceas to Mastering Complexity: Toward Adaptive Water Governance in River Basins," *Environmental Science & Policy* 23 (2013): 24–34; B. Chaffin, H. Gosnell, and B. Cosens, "A decade of adaptive governance scholarship: synthesis and future directions. Ecology and Society 19(3) (2014): 56. See also, J. Ruhl, "Regulation by Adaptive Management – Is It Possible?" 7 *Minnesota Journal of Law, Science & Technology* 21 (2005).

114 W. Adger, K. Neil, and E. Tompkins, "The Political Economy of Cross-Scale Networks in Resource Co-Management," *Ecology and Society* 10 (2) (2015). See also, R. Bixler et al., "Network Governance for Large-Scale Natural Resource Conservation and the Challenge of Capture," *Frontiers in Ecology and the Environment* 14 (3) (2016): 165–171; T. Morrison, "The black box of power in polycentric environmental governance," *Global Environmental Change*, 57 (2019); J. Raab, R.S. Mannak, and B. Cambre, "Combining Structure, Governance, and Context: A Configurational Approach to Network Effectiveness," *Journal of Public Administration Research and Theory* 25 (2015): 479–511; E. Klijn, B. Steijn, and J. Edelenbos, "The Impact of Network Management on Outcomes in Governance Networks," *Public Administration* 88 (2010): 1063–1082; M. Barnes et al., "Social networks and environmental outcomes," *Proceedings of the National Academy of Sciences* (2016); Ö. Bodin, B.I. Crona, "The role of social networks in natural resource governance: What relational patterns make a difference?" *Global Environmental Change* 19 (2009): 366–374; Ö. Bodin, A. Sandström, and B. Crona, "Collaborative Networks for Effective Ecosystem-Based Management: A Set of Working Hypotheses," *Policy Studies Journal* 45 (2017): 289–314.

115 A. Underdal, "Complexity and challenges of long-term environmental govern-ance," *Global Environmental Change* 20(3) (2010): 386–393.
116 R. Beunen & J.Patterson, "Analysing institutional change in environmental gov-ernance: exploring the concept of 'institutional work,'" *Journal of Environmental Planning and Management* 62(1) (2019): 12–29.
117 J. Patterson et al., 'Transformations towards sustainability'. Emerging approaches, critical reflections, and a research agenda," Earth System Governance Working Paper No. 33 (2019).
118 For a good description of mutualism, see, J. Green & J. Hadden, "How Did Environmental Governance Become Complex? Understanding Mutualism Between Environmental NGOs and International Organizations," *International Studies Review* 23(4) (2021): 1792–1812.
119 For the spider analogy, see, Ö. Bodin, "Collaborative environmental governance: Achieving collective action in social-ecological systems," *Science* (2017): 357.

4   Violence as a disease

An immune system against war

The problem: War is back – we are not ready

The early 1990s had a lot going for them. Besides some of the best hip-hop albums of all time, the post-Cold War period produced collective security arrangements amongst major powers that held for decades. Global treaties on the reduction of strategic arms, nuclear non-proliferation, and chemical weapons controls were signed for the first time in history. Amidst a flurry of international peace agreements, the UN Security Council issued more than 200 resolutions, established 15 new peace operations, and oversaw a rapid expansion of its influence globally.[1] Proponents of Western liberal order boldly declared the "end of history," and the inevitable spread of free-market democracy around the globe.[2]

That euphoric period is now over. And though it is not clear how the international system will reorganize itself in the long term, today's world is one of "multipolarity" and competition, not collaboration. Power is spread across many actors and new blocs of contestation, while any semblance of unity of purpose within the multilateral system appears to have evaporated.[3] National security doctrines of major powers speak of growing geostrategic competition, as military expenditures set a new record in 2022.[4] The arms control and military transparency frameworks that helped to maintain relative equilibrium amongst major powers for 30 years are disintegrating, leaving uncertainty in their place.[5] As new escalation points appear around nuclear weapons, emerging technologies, and outer space, the risks of large power confrontation seem to have grown significantly, while the forums for de-escalation are moribund or extinct.

This crisis in global security governance coincides with (and fuels) a worrying set of conflict trends. Deaths from violent conflict increased a staggering 96 percent in 2023, with 79 countries experiencing higher levels of conflict than previous years.[6] Internal wars are becoming increasingly internationalized, with 91 countries now experiencing conflict involving external fighters. The rate of relapse of wars also has been steadily on the rise – as of today, roughly 60 percent of conflicts that reached a peace agreement have already fallen back into war.[7] Add in the growing security implications of climate change, risks posed by emerging technologies, and rapidly rising inequalities worldwide, and the factors driving us towards violent conflicts are clearly

DOI: 10.4324/9781003506386-5

proliferating. Put simply: war is not only back – it seems to be expanding and becoming harder to resolve.[8]

My core argument here is that *there is a mismatch between the complex, interrelated conflict dynamics of today and our global security governance regimes*. Violent conflicts in this century are fought by many different actors, at multiple levels, with a wide variety of instruments. They are often caused by deeply rooted social, economic, and political factors that are difficult to resolve via traditional state-driven, top-down structures. They tend to move across hierarchies, blending geopolitical dynamics with local ones. And, as a result, they traverse space and time in dynamic and surprising ways. Look at how the social uprisings of the Arab Spring became a regionally-based conflict in Syria, drawing in major powers and a range of mercenary/proxy groups, fueling the rise of ISIS, which has in turn appeared in the Sahel, Mozambique, and Southeast Asia. From Yemen to Myanmar to Gaza to Ukraine, today's violent conflicts demonstrate all the characteristics of a complex adaptive system. This is not a controversial point – scholars have investigated the complexity of security dynamics in a wide range of settings for a long time.[9]

However, *our security architecture has been consciously kept complicated, not complex*.[10] Consider the entities tasked with addressing global security risks. Bodies like the UN Security Council are not only exclusively the domain of (a very few) states but are also structurally cut off from the major financial, social, human rights, environmental, and development institutions.[11] Similarly, the regimes we have developed to regulate the risks of strategic weapons, biological threats, cyberthreats, and weaponized technologies are intentionally isolated from each other and from the rest of the multilateral system. When it comes to the deeper drivers of violent conflict – inequality, poor governance, criminality, underdevelopment, lack of accountability, political and economic exclusion – our governance architecture is scattered and largely left to national governments to sort out on their own.

The result of this highly fractured, exclusive architecture is that our security governance systems are slow, fragile, and unable to respond to new dynamics. Unlike complex systems, which tend to have a resilience to major shocks, we live in fear of a small change that could cause a collapse of our security systems. The US withdrawal from the Iran nuclear deal could have triggered a major escalation, with little capacity in the international system to constrain it. Russia's invasion of Ukraine caused a massive ripple effect across the world, while the Security Council sat paralyzed by the veto. The war between Israel and Hamas has pushed the entire Middle East region to the brink of all-out war, while major powers quibble over the wording of ceasefire texts in an increasingly irrelevant Security Council chamber.

Our security architecture has also failed to address deeper drivers of violence. The past five years have witnessed a steady shift towards securitized, authoritarian forms of governance in many parts of the world, driving even greater levels of inequality and exclusion. But these changes happen largely below the international radar, manifesting as growing crime rates, or social unrest, or increases in domestic violence rates. Our complex socioeconomic systems move us towards the next round of violent conflicts, while our fragmented, rigid governance systems are unable to adapt. Unless we find better solutions, we may spend the next several decades hovering on the verge of a world of wars, our geopolitics defined by brinksmanship and an inability to react to emerging risks.

The big proposals for improving global security governance outlined below could help to address some of these shortcomings. Expanding the Security Council might broaden the playing field a bit and potentially dilute the power of veto-wielding members (though not much). Building stronger regional constellations of actors might create a bulwark against some of the larger risks on the horizon. And the efforts to bolster more local, upstream forms of conflict prevention across the multilateral system offer promising avenues towards a more interconnected security response. But each of these proposals on its own is unlikely to resolve the more fundamental problem of "fit" between the complex systems that drive violent conflict and our siloed security institutions.

Here, complexity thinking suggests we start with the strong attractors to conflict present in our system. These are the gravitational forces within our social, political, economic, and cultural systems that push us towards violent conflict. The global governance discussion then becomes about generating a counterbalance to these attractors, building new centers of gravity, and ultimately creating a political landscape that encourages a shift away from securitization and militarization. As described below, this leads to some surprising ideas for how we might respond to the coming risks of violent conflict.

Three ideas: Go big, go to the club, go local

There are diverse proposals for improving our global governance of security which can be clustered into three main types: (1) fixing things at the top (going big); (2) getting groups of states to take action together (going to the club); and (3) going local by empowering more locally and regionally grounded responses to insecurity.

Idea 1: Go big

The starting point for almost every discussion on global governance is the historical moment of 1945. Rising from the ashes of World War II, the UN was born as an institution explicitly designed to prevent great power conflict. It is no coincidence that the permanent five members of the Security Council are the major nuclear powers of that era, and it is the explicit purpose of the UN to protect the territorial integrity from aggression by any of its members. But, as the usual conversation goes, things have changed, and the multilateral system must change with it. Some version of "we cannot address today's threats with a 1940s organization" is behind nearly every reform effort.

The most obvious place to start is the Security Council, the apex actor for addressing threats to international peace and security. Composed of five permanent and ten non-permanent members, the Council is one of the most exclusive clubs in the world. Council reform typically encompasses three main areas: (1) expanding membership (permanent and non-permanent seats), (2) the question of the veto power of the P5 members, and (3) the relationship between the Council and the General Assembly.[12] Council reform has been squarely on the agenda since Secretary-General Boutros-Ghali's 1992 Agenda for Peace and the 1993 creation of the Open-Ended Working Group tasked with identifying options for reform.[13] Over the past 30 years, a wide range of formulas have been offered, most focused on either a small expansion of the permanent seats, or a more substantial increase in the non-permanent seats, helping to better reflect the geopolitical realities of today.[14] In his 2022 and 2023 speeches to the UN General Assembly, President Biden called for a renewed effort at Council reform, while the High-Level Advisory Board on Effective Multilateralism proposed that the 2024 Summit of the Future should open a Charter review conference on the topic of Council reform.[15]

Given the low likelihood of achieving reforms in the short term, a range of alternative proposals have been made, including: (1) creating a Global Resilience Council to address the large number of threats to human security not covered by the Security Council; (2) empowering the General Assembly to take more frequent and direct action in the case of threats to international peace and security; and (3) bolstering the capacities and mandate of the Peacebuilding Commission, potentially even transforming it into a Council.[16] Taken together, these ideas aim to empower and broaden the highest level governance institutions.

Idea 2: Go to the club

There is a growing trend of member states withdrawing from – or reducing support for – international security arrangements. This can be a visible decision by a major power, such as the US withdrawal from the Iran nuclear deal in 2018, or Russia suspending its participation in the nuclear arms treaty with the US. Or it can be the gradual movement away from multilateral forums for the resolution of ongoing conflicts, such as the decision to host Syria talks in Astana and Sochi, or Mali's rejection of a UN peace operation in favor of bilateral military support. Or it can be the willingness to let international security institutions grind to a halt, such as the lack of progress in the Conference on Disarmament, or the Nuclear Non-Proliferation Treaty, or the diminishing participation in the UN registries designed to build greater transparency and trust in terms of security risks (and how many of you have heard of UNMILEX or UNROCA, the UN's military registries?).

Some of the withdrawal from multilateral security arrangements reflects the populist moment in which we live. Trump's "America First," or Modi's

"India First," or Putin's aggression against Ukraine all speak to a growing push for nationally-driven, isolationist paradigms of global affairs. I had thought of a separate category here called the "go home" idea, reflecting this abandonment of internationalism and focus on domestic policy. This remains a worrying trend.

But more relevant for international security governance is the reconfiguration around "clubs." A "club" in this context refers to a group of states that have come together around a common purpose, while not necessarily strategically aligned on all matters. Whether NATO's response to Russia in the Ukraine, a push for more AU-led peace support operations in Africa, G7 announcements about global security, the growing use of "plurilateral" or "minilateral" agreements within the WTO, or the BRICS countries' common positions security, the club appears to be the main outcome of geopolitical fracture.[17] And many of the biggest initiatives on global security today are based on the idea of a club taking first action, paving the way for others to join.

Idea 3: Go local

Faced with low prospects of fixing the system at the top and an increasingly difficult geopolitical terrain, the past ten years have witnessed an attempt to push security governance downwards, characterized by two clusters of proposals. The first can be thought of as regional outsourcing: transferring greater authority and resources to regional bodies that may be better placed to respond to conflict risks and build better governance in fragile settings. This is not a new idea. Chapter VIII of the UN Charter envisages involvement of regional bodies in the maintenance of international peace and security, including specific provisions for the Security Council to authorize regionally-led peace operations. Successive high-level reports have stressed the special importance of granting greater strategic authority and resources to regional bodies – especially the African Union – and the recently-published *New Agenda for Peace* proposes that the AU be given access to the UN's assessed contributions for peace support operations.[18] The idea here is that regional organizations are closer to the realities on the ground, more likely to hold legitimacy with conflict actors, and able to maintain a longer-term engagement for the drawn out processes of building strong governance capacities to sustain peace.

This line of thinking underscores perhaps an even more significant push downwards, towards more local approaches to conflict resolution and peace-building. This so-called "local turn" or "bottom-up" approach to peace and security has manifested in a shift towards initiatives to empower communities to address conflict dynamics themselves.[19] Here, local actors are the "primary architects, owners and long-term stakeholders" of peace, and success is determined not by top-down criteria, but via local "frameworks."[20] In fact, "the local" has become one of the most frequently-repeated keywords across development, peacebuilding, and peacekeeping interventions globally.[21] The term "local" appears 46 times in the landmark Brahimi Report of the UN, 382 times in the 2011 World Development Report, and is by far the most common refrain I've heard after working for 15 years in the UN system.[22]

Part of the local turn is about conflict prevention, acting early to stop risks before they get out of hand. When asked what his top three priorities were upon taking office, Secretary-General Guterres replied, "Prevention, prevention, prevention." He is the third successive SG to make prevention a top priority, and we can go back to the days of Dag Hammarskjöld to see that preventing violent conflict is at the heart of global governance of security. Over the past five years, the most important set of proposals has been made around what experts call "upstream" or "structural" prevention. This refers to identifying the deeper social causes of violent conflict – things like ethnic divisions, inequality, poverty, unfair access to resources – and ramping up programming to address these "root causes." The key theory of change here is "if we can improve national and local governance capacities to meet the needs of communities, the risks of violent conflict will be reduced."

These three clusters of proposals are very different from each other, but they tend to share a similar set of beliefs about how change happens. The core assumption is that state failure and poor governance are the heart of the problem. Chronic violence, poverty, and corruption are not merely signals of underdevelopment and bad governance – they are "the single most important problem for world order."[23] From a global governance standpoint, ungoverned or poorly governed space is the "black hole" from which terrorism, poverty, refugees, and other risks emanate, a "weak link" in our world order.[24] Fixing bad governance at the local source and shoring up these weak links is the solution.

This preoccupation with fixing failed states has driven a massive industry to improve and extend state governance capacities since the early 1990s.[25] In Afghanistan, the US spent more than $100 billion to rebuild state institutions after the 2001 invasion. International support to Somalia runs in the billions per year.[26] And the UN Security Council has diverted massive portions of the UN's roughly $7 billion peacekeeping budget to state-building in places like the Democratic Republic of the Congo, Mali, Central African Republic, and South Sudan. These investments demonstrate a "peace as governance" mindset with an overwhelming focus on building up the capacities of state institutions to deliver security and basic services to its populations. As David Chandler succinctly put it: peacebuilding = state-building = institution-building.[27] This paradigm is neatly captured in the New Agenda for Peace's call for every country in the world to develop national prevention strategies to "reinforce State institutions, promote the rule of law and strengthen civil society and social cohesion."[28]

What's wrong with these proposals? Apart from their long track record of failure, nothing per se. But there is a reason every conversation I've had on peace and security in the past three years has ended with a shrug and some version of "but we know this isn't really going to solve the bigger problem." As Jan Pospisil succinctly notes, "there is a remarkable inertia in liberal peace."[29] Continually focusing on building towards a liberal model of good governance seems to have become an act of endless deferral, an acceptance that we are going to fail no matter what.[30] There is another way.

What can complexity thinking offer global security governance?

If we think of global security governance as a machine that needs fixing, then it makes sense to tinker with the pieces, or even replace some of them. Adding some members to the Security Council, putting some more money into the Peacebuilding Commission, strengthening national/local governance institutions, all sound like reasonable proposals. And if we think in linear terms of conflict arising from poorly governed or undergoverned spaces, then it also makes sense to try to fix the problem by supplying capacities and investments in governance institutions. But if we think of violent conflict as part of a complex adaptive system, then the discussion shifts towards adaptive governance. Here we need to ask what the underlying rules and patterns of the system are, how we can gradually alter the gravitational pulls away from violence, and how we might need to constantly adapt our responses to new shocks.

Attractors of conflict

Think of the outbreak of war as the result of a positive, escalatory feedback loop. Opposing parties see the other side in increasingly zero-sum terms, creating a set of reactions and response patterns that grow over time. As the "enemy" is defined solely as a threat, options narrow, groups become trapped in a feeling of irreversibility, the capacities to walk back from the brink become constrained. This narrowing of thoughts, feelings, and actions is what Peter Coleman calls the "attractor landscape" for conflict. It describes how a complex dynamic system can evolve from a wide range of possible outcomes into a highly polarized one where conflict is much more likely. Attractors "channel mental and behavioral experience into a narrow range of malignant (but coherent) states."[31]

The genocide in Rwanda is an example of how quickly a complex social system can become polarized and plunge into mass violence. After decades of gradually increasing hostilities between Hutus and Tutsi, early 1994 witnessed a snowball effect of animosity between the groups, where inter-ethnic hatred quickly escalated and overwhelmed the capacities of its leaders to bring the system back into balance. We see somewhat similar dynamics in the US today, where the deeply entrenched political positions of the Republicans and Democrats offer fewer and fewer opportunities to find a middle ground, and where every gain of one side is seen as a loss to the other.[32] And we see it on the world stage, where polarization between the

US and China has created an escalatory dynamic that may push them into conflict over Taiwan.[33]

I think of a *strong* attractor for violent conflict as one where a destructive threshold has been crossed, where the number of options for de-escalation has been reduced, and where the positive feedback loops overwhelm the negative ones. In these situations, the emergence of stable attractors indicate that the system is actually self-organizing around violence. This dynamic occurs across hierarchies from individual animosity to group hatred to official state positions. It is able to cascade up and down levels and becomes a sort of form of communication amongst actors. And it means that systems in conflict tend to return to conflict over time, circling back to their strong attractors even if momentarily interrupted (by a peacekeeping operation, for example).[34]

In my work in eastern Congo and South Sudan, I would often hear people speak of this strong gravitational pull of violence in their lives, and the sense of inevitability they felt. One South Sudanese woman told me, "We might go many months in peace, but we know that as soon as there is any new event like a heavy storm, or some cattle go missing, or the price of oil changes, that's when the violence starts again."[35] She was describing a social system with a strong attractor around violence: when it experiences even a small disruption, violence is the way the system returns to equilibrium.

Conflict attractors

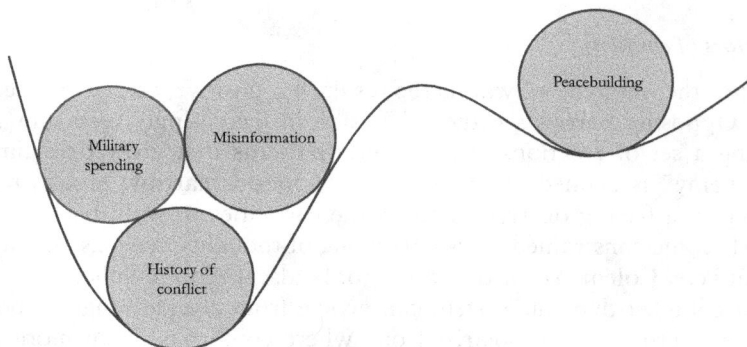

Shifting conflict attractors

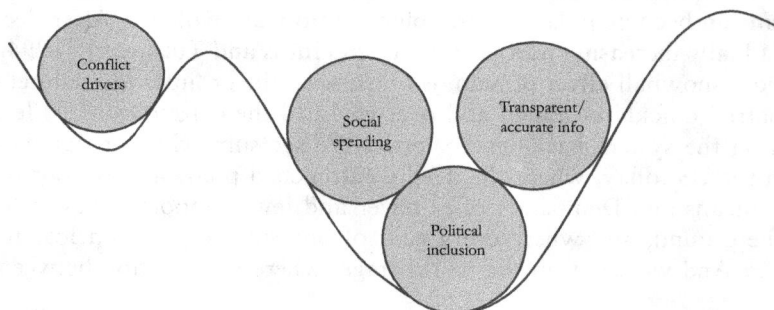

This understanding of conflict dynamics has tectonic implications for how we think of our global security responses. It suggests that we should pay much more attention to the following functions of our governance systems:

1. *A reset button*: Complex systems are especially sensitive to the conditions of their early formation. Think of young children taught to believe something and how hard it is to dislodge that early belief. Similarly, if one country is organized around an endless opposition to another (India vs. Pakistan, US vs. Russia, Israel vs. Palestine), that polarization will tend to collapse the range of options towards conflict. Finding ways to generate a "reset" or a large disruption in those conditions can be a crucial way to break conflict attractors.[36]

2. *A counterbalance*: Weakening the effect of a conflict attractor is not enough. We need to create a new, heavier gravitational pull that draws activity towards it. This can mean investing in "peace positive" activities with a proven track record, or connecting actors and institutions in a way that generates new incentives. At the very least, it means studying settings that have managed to avoid a descent into conflict, to understand what they are getting right. And finding ways to reorient the flows of resources (money and political energy) so they begin to cluster around non-violent actors and processes.

3. *Disrupting bad information loops*: Sometimes a system will fall into a pattern of reinforcement of bad patterns, in part due to faulty information or misperceptions. A landmark study of Israeli and Palestinian perceptions demonstrated that each side thought the other side's perceptions were worse than reality, in part because the information they had about the other side was distorted by the media and their own echo chambers.[37] This is typical: when we lack a constant feedback loop of accurate information, we tend to fall into our worst assumptions. At a global level, we see this playing out in escalatory rhetoric amongst major powers, while they simultaneously retreat from the agreements that allow for good information flows. Building forums and processes that generate solid, transparent information to all actors is central to building trust and a shared basis for decision-making and crucially important to global governance.

4. *Going viral*: Complex systems evolve across hierarchies as change in one part of the system rapidly affects the rest of it. This can look like a pandemic expanding from a health crisis to one that destabilizes financial and political domains, too. It can look like a populist movement in one country suddenly becoming a global trend. Complexity demands that we think of how small changes can "go viral," spreading rapidly across time and space. It suggests that we can "entangle" our peace efforts in the root structures of societies.[38] And it also pushes us to think of violence more like a disease that can metastasize, infecting our social and political systems.

What do these insights from complexity mean for the specific proposals on the table today? What can we do next? The remainder of this chapter explores some specific ideas, directions, and proposals that could emerge (pun intended) from an application of complexity thinking to global security governance. They are not meant to endorse a particular proposal, but to give a sense of the interesting and often counterintuitive directions we can explore with complexity.

Spokes and motion, not hubs

Reforming the Security Council, or bolstering the Peacebuilding Commission, or creating a new more inclusive body to address security threats all share a common paradigm: we need to get more actors involved at the center. The same is true of many of the (laudable and important) proposals to increase civil society and youth representation on major UN bodies. "We need more people around the table," is a common refrain. And this makes sense: expanding the Security Council to include permanent members from Africa would add much-needed legitimacy to a body that spends most of its time focused on the African continent. And though it would do nothing to address the main obstacle to Council action – the use of the veto by its permanent members – an expanded membership could help to create a counterbalance to it. But there is also a risk that adding more members might just add weight to existing polarization: some countries would be added on "Russia and China's side" and some on the "US, UK, and France's side." I have spoken to many of those involved in Council reform processes – all speak of this risk.

Complexity thinking recognizes the importance of strong, inclusive nodes within systems, but also pushes us to think of more distributed approaches to governance. Here, we can use complexity to reframe the Security Council reform debate. Instead of focusing solely on getting more actors into the Security Council – strengthening it with numbers – perhaps we should be more concerned with distributing security governance mandates and capacities outward across the system. After all, the Security Council was designed to prevent a direct aggression between great powers, not necessarily the kinds of internationalized civil wars we see today. Rather than asking the Security Council to do more, maybe we should keep it in its lane and focus on empowering others to drive more of the action.

What might this look like in practice? Broadly, it could take the form of *institutional deference*, where the Security Council gradually recognizes a more lead role of other actors in addressing non-traditional security threats.[39] Here are some concrete ideas, building on proposals already out there:

- *Empowering the General Assembly as a concurrent security actor.* The 1950 Uniting for Peace resolution stands for the principle that the General Assembly can act when the Security Council is unable or unwilling to respond. This resolution has been underutilized, though recent years have seen an attempt to revitalize it, and also to use the General

Assembly more creatively to hold the Security Council accountable for its inaction.[40] But the General Assembly also has a longstanding (if not well known) set of practices to address international insecurity, including deployment of mediators, establishment of peace operations, mandating of special envoys, and creation of accountability mechanisms such as sanctions and investigations.[41] One potentially fruitful pathway would be to more specifically empower to use these tools, not as a last resort after the Security Council fails, but as part of its daily work. The 2023 General Assembly resolution on revitalizing the body's work suggests that it might be open to exploring a more direct role on conflict prevention and resolution.[42] We could start there.

- *Turning subsidiarity upside down.* While a slippery subject, subsidiarity is generally understood as a presumption that the lowest level within a hierarchy should take the lead.[43] Weak subsidiary means that the presumption is easily overruled, allowing authority to move upwards; strong subsidiarity places a higher threshold for deciding to escalate decision-making within a system.[44] But in general, subsidiarity aims to resolve issues at the lowest possible level. Within global security governance, we not only have a weak and narrow use of subsidiarity, but authority starts at the top. The UN Security Council (at the top) has "primary" responsibility for international peace and security, and its authority can be delegated downward to regional organizations by its own decision (or occasionally when it fails comprehensively to act).[45] A good example of this is the 2023 New Agenda for Peace, which proposes that the AU be delegated access to UN resources for AU peace operations authorized by the Security Council (again, top down). Unfortunately, this means that the body which has proven itself chronically unable to act (the Security Council) must act to trigger subsidiarity. Complexity thinking suggests starting with more distributed authorities, giving regional organizations (and maybe local actors) a more direct and resourced role in driving responses to conflict risks from the outset. What if, for example, the Security Council's decisions on African peacekeeping were first discussed within the AU and based upon a proposed resolution by the AU Peace and Security Council? Or what if there was a standing resolution that authorized regional organizations to take a much broader range of security actions on their own, essentially delegating authority and resources ahead of time? These are not necessarily the exact proposals needed, but starting to turn the subsidiarity issue upside down seems like a sensible place to begin. And it could be part of the "reset button" needed to move us into a different kind of conversation about security.
- *Banking on peace.* When the UN/World Bank Pathways for Peace report came out in 2018, I thought it would be the beginning of a strategic partnership between the two organizations (not even really two, because the World Bank is part of the UN). The report clearly identified a set

of common drivers of violent conflict and seemed to point the way to a collaborative approach to preventing it, with the World Bank and UN joined at the head and the hip. This has not happened. Apart from some light coordination at working level and some in-country joint analysis, there is no common strategic vision driving the UN and World Bank's work on violent conflict. Developing one would help to align the large International Financial Institution funding flows more directly with agreed priorities, moving resources in the right direction. As discussed in more detail below, redirecting resource flows away from the attractor basins of conflict – and having safeguards to prevent capture – can help to counterbalance the tendencies of systems to lapse into violence.

Ultimately, these kinds of ideas promote what complexity theorists call "convergence," where competing and hierarchically different spheres of authority can be brought around a common set of outcomes and approaches.[46] They might not be exactly the way forward, but they give a sense of the kind of discussions that complexity thinking could drive us towards.

Finally, it is worth flagging one of the most important insights from complexity thinking: *small changes to rhythms, spaces, and routines can have enormous impacts on systemic outcomes.*[47] There is fascinating and persuasive research showing that people have a much harder time maintaining violently opposed positions when they are taken out of their usual surroundings, made to walk around, or put in situations where they confront new experiences.[48] Those who study the Balkan crisis of the early 1990s will remember Richard Holbrooke's decision to bring Milošević to Dayton, Ohio and discuss the peace deal while walking beneath the wings of America fighter jets. This got Milošević quite literally out of his comfort zone and tilted the negotiations towards an agreement.[49]

Here, the Security Council reform discussion could be reframed by bringing the Council more frequently into direct contact with the actors, settings, and dynamics it is addressing. What if the Council held one out of every three meetings in the country it was discussing? Or if the Council traveled to Addis to hold its Africa meetings in the AU's premises? What if the Council's next deliberation on conflict-induced displacement in Syria was held on a bus traveling from Syria to Turkey, or walking around an IDP camp? How would a Council session within sight of the Rafah crossing between Gaza and Egypt change the discussion on humanitarian access? These ideas may sound far-fetched, but empirical research has shown that polarized dynamics can be strongly disrupted by changes of venue, shifts in the physical set up of actors, and even locomotion.[50]

One of the most common phrases in the Security Council is that it will remain "seized" of the matter. I often think of the Council as being "seized up," stuck in a static constellation of chairs around a circular table with their backs to the real world. Having sat in that chamber dozens of times taking notes (and occasionally dozing off amidst hours of prepared statements), I believe the physical space in New York has become an impediment to breaking the Council's deadlock. As Peter Coleman suggests, we may need to quite literally "get moving."[51]

Transparency as a feedback loop

International institutions play a range of functions in global governance, one of which is the consolidation and transmittal of information. The START treaty between the US and Russia contained a robust "data exchange" provision, along with verification mechanisms and a bilateral consultative commission. This allowed for constant exchange of information between the two countries, reducing the risks of miscalculation around the use of strategic weapons and keeping a wider range of options on the table. Similar possibilities for sharing information about security developments and weapons are central to the UN Conference on Disarmament, the Biological Weapons Convention, and the Chemical Weapons Convention. In fact, there are entire UN bodies dedicated to registering and tracking weapons.[52]

The decline in use of these bodies and the disintegration of major security treaties – like the Iran nuclear agreement and the START treaty – is bad in itself, but also reduces the prospects for information flows amongst actors. Specifically, the lack of common, scientifically vetted sources of information opens the door to more malignant sources of misinformation and disinformation. Imagine a scenario where a deep fake of Putin announces a nuclear attack on the US, or where social media is suddenly viral with announcements of a Chinese invasion of Taiwan.[53] What forums do we have to correct this potentially catastrophic misinformation? We are increasingly like a colony of antennae-less ants, unable to exchange information to produce a collectively beneficial response.

One of the insights from complexity thinking is that actors with insufficient information tend to overreact, to "go ballistic" in the face of crises.[54] In cloudy, uncertain moments, we often assume the worst, jump straight to worst-case scenarios, and act accordingly. Uncertainty and lack of information become a positive feedback loop, driving us towards escalation. In contrast, systems that enable flows of accurate and trusted information across levels and communities are far less likely to experience disproportionate, violent overreactions.[55]

This suggests we should be placing far more attention and resources on building forums for information exchange and transparency within our global governance architecture. In addition to trying to revitalize existing mechanisms, here are three concrete ideas:

1. *A security feedback loop.* A security transparency platform could bring together information from existing arms control bodies, a range of scientists and security experts, and resources to track and generate high-quality information on security. Such a platform could build consensus

on trends, increasingly knowledge on potential risks, and offering a way to reduce risks in real time. We often speak of a red telephone to connect world leaders in times of crisis. That red phone should be complemented by amber and green ones, less crisis-oriented channels of information-sharing about military capacities, risks, and intent that can form a sort of daily exchange. Even bodies like the now-defunct US/Russia START treaty offered ways to share such information. At a minimum, investing more in information exchange and transparency might reduce some of the worst feedback loops of misinformation and disinformation.[56]

2. *Unblock information flows across the UN system.* Different parts of the UN system produce a staggering amount of information. A lot of it is very dull, but a surprising amount is relevant to our understandings of security risks. The Food and Agriculture Organization and World Food Programme's data on food insecurity, for example, paints a detailed and very accurate account of where the next food-driven shocks might escalate into violence (in fact, whenever I do field research, I try to start with the food people – they have a much better sense of conflict dynamics than most political officers). UNEP's Global Environmental Outlook (GEO) has an enormous amount of information relevant to climate-driven security threats, though few people I have met have read all 708 pages of the latest edition of the GEO report. The UN Human Rights Council produces massive amounts of empirical data on rights violations, trends in violent extremism, digital threats, and repression of communities, all of which could be part of an early warning system for violent conflict. UN peacekeeping has an enormous repository of data drawn from its operations, almost none of which is shared beyond the Department of Peace Operations. In some cases, this information is accessible but siloed. In others – such as the Security Council's refusal to accept cross-fertilization of Human Rights Council information – it is actively blocked.[57] In an age of big data and digital capacities, there are technologically easy ways these lakes of information could flow together, generating an empirically strong basis for a common understanding of security dynamics.

3. *A right to truth?* Much of today's political discourse focuses on the right to free speech. And in an era of growing surveillance capacities and authoritarian tendencies, it is critical that free speech is protected. But just as you cannot shout "fire" in a crowded movie theater or burn a cross on your front lawn in the US, certain forms of speech are considered inflammatory and dangerous. Free speech has a limit and, though it's fuzzy, that limit is meant for our safety. This points to an interesting question: do populations have a right to scientifically-vetted information about issues that matter for our collective security and welfare? If, for example, we are wrongly told that Putin is going to fire a nuclear weapon towards the US and it triggers mass hysteria and deaths, should the authors of that misinformation be held responsible? Probably. But could we think more ambitiously about translating that limit into a

"norm of truth," a gradually evolving common understanding that some areas require an additional layer of independent fact-checking.

Again, these three ideas may not be precisely the models that should be adopted to address the problem of opacity in our global security governance. But they point in a direction that could help to unlock some of the more entrenched problems we see today. And they also suggest that we could be doing more to develop and spread a norm of transparency and communication around security, building towards a consensus that our collective safety requires a common, empirically-founded understanding of risks. As complexity scholars have shown, norms can cascade surprisingly quickly around the world, feeling like "the way we've always done it" in a remarkably short time.[58]

From fixing to re-landscaping

The world can be thought of as both a physical and an imaginary landscape. In the physical world, water falls on the sides of mountains and runs down towards sea level. In our socioeconomic system, resources (money and political energy) flow towards the basins of attraction, the areas with strong gravitational pull. These basins tend to get deeper, with a stronger pull, when our systems are stressed. A good example of this is the war in Ukraine, which generated a strong shock around the world. Faced with Putin's saber rattling, a massive humanitarian catastrophe, and an unequivocal violation of the international prohibition on aggression, global military spending skyrocketed. Increases in military spending of course occurred in Ukraine's neighbors, but the largest increases were in the US, India, and China, far from the immediate theater of war.[59] The strong attractor of militarization kicked in.

I found a worrying parallel when I began looking at the UN and World Bank's peacebuilding programming, tracking where the resources ended up. Over and over, we encountered peacebuilding projects with the stated goal of addressing the underlying conflict drivers of inequality and political grievances. This should have meant that money and political support flowed outward from the center, supporting communities in neglected peripheries. But we found that resources were repeatedly getting stuck in the center, captured by a small political elite, and often by the military.[60] As Oisín Tansey and Sarah von Billerbeck have observed, this strong tendency of elite capture demonstrates how peacebuilding can unintentionally enable authoritarianism, with the consequence of locking in exactly the securitized dynamics it is trying to combat.[61]

Rachel Kleinfeld's wonderful book, *A Savage Order*, adds a layer to this set of insights. Not only does violence move like a disease across societies, but we have a strong tendency to respond with increasingly securitized responses to it. Faced with growing rates of violence, governments often strengthen the hand of their security forces, making them less accountable and more brutal. This in turn has the effect of normalizing violence and reducing societal inhibitions around resort to violent, criminal behavior. Middle classes, fearing spread to their communities, tend to encourage a heavier-handed security response, which amplifies the positive feedback loop of violence in society. By prioritizing and resourcing security, we enter a vicious cycle where a transition to peace may require a reset button or some other strong jolt.

What does this mean for the big proposals and ideas for improving global security governance? First, we need to worry about the strong attractor of militarization and security sector capture. We cannot assume that just aiming at equitable settlements will be enough; there is a high chance that our good intentions will be distorted. The (good) ideas of adding more funds to peacebuilding, or expanding the mandate of the Peacebuilding Commission, or even creating a Peacebuilding Council will need to be accompanied by a specific effort to counterbalance the gravitational pull of securitization. Here are some ideas:

- *A peacebuilding prism*: What if the UN's peacebuilding architecture were set up like a prism, reflecting resources away from militarization and towards the kind of social spending that tends to address the deeper causes of violence? The Peacebuilding Commission could more explicitly track how resources flowed in conflict settings, with benchmarks around demilitarization and incentives for those settings that demonstrated trends towards more social spending. You see the idea: create stronger gravitational pulls away from the kind of securitization cycles that drive us ineluctably towards violence.
- *An authoritarianism disruption – local elections*: Authoritarian systems tend to drive resources and power to the center, including by co-opting institutions of the state.[62] The result is often a highly-militarized state focused on protecting itself from threats. This means that our typical formulas for addressing conflict risks – building up rule of law institutions, supporting police, funding national elections – all have a strong tendency to become captured by authoritarian systems.[63] Once in place, authoritarian regimes can be extraordinarily resilient, becoming deeply entrenched and difficult to dislodge even over long periods of time.[64] Ironically, international interventions in these settings appear to mimic and reaffirm that strong centripetal force of authoritarian systems: we pour resources into state institutions that are flow-through points towards a small elite, and we focus all of our political attention on executive/presidential elections. This creates a winner-take all feel, where the international community is waiting for whoever wins the next (and often dubious) presidential election, forced to work with whoever takes the reins.[65] In contrast, the most positively disruptive activity would be to generate space for political plurality and meaningful contestation at the sub-national level. Investing in local elections

rather than putting all eggs in executive ones could have a far more disruptive effect.[66]

The same is true at the global level, where we need to weaken the strong attractor of militarization and elite capture. The Secretary-General's New Agenda for Peace has one potentially helpful idea: produce a report on the social and economic impacts of military spending.[67] That's a good start, but we could be more ambitious. Here's a complementary proposal:

- *A demilitarization conditionality*: Could the World Bank and International Monetary Fund have explicit conditions on their investments that limited security sector capture and incentivized social spending? Could a group of big donors commit to demilitarization and reductions in security sector spending as a top priority for their support? Could we begin to think of our global governance architecture as a sort of re-landscaping where we gradually fill in the sinkholes of military spending and start to dig out basins where greater resources will flow to social programming?

These are just some of the kinds of ideas that could move the conversation towards a better fit between our institutions and the problems we are trying to solve. Eventually, our governance systems may need to evolve to generate a "repeller" effect, where militarization is a social taboo, a steep hill in our attractor landscape that is difficult to ascend.[68]

An immunity to war

One of the most important insights in the past decade of peace and security research is that violence acts more like a disease than we may have thought. Studies have shown that high rates of domestic violence contribute to greater risks of civil war, that communities with a history of violence have a strong tendency to relapse into large-scale conflict, and that violence can spread like a virus across large geographic spaces.[69] "Bad" norms like dictatorship, political violence, and repression can spread as easily as "good" ones.[70] In fact, we can think of a set of "pre-existing conditions" that create a higher chance of catching the violence bug. High rates of inequality, political exclusion, and a legacy of colonial rule are certainly among the top precursors to violent conflict.[71] And violence may be more like dengue than chicken pox: once a community has experienced widespread violence, it does not necessarily develop an immunity to it, but rather may be more susceptible to a second, more serious bout. You do not want to catch dengue twice. Similarly, the scholarship on conflict relapse supports a conclusion that settings with a history of violent conflict are far more likely to experience it again, often worse than the first time.[72]

Adaptive approaches to peacebuilding, pioneered by Cedric de Coning, can be seen as an attempt to build up a societal immunity (resilience) to violent conflict. Adaptive peacebuilding adopts an explicitly evolutionary approach by (1) generating many initiatives together with local authorities, (2) monitoring the effects these initiatives are having, and (3) investing in those producing the desired result.[73] The idea here is to mirror natural selection: initiatives that have the intended impact are selected and resourced for the next round, those that fail are discarded. Proponents of adaptive peacebuilding are careful to avoid the pitfalls of treating conflict-affected societies as Petri dishes for experimentation, instead speaking of "structured learning process together with the society or community" involved.[74] Adaptive peacebuilding demands that local actors generate their own solutions for testing, not merely accept what is being offered by external intervenors.[75]

There are certainly challenges in applying adaptive peacebuilding at the global governance level. Most of the scholarship on adaptive peace envisions a one or more warring parties inside a country testing out approaches that may address the underlying conflict dynamics. In South Sudan, for example, the UN's options included investing in a new set of mobile courts, training police, and cantoning armed groups in separate camps. Over time, my sense was that there was much greater return on investment in the mobile courts than the more traditional activities of supporting cantonment and security sector reform. Similarly, in eastern Congo, I believe the UN's experiments with investing in greater capacities to adjudicate sexual violence have resulted in more change than much of its longstanding disarmament and reintegration programming.[76] The costs of trial and error may be significant, but the process of selection seems manageable.

It is much more difficult to imagine an iterative, adaptive approach to international security threats. There is no room for trial and error with nuclear weapons. There isn't really scope for the UN or any other group of actors to test out a variety of interventions to resolve the US/Russia stand-off, or mitigate the growing tensions around Taiwan. But I think the underlying ideas of adaptation, learning, and feedback loops show enormous promise. Forums for more transparent information flows could help to dislodge great power antagonists from cycles of distrust and escalation and prevent a collapse into polarization. Helping to shape the financial landscape to channel resources away from militarization could lead to enormous reductions in the risks of violence in the long term. And distributing more decision-making authority outside of stagnant institutional centers could add much-needed flexibility and nimbleness to our governance of security threats.

These examples bring us to the final thought experiment on global security governance. Think of the main multilateral institutions on security: the UN Security Council, the General Assembly, the First Committee, the Conference on Disarmament, the key treaty bodies on nuclear and biological weapons, the main regional actors like the AU Peace and Security Council and NATO. These institutions can be thought of as a pure and static reflection of member-state interests, a set of rooms where actors meet to articulate their positions and nothing more. "The UN is just a collection of Member States," one senior UN official told me. "We can't expect the UN to do more than what its membership wants." That may be legally true: our international legal order is based on the specific commitments of its member states. But conceptualizing international security governance as just a reflection of these interests consolidated in institutions means that when tensions escalate and when options begin to narrow, the scope for action narrows equally quickly.

Rather than think of our security governance institutions as locations where states express a limited set of commitments, perhaps we could re-envision them as a network designed to keep options open. Every time tensions rise and the risks of large-scale violence increase, the question we should ask is how to prevent what Peter Coleman calls a "collapse of multidimensionality." This means designing and using our institutions as flow-through points for information, forums to disrupt the strong tendency to militarize, a permeable membrane that continuously allows new ideas and options to flow in. This echoes Jan Pospisil's idea of "political unsettlement."[77] I think unsettlement could mean preventing the kind of gridlock that occurs when all our efforts go into institutionalizing agreements, instead keeping options open and information flowing at moments when parties tend to become rigid and polarized. This understanding of unsettlement recognizes that we cannot control the system, but we can help it to avoid getting stuck in the same cycles and entrenched patterns that characterize today's security discussions. If violence is like a disease that can metastasize, shift, and grow, then our security responses need to look and feel more like an immune system that continuously produces antibodies to slow its spread until a good match is found and the disease can be beaten back.

Notes

1 D. Malone & A. Day, "The UN at 75: How Today's Challenges Will Shape the Next 25 Years. *Global Governance: A Review of Multilateralism and International Organizations,* 26(2) (2020): 236–250, available at: https://doi.org/10.1163/19426720-02602004.
2 F. Fukuyama, *The end of history and the last man* (New York: Simon and Schuster, 2006).
3 The New Agenda for Peace policy brief, available at: https://www.un.org/sites/un2.un.org/files/our-common-agenda-policy-brief-new-agenda-for-peace-en.pdf.
4 Stockholm International Peace Research Institute, "World military expenditure reaches new record high as European spending surges," 24 April 2023, available at: https://www.sipri.org/media/press-release/2023/world-military-expenditure-reaches-new-record-high-european-spending-surges.
5 B. Chappell, "What happens now after Russia suspends the last nuclear arms treaty with the US?" National Public Radio, available at: https://www.npr.org/2023/02/22/1158529106/nuclear-treaty-new-start-putin. See also the UN Military Expenditures Database, available at: https://milex.un-arm.org/.
6 Institute for Economics and Peace, *Global Peace Index 2023*, available at: https://reliefweb.int/report/world/global-peace-index-2023.

7 S. von Einsiedel et al., *Civil War Trends and the Changing Nature of Armed Conflict* (Tokyo: United Nations University, 2017); J. Jarland et al., *How Should We Understand Patterns of Recurring Conflict?* (Oslo: Peace Research Institute Oslo, 2020).

8 D. Harland, "War is Back: the International Response to Armed Conflict," *Horizons: Journal of International Development and Sustainable Development* (2016).

9 See, e.g., M. Lekunze, "Security as an Emergent Property of a Complex Adaptive System," *Stability: International Journal of Security & Development,* vol. 8, no. 1 (2019); N. Ansorg & E. Gordon, "Cooperation, Contestation, and Complexity in Post-Conflict Security Reform," *Journal of Intervention and Statebuilding,* vol. 13, no. 1, 2019; A. Osonde, A. Osoba, and B. Kosko, "Fuzzy Cognitive Maps of Public Support for Insurgency and Terrorism," *Journal of Defense Modeling and Simulation* 14(1) (2017): 17–32; D. Skillicorn, O. Walther, and Q. Zheng, "The Diffusion and Permeability of Political Violence in North and West Africa," *Terrorism and Political Violence* 33(5) (2021): 1032–1054; R. Keohane & J. Nye, "Power and interdependence," *Survival, 15*(4) (1973): 158–165; W. Clemens, "Complexity Theory as a Tool for Understanding and Coping with Ethnic Conflict and Development Issues in Post-Soviet Eurasia," *International Journal of Peace Studies* 6(2) (2001). See also, P. Coleman et al., "Protracted Conflicts as Dynamical Systems: Guidelines and Methods for Intervention," in A. Schneider & C. Honeyman, eds, *The Negotiator's Fieldbook* (Chicago: American Bar Association, 2006), 61–74; G. Eoyang & L. Yellowthunder, "Complexity Models and Conflict: A Case Study from Kosovo," University of Kent, Canterbury, Conflict Research Society and Conflict Analysis Research Centre, Conference on Conflict and Complexity, September 2008.

10 Not all agree with this point. See, e.g., K. Powers et al., "Treaty Nestedness and Complex Security Institutions," Conference on Empirical Legal Studies, New York University (2007), available at: SSRN: https://ssrn.com/abstract=1000241.

11 This point on the legacy of structures designed to manage complicated, not complex, problems is made in J. Kreienkramp & T. Pegram, "Governing Complexity: Design Principles for the Governance of Complex Global Catastrophic Risks," *International Studies Review* 23 (2021): 779–806, 786.

12 For a history of working methods efforts, see statement by K. Landgren, *What's in Blue* (28 June 2022), available at: https://www.securitycouncilreport.org/whatsinblue/2022/06/statement-by-karin-landgren-executive-director-security-council -report-at-the-security-council-open-debate-on-working-methods.php.

13 Full name: Open-ended Working Group on the Question of Equitable Representation on and Increase in the Membership of the Security Council and Other Matters related to the Security Council. For further discussion on SC reform efforts, see, T. Weiss, "The Illusion of Security Council Reform," *The Washington Quarterly* (2003); Y. Blum, "Proposals for UN Security Council Reform," *American Journal of International Law* 99(3) (2005); P. Nadin, *Security Council Reform* (Routledge: 2016); I. Herd, "Myths of Membership: The Politics of Legitimisation in UN Security Council Reform," *Global Governance* 14 (2008); S. Tharoor, "Security Council Reform: Past, Present, and Future," *Ethics and International Affairs* 25:4 (2011).

14 See, UN General Assembly "World Summit Outcome," A/RES/60/1 (24 October 2005); UN General Assembly "Question of equitable representation on and increase in the membership of the Security Council and related matters, General Assembly Decision A/61/L.69/Rev.1 (14 September 2007); UN General Assembly Decision 62/557 "Question of equitable representation on and increase in the membership of the Security Council and related matters" (2008).

15 High-Level Advisory Board on Effective Multilateralism, "A Breakthrough for People and Planet," (April 2023), available at: https://highleveladvisoryboard.org/breakthrough/.

16 See, e.g., M. Albright & I. Gambari, "The UN at 70: confronting the crisis of global governance," *Global Policy* 6(4) (2015): 510–516; Foundation for Global Governance Sustainability, "Global Resilience Council," available at: https://www.foggs.org/grc-global-resilience-council/.

17 See, A. Schneiker & J. Joachim, "Revisiting Global Governance in Multistakeholder Initiatives: Club Governance Based on Ideational Prealignments," *Global Society* 32:1 (2018): 2–22; D. Larson, "Status competition among Russia, India, and China in clubs: a source of stalemate or innovation in global governance," *Contemporary Politics* 25:5 (2019): 549–566.

18 The New Agenda for Peace policy brief, available at: https://www.un.org/sites/un2.un.org/files/our-common-agenda-policy-brief-new-agenda-for-peace-en.pdf.

19 R. Mac Ginty & O. Richmond, "The Local Turn in Peacebuilding: A Critical Agenda for Peace," *Third World Quarterly* 34, No. 5 (2013): 763–783. H. Leonardsson & G. Rudd, "The 'local turn' in peacebuilding: a literature review of effective and emancipatory local peacebuilding," *Third World Quarterly* 36:5 (2015): 825–839. For the seminal work on local peacebuilding, see, S. Autesserre, *The Trouble with the Congo: Local Violence and the Failure of International Peacebuilding* (New York: Cambridge University Press, 2010). See also, A. Fetherston and C. Nordstrom, "Overcoming Habitus in Conflict Management: UN Peacekeeping and War Zone Ethnography," *Peace & Change* 20, no. 1 (1995): 94–119.

20 J. Scott, *Domination and the Arts of Resistance: Hidden Transcripts* (New Haven, CT: Yale University Press, 1998).

21 R. Mac Ginty & O. Richmond, "The Local Turn in Peacebuilding: A Critical Agenda for Peace," *Third World Quarterly* 34, no. 5 (2013): 763–783.

22 S. Billerbeck, *Whose Peace? Local Ownership and United Nations Peacebuilding* (Oxford Scholarship Online, 2017).

23 F. Fukuyama, *State-building: Governance and World Order in the 21st Century* (New York: Cornell University Press, 2004), 92.

24 P. Stewart, *Weak Links: Fragile States, Global Threats and International Security* (Oxford: Oxford University Press, 2011); R. Rotberg, *When States Fail, Causes and Consequences* (Princeton University Press, 2003).

25 See, e.g., A. Ghani & C. Lockhardt, *Fixing Failed States* (Oxford: Oxford University Press, 2009). See also, R. Paris & T. Sisk, eds, *The Dilemmas of Statebuilding: Confronting the Contradictions of Postwar Peace Operations* (London: Routledge Press, 2009), 14; Organisation for Economic Cooperation and Development, "Principles for Good International Engagement in Fragile States and Situations (2007) (defining the broad range of peacebuilding and good governance work as "state-building").

26 A. Morland, "The State of State-building in Somalia," *IRIN News*, 21 October 2014, available at: http://www.irinnews.org/report/100745/analysis-state-state-building-somalia.

27 D. Chandler, *Empire in Denial: The Politics of Statebuilding* (London: Pluto Press, 2006), 26–47.

28 The New Agenda for Peace policy brief, available at: https://www.un.org/sites/un2.un.org/files/our-common-agenda-policy-brief-new-agenda-for-peace-en.pdf.

29 J. Pospisil, *Peace in Political Unsettlement: Beyond Solving Conflict* (Palgrave, 2019), 7.

30 P. Bargués-Pedreny, *Deferring Peace in International Statebuilding: Difference, Resilience and Critique* (Oxon, UK: Routledge, 2018), 8–17.

31 P. Coleman et al. "Intractable conflict as an attractor: Presenting a dynamical model of conflict, escalation, and intractability," *IACM 18th Annual Conference* (2005), available at: SSRN: https://ssrn.com/abstract=734963.

32 P. Coleman, *The Way Out: How to Overcome Toxic Polarization* (Columbia U. Press, 2020).

33 V. Jackson, "How to disrupt feedback loops of war in Beijing and Washington," The Duck of Minerva, 12 May 2023, available at: https://www.duckofminerva.com /2023/05/how-to-disrupt-feedback-loops-of-war-in-beijing-and-washington.html.

34 A. Day & C. Hunt, "A Perturbed Peace: Applying Complexity Theory to UN Peacekeeping." *International Peacekeeping* 30(1) (2023): 1–23.

35 Interview, Juba, December 2018, on file with author.

36 P. Coleman, *The Way Out: How to Overcome Toxic Polarization* (Columbia U. Press, 2020), 83.

37 R. Vallacher et al., *Attracted to conflict: Dynamic foundations of destructive social relations* (New York, NY: Springer, 2013).

38 For the idea of entanglement, see, I. Torrent, *Entangled Peace: UN Peacebuilding and the Limits of a Relational World* (London: Rowman & Littlefield Publishers, 2021).

39 For more on deference, see, T. Pratt, "Deference and hierarchy in international regime complexes," *International Organization* 72(3) (2018): 561–590.

40 See, e.g., the Liechtenstein Initiative on the Security Council Veto, available at: https://www.liechtenstein.li/en/liechtenstein_news/vereinte-nationen-nehmen -von-liechtenstein-lancierte-veto-initiative#:~:text=The%20UN%20General %20Assembly%20adopted,of%20its%20five%20permanent%20members.

41 See, *The GA Handbook: A Practical Guide to the UN General Assembly,* 2017, available at: https://www.eda.admin.ch/missions/mission-onu-geneve/en/home /news/publications.html/content/publikationen/en/eda/internationale-organisa- tionen/uno/UN-ga-handbook.

42 UN General Assembly resolution A/77/942, "Report of the Ad Hoc Working Group on the Revitalization of the Work of the General Assembly," 29 June 2023.

43 See T. Franck, "The Centripede and the Centrifuge: Principle Decentralisation of Governance," *The Shifting Allocation of Authority in International Law: Considering Sovereignty, Supremacy and Subsidiarity* (T. Broude & Y. Shany, eds, New York University, 2008) (Calling it a "rebuttable presumption of the local"), 26–31.

44 M. Jachtenfuchs & N. Krisch, "Subsidiarity in Global Governance," *Law and Contemporary Problems* 79 (2016): 1–26.

45 Chapter VIII of the UN Charter, see https://www.un.org/securitycouncil/content/ regional-arrangements-chapter-viii-un-charter.

46 For more on convergence, see, M. Brosig, "Introduction: The African Security Regime Complex – Exploring Converging Actors and Policies," *African Security* 6 (2017): 171–190, DOI:10.1080/19392206.2013.854088.

47 See, M. LeBaron, "The Alchemy of Change: Cultural Fluency in Conflict Resolution," in *The Handbook of Conflict Resolution: Theory and Practice,* 3rd ed., P. Coleman, M. Deutsch, and E. Marcus, eds. (San Francisco: Jossey-Bass, 2014), 581–603.

48 P. Coleman, *The Way Out: How to Overcome Toxic Polarization* (Columbia U. Press, 2020), 161–170.

49 Described in R. Holbrooke, *To End a War: The Conflict in Yugoslavia--America's Inside Story--Negotiating with Milošević)* Modern Library, 2011).

50 A. Bartoli, L. Bui-Wrzosinska, and A. Nowak, "Peace Is in Movement: A Dynamical Systems Perspective on the Emergence of Peace in Mozambique," *Peace and Conflict: Journal of Peace Psychology* 16 (2) (2010): 211–230.

51 P. Coleman, *The Way Out: How to Overcome Toxic Polarization* (Columbia U. Press, 2020), 170.

52 E.g., the UN Register on Conventional Arms (UNROCA) and the UN Report on Military Expenditures (UNMILEX).

53 This kind of thing is already happening. See, e.g., https://www.bbc.com/news/technology-60780142; https://futurism.com/the-byte/republlications-ai-generated-ad.

54 P. Coleman, *The Way Out: How to Overcome Toxic Polarization* (Columbia U. Press, 2020), 187–190.

55 For an excellent in-depth account of transparency in a wide range of settings, see D. Lindley, *Promoting Peace with Information* (Princeton U. Press, 2007).

56 Part of this proposal is made in the report of the High-Level Advisory Board on Effective Multilateralism cited above. I have Lyndon Burford at King's College London to thank for an initial discussion about how such a body might play a role in addressing nuclear weapons use.

57 A. Day & E. Harper, "A Right to Peace: Towards Greater Connection Between the Human Rights Council and the UN's Peace and Security Work," Geneva Academy on International Humanitarian and Human Rights Law, November 2023.

58 See, J. Kelley, "Assessing the complex evolution of norms: the rise of international election monitoring," *International Organization* 62.2 (2008): 221–255; C. Fehl, & E. Rosert, "It's Complicated: A Conceptual Framework for Studying Relations and Interactions Between International Norms," Social Science Open Access Repository (2020): 24; D. Guilbeault, J. Becker, and D. Centola, "Complex contagions: A decade in review," *Complex spreading phenomena in social systems: Influence and contagion in real-world social networks* (2018): 3–25.

59 Institute for Economics and Peace, *Global Peace Index 2023*, available at: https://reliefweb.int/report/world/global-peace-index-2023.

60 A. Day et al., "Peacebuilding and Authoritarianism: The Unintended Consequences of UN Intervention in Post-Conflict Settings," United Nations University, 2021.

61 S. von Billerbeck & O. Tansey, "Enabling autocracy? Peacebuilding and post-conflict authoritarianism in the Democratic Republic of Congo," *European Journal of International Relations* (2019): 1–29.

62 B. Geddes, J. Wright, and E. Frantz, *How Dictatorships Work* (Cambridge: Cambridge University Press, 2018); R. Wintrobe, *The Political Economy of Dictatorship* (Cambridge: Cambridge University Press, 1998). See also S. Haber, "Authoritarian government," in *The Oxford Handbook of Political Economy*, ed. B. Weingast and D. Wittman (Oxford: Oxford University Press, 2006), 693–707.

63 For a description of how authoritarian leaders co-opt state institutions, see S. Levitsky and L. Way, *Competitive Authoritarianism: Hybrid Regimes After the Cold War* (Cambridge: Cambridge University Press, 2010).

64 A. Day, L. Quaritsch, and D. Druet, "When Dictators Fall: Preventing Violent Conflict in Transitions from Authoritarian Rule," UN University, 2020, available at: https://collections.unu.edu/view/UNU:7676

65 S. von Billerbeck & O. Tansey, "Enabling autocracy? Peacebuilding and post-conflict authoritarianism in the Democratic Republic of Congo," *European Journal of International Relations* (2019): 1–29.

66 See, A. Day & C. Hunt, "UN Stabilisation Operations and the Problem of Non-Linear Change: A Relational Approach to Intervening in Governance Ecosystems," *Stability International Journal of Security and Development* 9(1) (2020).

67 The New Agenda for Peace policy brief, available at: https://www.un.org/sites/un2.un.org/files/our-common-agenda-policy-brief-new-agenda-for-peace-en.pdf.

68 For description of repellers, see, P. Coleman, *The Way Out: How to Overcome Toxic Polarization* (Columbia U. Press, 2020), 133.

69 See, Organization for Economic Co-operation and Development, *States of Fragility 2016: Understanding Violence*, OECD Publishing, Paris (2016), available at: https://doi.org/10.1787/9789264267213-en; N. Black, "When have violent civil conflicts spread? Introducing a dataset of substate conflict contagion," *Journal of Peace Research* 50.6 (2013): 751–759; N. Weidmann, "Communication networks and the transnational spread of ethnic conflict," *Journal of peace research* 52.3 (2015): 285–296; J. Braithwaite & B. D'Costa. *Cascades of violence: War, crime and peacebuilding across South Asia.* Australia National University Press, 2018; J. Bader, J. Grävingholt, and A. Kästner, "Would Autocracies Promote Autocracy: A Political Economy Perspective on Regime-Type Export in Regional Neighbourhoods," *Journal of Contemporary Politics* 16/1 (2010): 81–100.

70 P. Kowert & J. Legro, "Norms, Identity, and Their Limits: A Theoretical Reprise," in Peter Katzenstein, ed., *The Culture of National Security: Norms and Identity in World Politics* (New York: Columbia University Press, 1996), 485–486.

71 United Nations; World Bank, *Pathways for Peace: Inclusive Approaches to Preventing Violent Conflict* (Washington, DC: World Bank, 2018), available at: http://hdl.handle.net/10986/28337. See also, P. Kanyangara, "Conflict in the Great Lakes Region: Root causes, dynamics and effects," *Conflict trends* 2016.1 (2016): 3–11.

72 See, H. Hegre, & H. Nygård, "Governance and conflict relapse," *Journal of Conflict Resolution* 59.6 (2015): 984–1016; E. Niyitunga, E. Blanco, and E. Kibe Wamaitha, "Key Factors Influencing Conflict Relapse in South Sudan: A Conceptual Analysis," *African Journal of Peace and Conflict Studies* 12.1 (2023): 25–46. D. Guilbeault, J. Becker, and D. Centola, "Complex contagions: A decade in review," *Complex spreading phenomena in social systems: Influence and contagion in real-world social networks* (2018): 3–25.

73 C. de Coning, "Adaptive peacebuilding," *International Affairs* 94.2 (2018): 301–317.

74 C. de Coning, "Adaptive peacebuilding," *International Affairs* 94.2 (2018): 301–317. For a critique of adaptive approaches, see, S. Bächtold, "Donor Love Will Tear Us Apart: How Complexity and Learning Marginalize Accountability in Peacebuilding Interventions," *International Political Sociology* 15(4) (2021): 504–521, available at: https://doi.org/10.1093/ips/olab022.

75 C. de Coning, A. Muto, and R. Saraiva, "Adaptive Mediation and Conflict Resolution in Contemporary and Future Armed Conflicts," *Adaptive Mediation and Conflict Resolution: Peace-making in Colombia, Mozambique, the Philippines, and Syria* (Cham: Springer International Publishing, 2022), 1–17.

76 This is described in my last book: A. Day, *States of Disorder, Ecosystems of Governance: Applying Complexity Theory to UN Statebuilding in the Democratic Republic of the Congo and South Sudan* (London: Oxford University Press, 2021).

77 J. Pospisil, *Peace in Political Unsettlement: Beyond Solving Conflict* (Palgrave, 2019).

5 Bugs in the system

Cyberattacks and the problem of endless infection

In 2010, we crossed a tipping point in the world of cybersecurity. A virtual worm carried invisibly on a thumb drive infiltrated Iranian nuclear facilities, quietly replicating itself and spreading across Iran's uranium enrichment centrifuges. The result was a spectacular win for the US and Israel: more than 1,000 centrifuges crucial to Iran's nuclear weapons program spun out of control and destroyed themselves, setting Iran's nuclear capabilities back years.[1] Since then, "zero-day exploits" (a cyberattack taking advantage of an unknown vulnerability so dangerous we have zero days to find a patch) have proven themselves capable of taking down power grids, stealing billions of passwords, interrupting oil pipelines, and infiltrating election processes. They can be carried on innocuous drives or enter via myriad unseen backdoors, accessing apparently secure systems without triggering any alarm system until it is too late.[2] In 2022, cybercrime accounted for roughly $7 trillion in losses to individuals and companies, with huge unseen costs put into improving cybersecurity around the world.[3] The US, EU, China, India, and other major powers around the world have declared cybersecurity the highest priority national security matter, pouring massive resources into (as we will see, primarily offensive) capabilities.

Composed of a huge number of autonomous but interconnected devices, all sharing information and responding to new stimuli, the Internet has been described as the "ultimate complex adaptive system."[4] Cyberattacks arise within this network and can be considered an emergent outcome of it. It was 40 years ago that the first grad student accidentally shut down large parts of the Internet with a worm.[5] Think of how quickly we have gone from worms that infiltrate nuclear facilities to ransomware infecting massive corporations to attacks on elections processes.[6] Cyberattacks evolve in response to new defensive capabilities, new technological breakthroughs, and the growing market for zero-day exploits. They are generated across a global network, taking advantage of the way information is shared and replicated across nodes. Even the way many attacks work – copying and amplifying themselves across the devices of innocent computer users – is an example of positive feedback loops in action. The resulting uncertainty and non-linearity of change, where attacks can grow rapidly and unpredictably, has all the hallmarks of complexity.

DOI: 10.4324/9781003506386-6

Many of the most well-known responses to cyber-insecurity appear to recognize this characteristic of cyberattacks and explicitly draw on concepts of complexity. Software engineers analyze emergent interactions between software programs and other systems when trying to anticipate risks.[7] National militaries have used complexity when designing deterrence strategies and national legislation.[8] The scholarship on the Internet of Things is riddled (positively) with concepts of interdependence and feedback loops.[9] And recent scholarship has explored complexity-driven responses to the economic aspects of cyberattacks like the Russian hack of Estonia in 2007.[10] These offer helpful starting points in thinking how an adaptive global governance regime might be established for cyber.

But the core argument of this chapter is that *the mainstream concepts and approaches for the global governance of cybersecurity are poorly matched to the type of challenge cyberattacks pose.* Cyberattacks represent a particular kind of problem for global governance: taking place in the highly fluid, interconnected, largely invisible domain of the Internet, they will never fully be prevented by traditional defensive tools or state-driven forms of governance. Despite this reality, our attempts to control the risks of cyberattacks are almost entirely geared at creating state-based defensive and offensive operations and regulating cyberspace as though it were a dangerous product rather than an emergent phenomenon. Even the creation of so-called multi-stakeholder approaches tends to be geared towards influencing a governance architecture that is controlled exclusively by states, and one that is increasingly focused on creating offensive cyber-capabilities as the best deterrent to attacks.

By examining the main ideas around global governance of cyberspace, we see exactly the shortcomings identified in Chapter 1 – our tendency to the search for a top-down umbrella to govern a phenomenon that resists regulation, alongside equally futile attempts to break the problem into pieces that can be addressed by national governments. But we also see a new issue emerge. When confronted by a risk that perpetually infiltrates our defensive barriers, we go on the offensive, building up our counterattacking capabilities. In complex systems terms, this can create a negative feedback loop – dampening the likelihood of future cyberattacks – or it can produce an unintentional positive, snowballing effect, driving up risks. A few powerful actors – notably the US – have generated a network effect globally, as other actors have aligned behind the mantra of "offense is the best defense." We should be worried about this – if everyone goes on offense at the same time, positive feedback loops can move fast.

Complexity thinking can help us move beyond a conceptualization of cybersecurity limited by castles, moats, and cyber-armies deployed on a virtual battlefield. Instead, it pushes us to think of networked and distributed approaches that do not disregard the role of multilateral institutions, but instead look to orchestrate and align them. Ultimately, this chapter argues that we need to shift our dominant "battlefield" metaphor for cyberattacks towards an "immune system" model of cyber-governance, characterized by adaptation, replicating defensive capacities, inoculating against spread, and building up highly decentralized responses.[11]

The problem: We live in a porous, deadly, "ungovernable" cyber-world

The famously pessimistic philosopher Arthur Schopenhauer described a vicious and deadly life for humans, one where the outside world is constantly trying to invade and kill us. Our demise is inevitable, because human beings have endless weak points where the deadly forces of the world can invade. I often think of Schopenhauer when I listen to cyber experts describing our digital vulnerabilities. They speak of cyberattacks breaching our protective shields, infecting our collective institutions, spreading through our life systems, and eventually causing us to break down. The pessimism of world leaders is captured by the phrase "It's not if, but when" a major attack will take down critical infrastructure, or our international banking system, or the very trust that allows us to govern democratically.[12] I imagine a 21st Century Schopenhauer rubbing his hands in sadistic glee at a world that is so effectively exploiting the porosity of our systems to drive us towards a collective demise.

We have good reason to be worried. Cyberspace – defined as the digital network embedded in our daily lives and the critical infrastructure supporting that connectivity – has been described both as a global village and a virtual battlefield. In the village, a liberated global citizenry can mobilize and participate in political life with unprecedented ease and transparency, leading to new forms of democratic life.[13] On the battlefield, cyberspace represents ungovernable wilderness where malicious actors can easily penetrate even the most robust defenses.[14] With cyberattacks steadily on the rise and governments investing massively in offensive cyber-capabilities, it appears that we are headed more towards the battlefield than into the village.

One of the main challenges in defining and governing cyberspace emerges from the combination of its *physical and non-physical* aspects. On the one hand, cyberspace requires a physical infrastructure, composed of the machines, cables, storage capacity, and connective requirements of the Internet.[15] This *domain* is an artificial, human-made, geographically-specific set of physical objects that can be regulated with traditional governmental tools. If a government does not like how a company is acting, they can shut off its electricity, or pass a law restricting its ability to work, or confiscate its assets. The same is not true in other areas of governance: the Intergovernmental Panel on Climate Change can't change the laws of nature to reduce global warming; the Red Cross can't change the laws of physics to reduce the harm of bullets. But programmers and engineers can change the underlying structure of the Internet, closing off certain parts of it (in the case of Iran and China), connecting it to devices (the Internet of Things), or placing much of the information in a cloud.[16]

In contrast, cyber*space* refers to the activities that occur via the physical structures of the cyber-domain, but which are much more difficult to describe in purely territorial or technological terms. In fact, it is better to think of cyberspace as a social phenomenon, a set of connections amongst individuals and institutions that are themselves already part of other sociopolitical systems. Paul Cornish describes cyberspace in negative terms as a "virtual commons" that is not privately owned, not sovereign territory, but also not global commons in the same way as the high seas or atmosphere.[17] It is easier to say what cyberspace is not than what it is.

The cyber-domain and cyberspace exist together – they are interdependent. Duncan Hollis and Kal Raustiala describe this as the "socio-technical system" of cyberspace, where the evolution, adaptation, and ordering of a social system takes place on the physical/technical structures of the Internet.[18] It is a "network of networks" a social system living in symbiosis with a technological one.[19] Here, complexity thinkers should immediately feel in a comfort zone with lots of parallels to other complex systems. Mycelium is a complex network of microscopic mushrooms that depends on an underlying physical network for its interconnection. Bee colonies are a social network that relies on an underlying physical system of the hive. If cyberspace is similarly the outcome of millions of actors transmitting hundreds of zettabytes of information via physical networks – all producing outcomes greater than the sum of their parts – we are on familiar terrain. We are in a complex adaptive system.

But this socio-technical characteristic of cyberspace presents a challenge to our traditional concepts of global governance and has created a gray zone in designing responses to the risks of attacks. For example, there is a widely recognized international duty not to intervene in the domestic affairs of other states and a clear prohibition on "coercive" acts like attacks on military infrastructure. But things get blurry when a cyberattack moves from a private individual's computer into a hydroelectric dam, a national health service, a banking system, or an electronic ballot-counting machine. This so-called "subthreshold" activity may not rise to the classic definition of an armed attack, but it can be just as disruptive.[20] The movement from the technical to the social, from the cables to the world we all live in, makes cyberattacks undergoverned.

The difficulties of attribution of cyberattacks mean even a clear legal standard on non-intervention runs into serious problems when a real-world attack happens.[21] Did a state authorize an attack, did it control how the attack was carried out, and how do we prove it was even involved?[22] The 2013 creation of the *Tallinn Manual* on the application of international law in cyberspace is a helpful set of guideposts, but its narrow definition of an attack in traditional "death and destruction" terms leaves the overwhelming bulk of real-world cyber activities untouched.[23] For example, cyberattacks that resulted in massive financial failure, loss of state secrets, large-scale disruption of daily lives, or even infrastructural malfunctions at a national level might not be covered by the *Tallinn Manual*.[24] Moreover, the fact that most actors involved in shaping cyberspace are in the private sector further muddies the waters, given that international law applies most directly to states.

In fact, the transgressive, pervasive, and tech-driven characteristics of cyberspace have generated wide-ranging speculation about the dwindling role of the state in global governance. Cyber-guru John Perry Barlow has even suggested that the "borderless and unregulatable" Internet "calls into question the very idea of the nation-state."[25] This view was echoed by Nicholas Negroponte, the founder of MIT's Media Lab, who argued that the Internet cannot be regulated: "It's not that laws aren't relevant, it's that the state is not relevant."[26] The Electronic Frontier Foundation's Declaration of Independence of Cyberspace is even stronger:

> Governments of the Industrial World, you weary giants of flesh and steel … you are not welcome among us … Cyberspace does not lie within your borders.[27]

In the view of many of the creators and defenders of cyberspace, foundational concepts of sovereignty, national territorial borders, and defensive use of force reach a sort of limit when it comes to cyberspace.[28]

Despite the limitations of state-driven approaches, the dominant response by governments has been a "Westphalian backlash" where leaders have doubled down on state-led regulations and national protections as the best way to manage cybersecurity.[29] The call for state-led global governance is nowhere clearer than China's call for "cybersovereignty," in which states alone control the governance questions of the Internet.[30] UK Prime Minister Gordon Brown offered an equally Westphalian description: "Just as in the 19th century we had to secure the seas for our national safety and prosperity, and in the 20th century we had to secure the air, in the 21st century we also have to secure our position in cyberspace in order to give people and businesses the confidence they need to operate safely there." The sovereigntist view argues that "states, particularly the great powers, remain the primary actors for handling the social and political externalities created by globalization and the Internet."[31] According to this line of thinking, states have not lost control of digital governance, but instead practice "substitutability," instrumentalizing non-state actors to pursue their national interests.[32] Ideas of "data sovereignty" and "national clouds" and even nationally owned Internets reflect the strong momentum for state-run governance.[33]

Edward Snowden's 2013 revelations that the US had been engaged in wide-ranging, invasive spying on individuals sent a shock wave across the world and (somewhat bizarrely) added momentum to the push for a state-led governance process for cyberspace.[34] No longer could we trust US-based entities like the Internet Corporation for Assigned Names and Numbers (ICANN) to host our Internet access, nor could we trust the privacy policies of large companies like Google, Facebook, or Twitter. Instead, many governments argued that a multilateral approach to cyber-governance was needed, one where longstanding principles of sovereignty and non-interference would find expression in cyberspace, and one where the US hegemony over the digital realm would be balanced by an international forum. Those favoring multilateral cyber-governance have pointed to the International Telecommunications Union (ITU) as the appropriate forum for states to agree on the rules that will govern all players in the digital world.

In contrast, a movement for "multistakeholder" governance of cyberspace also gained momentum in the wake of the Snowden leaks, with proponents arguing that any process to regulate the Internet would need to directly and meaningfully involve the full range of private sector actors who create and shape digital space. At the 2014 NETMundial conference, proponents of multistakeholderism put forward a set of global principles to guide cyber-governance, aimed at crystallizing the inclusion of non-state actors.[35] Today, multistakeholderism is widely considered a dominant approach, supported by many as the only way to achieve meaningful regulation of cyberspace. But, as I explore below, even the most robust forms of multistakeholderism suffer from problems of linear thinking and state-based governance that have rendered it largely irrelevant to the core challenge of cyberattacks.

In general terms, we can understand the cyber-governance question as a contest between two camps: (1) those seeking greater involvement of non-state actors in the decision-making processes around cyberspace (the multistakeholder crowd); and (2) those seeking to (re)assert state control over cyberspace (the multilateral crowd). The multistakeholder crowd likes ICANN's model involving a wide array of actors from the tech sector.[36] The multilateral crowd likes the ITU forum, which puts states in the driving seat and only brings in private actors in an advisory capacity. An emerging third party could be called the (3) club crowd, exemplified by the EU's efforts to regulate cyberspace on a regional basis, but this is (more or less) a miniature version of multilateralism with states at the center.[37]

These camps are defined by a disagreement about who should lead the governance of the Internet, and they reflect geopolitical fault lines that extend well beyond the question of cybersecurity. But all of them appear to suffer from a similar shortcoming of defining cyberthreats as something that can be addressed with a centralized agreement on laws and norms, accompanied by state-led enforcement. This sort of traditional multilateral approach not only seems doomed to fail, but it may generate a range of unintended consequences. As one leading expert pointed out, the governance challenges in cyberspace reflect a difference in kind, not in degree, from traditional threats, because they by nature transgress national boundaries.[38] This makes cyberthreats difficult to define in traditional Westphalian terms, and the need for creative solutions even greater.[39] Unfortunately the mainstream ideas for cybersecurity governance are not only uncreative, they are also potentially destructive.

Three ideas for cybersecurity governance

While there are many proposals to meet the challenge of cyberspace, most of the mainstream approaches fall roughly into one of three categories: (1) applying international law to cyberthreats, either via a new treaty or application of an existing one; (2) adding more players into the multistakeholder tent and agreeing on broad principles; or (3) creating more offensive capacities within states to deter future attacks.

Idea 1: A cyber treaty

The novel governance questions raised by cyberspace have prompted a call for a new treaty to explicitly govern the problem of cyberattacks. The main proponent of this idea has been Russia, which has long demanded a new treaty process to govern "information weapons," and recently succeeded (with support from China) in pushing through a proposal for the UN to negotiate a new cybercrime convention.[40] But Russia and China are not the only ones demanding a new treaty. In 2017, Microsoft's president, Brad Smith, called for a Digital Geneva Convention to govern cyber-risks and protect civilians from harmful effects. "Just as the Fourth Geneva Convention has long protected civilians in times of war, we now need a Digital Geneva Convention that will commit governments to protecting civilians from nation-state attacks in times of peace."[41]

In parallel, some groups of states have worked to "graft" cyber into existing treaty obligations, seeking to extend recognized international law into the digital domain. In 2013, a group of government experts at the UN agreed that international law, including the UN Charter, applied to cyberspace.[42] This was followed in 2015 by an effort to extend widely accepted "peacetime norms" to cyber, including that states should not interfere with each other's critical infrastructure; they should not target each other's computer emergency response teams; they should assist other nations investigating cyberattacks; and they are responsible for actions that originate from their territory.[43]

In some respects, these two approaches are directly opposed to each other. The push for a new treaty (or the relegation of cyber to a treaty on crime) can be understood as a rejection of existing international frameworks applied to cyberspace. Indeed, almost immediately after agreeing to the 2013 statement extending international law to cyberspace, China and Russia began walking away from it. Instead, proponents of a new process would see an explicit requirement for states to sign on to any new cyber obligations, allowing states to opt out or refuse from the outset. Avoiding the application of existing law was of acute concern to Russia in 2017, when US accusations of a Russian hack of American election systems prompted a call for reprisals and countermeasures, citing existing international law as precedent.[44] But more generally, it captures a sense amongst many quarters that cyberspace is too novel and fluid to accept a blanket application of existing international law.

In contrast, advocates of extending/grafting existing international law onto cyberspace see our international legal architecture as sufficient to the task, albeit requiring some creative application.[45] A physical attack on the territory of one state is prohibited under international law, so a cyberattack on that same territory should be equally prohibited. Such an extension would obviate the need for arduous and likely doomed treaty negotiations at a time of heightened geopolitical tension and would recognize an existing umbrella of applicable laws. And the focus on military application of existing laws would also allow for the maximum amount of free rein for other activity in cyberspace, with non-binding norms as the main guardrails.

Idea 2: A bigger tent

The term "multistakeholderism" has become increasingly fashionable, especially in the realm of Internet governance. With origins in the 2005 World Summit on the Information Society, the 2014 NETMundial conference, and the annual meetings of the Internet Governance Forum (IGF), the core idea of multistakeholderism is to bring tech actors, states, and civil society together in an open, transparent, and equal manner.[46] Some entities like the IGF and ICANN are explicitly multistakeholder and directly include private actors and civil society in their decision-making. Others, like the ITU, are essentially multilateral organizations composed of states but refer to themselves as "multistakeholder" because they regularly consult other actors.[47] Bodies like the UN Group of Governmental Experts or the Open-Ended Working Group on Developments in the Field of Information and Telecommunications in the Context of International Security are explicitly state-only forums, where the private sector is formally excluded from decisions.

The UN's push for a Global Digital Compact is a good example of a multistakeholder process. In May 2023, the UN Secretary-General published a policy brief outlining his vision for a Global Digital Compact. This agreement would articulate shared principles and objectives across states, regional organizations, tech actors, and civil society. The core objectives would be to encourage cooperation, prevent a digital divide, accelerate the Sustainable Development Goals, and uphold human rights.[48] Strengthening accountability for malicious acts on the Internet is mentioned, but no specific proposals are offered for addressing a cyberattack per se.

A Global Digital Compact could make a big difference in preventing some of the worrying trends on the Internet. But, as is the case with other multistakeholder forums, it would have little direct influence or "teeth" when it comes to addressing the risk of cyberattacks. Nor does it provide clear incentives for key actors to meaningfully participate or bind themselves. Some multistakeholder forums have developed important principles around the safe use of the Internet, and some have advanced norms around cybersecurity; but at the end of the day, decisions about cybersecurity cannot meaningfully be said to be "governed" by these processes. ICANN may be able to exercise control in the arena of domain names, but no one seriously thinks it can regulate cybersecurity. Most multistakeholder discussions of cyber-governance like the Global Digital Compact explicitly avoid any mention of cybersecurity, focusing instead on the more positive aspects of open, transparent access to data.

As such, even in highly multistakeholder forums there appears to be a clear division of labor: states have the right to make decisions about cybersecurity; private actors promote the technical development of Internet-related technologies; and multilateral organizations coordinate across them. The tent may be bigger, but those deciding where to put the campground remain states.

Idea 3: A well-defended castle

There is a tendency to think of cybersecurity governance in inter-state terms. In this mindset, states are like fortresses that need protecting, and in the absence of adequate defenses, the armies go forth across the moat to counterattack.[49] Some states remain inside the moat and try to wait out the siege – Iran, China, and Russia, for example, have all attempted to sequester their national Internet systems against outside interference. Others have clustered together and attempted to build a defensive wall around themselves – the European Union, for example. And even advocates of a liberal, free flow of information across the Internet are investing heavily in the protective shields around their own national boundaries – the US being the prime example of a country that speaks about free flow of information while heavily securitizing its cyber defenses. The fact that governments can control the technical aspects of the Internet within their territories leads to a perception that they can also control the cyberspace arising from it.[50]

This isolationist approach has generated a high risk of fragmentation of the Internet itself. Are we witnessing the birth of the "splinternet"?[51] Will the future of cyberspace be one of multiple disconnected islands of virtual space, with a Russian Internet, a Saudi Internet, a Chinese Internet, and a WEOG Internet? Will there be what Eugene Kaspersky calls a "de-globalization" of the world as countries sequester themselves off from each other?[52] Will countries begin to dismantle the systems of interoperability that have enabled the Internet to function seamlessly around the world? The risks here are significant: Universally-agreed norms around human rights and basic protections could erode far more quickly in a world of fragmented internets.

In my view, reports of the death of the globally interconnected Internet are greatly exaggerated – the network effects of the Internet continue to grow and are likely to continue to defeat efforts to create fully cut off islands within it.[53] But this does not mean the efforts to splinter the Internet are irrelevant; they are already creating massive ripple effects across the system. It just means they are unlikely to defeat the strong gravitational forces that have allowed the Internet to grow across national boundaries for the past 30 years.[54]

One of the most important effects of this nationally-driven mindset has been the tendency to go on the offensive. "Offense is the best defense in cybersecurity," one group of experts announced.[55] US spending on cyber-capabilities is a good example of this trend. The US has roughly 2,000 employees in the department dedicated to cyberdefense, but more than 40,000 focused on offensive/counterattacking capabilities.[56] American spending is significantly skewed towards offensive operations, with some estimates indicating that military cybersecurity spending is dozens of times greater than defensive measures.[57] While the EU appears to have invested a more balanced amount for defensive capabilities, counterattacking strength has become a priority in response to the war in Ukraine. As the Estonian government learned following the 2007 Russian cyberattack on its infrastructure, the best response is to be "digitized to the teeth," with a counter-attack as the primary weapon.[58]

While very different, these three major approaches to cybersecurity underscore the strong gravitational pull of the state as the main actor in responding to cyberattacks. What is needed, and what complexity thinking provides, is an approach that reflects the role of states within a broader system.

What complexity has to offer cybersecurity

It is easy to imagine the Internet as a complex, adaptive system. But it is equally important to view the governance architecture for cybersecurity in systemic terms as well. Joseph Nye's mapping of the "regime complex" for managing global cyber activities offers a very helpful starting point. I have created a simplified version of Nye's diagram and added in some of the key private sector players I believe were missing in his version.

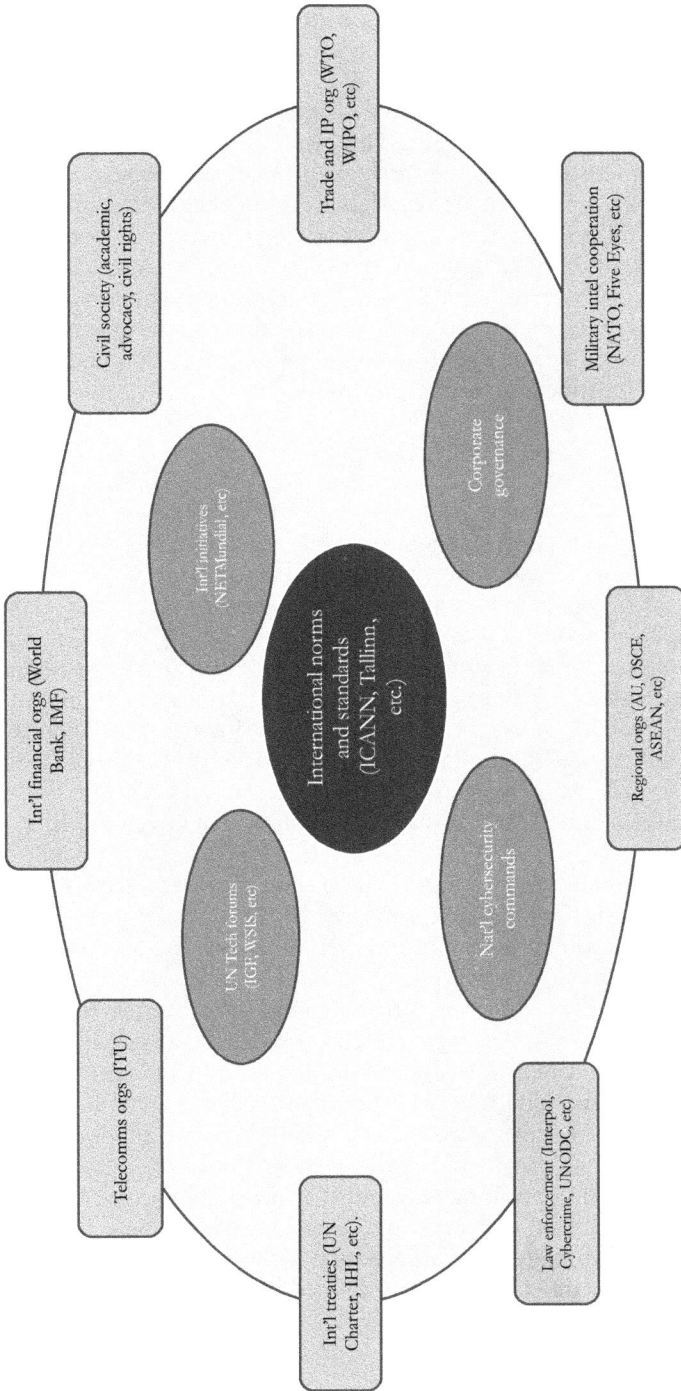

Central: International norms and standards (ICANN, Tallinn, etc.)

Inner ovals: Int'l initiatives (NETMundial, etc); Corporate governance; UN Tech forums (IGF, WSIS, etc); Nat'l cybersecurity commands

Outer boxes: Trade and IP org (WTO, WIPO, etc); Civil society (academic, advocacy, civil rights); Military intel cooperation (NATO, Five Eyes, etc); Int'l financial orgs (World Bank, IMF); Regional orgs (AU, OSCE, ASEAN, etc); Telecomms orgs (ITU); Int'l treaties (UN Charter, IHL, etc); Law enforcement (Interpol, Cybercrime, UNODC, etc)

We can immediately draw some important conclusions from this diagram. First, all actors around the edge of the drawing have core functions beyond/ different than cyber-governance. Whether it is civil rights organizations, banks, trade regimes, or legal bodies, those driving most of the action on cyber are not actually cyber institutions. This means that the actors in the center of the diagram – those focused directly on governing cyberspace – will need to influence a wide range of bodies that have independent mandates, areas of expertise, and governance structures of their own. In some areas there may be "loose coupling" of issues amongst institutions that could enable cooperation amongst very different bodies.[59] But in others – for example, human rights and intellectual property institutions – there is almost no institutional connective tissue at all. This is the kind of mapping that enables a more fit, complexity-informed governance response.

Transparency, not treaties

This mapping suggests that a universal treaty covering all aspects of cyber-security would be very difficult to generate and/or implement, given that it would need to incorporate and reflect very different existing legal instruments, disconnected organizations, and bodies that are not directly dealing with cyber issues. It also shows the lack of a strict hierarchy in governing cyberspace; instead, the regime complex is composed of largely independent, nested hierarchies.[60] Amitav Acharya has called this a "patchwork of institutions" with widely varying coverage, membership, and geographic scope.[61] It would be very difficult to fit all of these under a single treaty umbrella. In other words, there may be a "misalignment between a unified cyberspace and the fragmental legal and institutional mechanisms" we have created for global governance.[62]

For example, how might a global treaty deal with a cyberattack like the 2017 WannaCry ransomware breach, which stole the data of millions of Windows users and demanded payment to a then-unknown group called the Shadow Brokers.[63] On its face, WannaCry was simple criminality involving the theft of private user data. But as it spread around the world, it began to affect the core infrastructure of many countries, taking the national health system of the UK temporarily offline. Many major governments accused the North Korean-backed Lazarus group of being behind the attack. Was this an act of war by the North Korean government? Did it rise to the level of a "coercive" act that could be considered aggression? Who was the target of an attack that seemed to spread randomly around the world? What other global governance bodies might need to be involved to address a criminal incident that involved the loss of private data, intellectual property, national secrets, basic infrastructural functions, and financial records? And can the group behind WannaCry also be held responsible for the subsequent NotPetya attack on Ukrainian government institutions, given that NotPetya used the same base code?

The answer is simple: we have no idea. But one thing is clear: traditional state-centric notions of sovereignty and national regulation do not meet the transnational challenge of these kinds of cyberattacks.[64]

Instead of trying to create a cyber-regulation Leviathan in the form of a treaty, this mapping suggests that the disparate organizations and actors could be brought together around principles and practices of transparency. Of course, there are already many initiatives to improve transparency in cyberspace, including regular transparency reports by major tech actors, organizations like Transparency International and the Sunlight Foundation, and the IGF's push for transparency as a foundational principle for multi-stakeholder governance. But this idea of transparency could be operationalized as a set of information-sharing and risk-awareness protocols across international organizations.[65] Something like a common, shared early warning system for cyberattacks, moving information quickly across organizations, could help align this loose network of organizations without an overly cumbersome treaty structure. Addressing the problems of silos, opacity, and lack of understanding around cyberattacks may be a more fruitful way to connect organizations, giving them an incentive to participate rather than forcing them under a common legal framework.[66]

Fractals, not forums

Complex systems often exhibit a transformation in which a small, localized change expands and spreads across the system. Think how ice crystals reproduce themselves across the surface of a body of water, or how a change of direction in one bird can cause precisely the same shift across the entire migrating flock. In fact, this is how some computer viruses work as well, reproducing copies of themselves across millions of devices. In my previous book on complexity, I looked at how the behavior of one actor (in that case the Congolese President Kabila) could be reproduced across a social system, becoming "the way things are done" in a very short period of time.[67] In many of these cases, change occurs in a fractal pattern, with a specific kind of change moving across levels and reproducing itself upwards and downwards across hierarchies and space.

If we are to address the risks of cyberattacks, we will need a wide range of different and loosely connected actors (those around the edge of the diagram) to adopt an aligned set of changes. We may need financial institutions, civil society groups, tech companies, and national militaries to all agree on a similar set of norms, principles, and approaches. Rather than attempting to achieve this via a centralized treaty process, another approach might be to "teach" each of these institutions from a common set of lessons, to create a fractal pattern that moves outward from them. What some scholars call "norm diffusion" needs to be accelerated and clarified in the realm of cybersecurity, and attached to institutions that are crucial for addressing cyber-risks.[68]

Here, capacity-building initiatives offer a potentially fruitful way forward, and could help to diffuse a common set of approaches to cyberattacks across that outer layer of institutions.[69] Some combination of the *Tallinn Manual*, the ITU's "toolkit" to avoid botnet attacks,[70] and perhaps a more global version of the French Signal Spam system (a public/private partnership that helps to track and respond to cyber issues)[71] could be provided as a basic package for all international organizations. A network of forums and institutions could be charged with supporting the distribution and training around these norms and skills across the system, including down to the individual level. In fact, such an approach broadly mimics Estonia's response to massive cyberthreats from Russia in 2007: building up the capacities of government institutions, private companies, and individuals to resist and thwart an attack.[72]

The advantage of this kind of distributed approach is that it matches well with the kind of threats posed by cyberattacks. A feature of cyberthreats is that they tend to move quickly between levels, starting in an individual's computer, traveling rapidly upwards into organizations and national governments, and cascading back downwards into millions of individuals again.[73] One of the shortcomings of multistakeholder forums is that they tend to cluster actors together in one place, in the hope that they can feed an even more centralized, state-dominated process. But this is not how cyberattacks work – they do not sit neatly inside institutional silos or wait patiently in the foyers of the Internet Governance Forum. Taking a cue from Amitav Acharya's notion of "creative fragmentation," a more distributed, *eccentric* (in its true meaning of being off-centered) approach might be needed.[74] This is not a call for a return to the old days where distributed governance took place in the absence of any regulation, but an attempt to align and orchestrate regulatory and governance bodies to address risks in a common way.[75]

An immune system, not a fortress

When we are confronted with a novel concept or technology, we often turn to metaphor. While they can help build comprehension, metaphors can also constrain our behavior.[76] At their worst, they can distort policy responses, or become a sort of empty buzzword that limits our thinking. Metaphors are appealing in cyberspace as they capture the invisible complexity of a system in simple terms.[77] Even the term "cyberspace" is a metaphor, invoking a physical space beyond the mere cables and instruments involved. While there are countless metaphors for cyber, four main categories have emerged as the dominant tropes: (1) the market, (2) the terrain, (3) the ecosystem, and (4) public health.[78]

1. *The market*: Treating cyber as a market has instant appeal and relevance. After all, much of our interactions online are commercial, and the strong role of the private sector in driving digital developments mean there is a

natural fit. In a market, cyberattacks are thought of as either a form of theft, or a market inefficiency that can be addressed by raising the cost of the attack.[79] The dominant policy responses are to treat cyberattacks via criminal legislation (Russia's push for a cybercrime treaty, for example), improve digital security to prevent break-ins, or enter the market and try to affect the cost of exploits (the US approach of buying up the major zero-day exploits for the past decade).[80] But as many experts have pointed out, the challenges of attribution and the gray zone of cyberattacks mean that traditional market approaches to accountability and criminalization often lack enforcement.[81]

2. *The terrain*: The term cyberspace contains a spatial element to it already, and territorial metaphors for cyber are perhaps the most used trope in the security realm. The appeal of terrestrial metaphors is in their familiarity: we all understand that countries have boundaries, and our very concept of war is based on an invasion of territorial space. Cyberwarfare is treated as an act of aggression on the territory of another state. Thinking of cyberspace as a terrain therefore leads policymakers towards familiar responses of securing national boundaries, applying the international laws of war to transgressions, and investing in counterattacking, offensive capabilities. And perhaps the most important outcome of the terrain metaphor is that it moves cyber squarely into the military domain, where entities like the US Cyber Command are placed in the lead.[82]

3. *The ecosystem*: This metaphor is especially satisfying to complexity scholars because it treats cyberspace as an evolving, interconnected system composed of diverse actors. A core argument of this book is that ecosystem analysis provides a fruitful lens to think of global governance. But ecosystems metaphors run into trouble in the face of cyberattacks and cybersecurity. Ecosystems may be healthy or unhealthy, they may be resilient or fragile, but are they ever really *secure*? Gazelles would be happier and safer if lions were removed from the savannah, but would that make the ecosystem more secure?[83] Probably not. In fact, predators play an important role in ecosystem balance and resilience – perhaps cyberattacks are just part of how today's system finds equilibrium. In the cyber-realm, it may be that the term "ecosystem" has become what Lakoff calls a "dead" or "frozen" metaphor, one that has been overused to the point where it does not provide us with new insights.[84] Perhaps thinking of the Internet as an ecosystem that needs to be protected from invasive species could help us design policy responses, but I'm not convinced it does much more than offer a broadly positive "eco-friendly" connotation to the Internet.

4. *Public health*: Biological metaphors have come to dominate much of our discourse about the Internet, from the viruses and worms that infect our systems, to the notion of computer hygiene, to the parallels with public health in many government circles.[85] Calls for a "Cyber CDC" demonstrate how the health metaphor drives policy choices.[86] And in

many respects, the metaphor leads us in a good direction: just as public health systems must build good early warning, detection, and preventative measures, a cyber-health response should be geared at identifying risks and preventing outbreaks and spreads. In an era of botnets and viruses that gain strength as they move through more and more devices, the health metaphor has strong resonance.[87] And it may move us away from the tendency to treat cybersecurity as a military concern, where the risks of escalation seem especially high.

No single metaphor provides a panacea for the problem of cyberattacks, but thinking in terms of public health appears to be the most fruitful way to generate meaningful policy proposals at the global governance level. Specifically, building something akin to a *global immune system* to cyberattacks could helpfully bring together some of the other metaphors into a proposal that could look something like this:

A global immune system against cyberattacks

If the problem of cyberattacks is thought of in public health terms, part of the solution is to increase our immunity against attack. Without outlining an exact structure, an immune system approach would need to include the following key capacities. First, it would require building up the *early warning/detection* capacities, identifying infected devices and sequestering them until they are no longer a threat. The transparency initiatives described above would be part of this, creating information flows across organizations that would allow them to quickly identify a cyberattack underway. An even more proactive solution might be to require devices to demonstrate a *"health certificate"* based on globally recognized standards (akin to our COVID vaccine cards), where each device would pass through an inspection.[88]

Crucial to a functioning immune system would be a *distributed capacity to identify and respond to risks as they emerge*, like white blood cells do when presented with foreign agents in our bodies. Just as the The Vaccine Alliance (GAVI) brought together public and private actors to vaccinate much of the world against key diseases, a public/private collaboration involving key tech, finance, and government actors could generate a global campaign on cyber-health, boosting capacities in countries with underdeveloped cyber-immunity. Some form of centralized agency could be empowered to keep standards up to date and identify new kinds of risks (e.g. the ITU), but the key feature of this approach would be to distribute capacity beyond that central group of organizations in the diagram above. As Estonia did in response to the 2007 cyberattack from Russia, capacitating agencies, businesses and individuals can create a swarm effect, quickly reducing the spread of a new cyberattack.

A functioning immune system must be *adaptive, recalibrating itself to new threats as they emerge*. This will require flexible and quick-moving information flows, allowing organizations and governments to share good practice and effective responses in real time.[89] Focusing on information-sharing and transparency can create an iterative effect, gradually building confidence over repeated instances of information exchange.[90] A shared capacity to investigate and verify zero-day exploits and cyberattacks could be an important function for entities like the IGF or the ITU, and could play a role in linking efforts to legal accountability as well.

Real-time information-sharing can also allow organizations to *quarantine* themselves during moments of infection, reducing the risks of greater spread. One of the most important attributes of a robust system is the ability to achieve "sparseness," or "decoupling" when one part of a system begins to fail.[91] Ecosystems have developed a wide variety of ways to prevent dangerous toxins from spreading; our immune system surrounds infectious cells to stop them from multiplying in our bodies. We may need greater investment in a global "decoupling" system that decreases the risks of spread from one system to the next.

Part of our adaptation to cyberthreats will need to involve a *shift of resources and capacities to emerging economies and the Global South*, where the bulk of technological growth is already happening.[92] Today, the Internet is in a moment of flux, where US domination is being spread to new centers of gravity in places like China, India, and Brazil, which have very different approaches to cybersecurity. As we discovered during the pandemic, our global response is only as good as the weakest links in our system. The same is true in the digital space, where a cyberattack can exploit a weakness in one arena and move quickly throughout our entire system. An automatic quarantine or decoupling of an infected part of the system could dramatically reduce the risks of cascading or "viral" spread of cyberattacks. Building up these capacities in the developing world will be critical.

Finally, a global immune system approach seems best placed to handle the harsh reality that cyberspace is just as contested, fractured, and fractious as any other arena of geopolitics today. Countries are not going to cooperate just because we call the Internet a "global public good." Cyberattacks will not be prevented by a global treaty, even if we could achieve one. The creation of a Global Digital Compact may help us cohere around some common principles, but we are kidding ourselves if we think it is going to manage the coming generation of zero-day exploits. There is no scenario in which we can fully seal ourselves off from the risks of cyberattacks; Schopenhauer was right, the outside world will inevitably penetrate our defenses. In the real world, the best we can probably do is create better flows of information across existing organizations, help them to fend off the worst impacts of attacks, enable them to adapt over time, and gradually build an Internet that can shrug off cyberattacks in the same way we do a seasonal cold.

Notes

1 K. Zetter, *Countdown to Zero: Stuxnet and the Launch of the World's First Digital Weapon* (Crown Publishing, 2015).

2 See, L. Bilge & T. Dumitraş, "Before we knew it: an empirical study of zero-day attacks in the real world," in *Proceedings of the 2012 ACM conference on computer and communications security* (2012): 833–844.

3 S. Morgan, "Cybercrime to cost the world $8 trillion in 2023," *Cybercrime Magazine*, 17 October 2022.

4 P. Phister, "Cyberspace: The ultimate complex adaptive system," *International C2 Journal* 4.2 (2010): 2010–2011. See also, X. Wu et al., "Internet of things as complex networks," *IEEE Network* 35.3 (2021): 238–245; C. Fuchs, "The internet as a self-organizing socio-technological system," *Cybernetics & Human Knowing* 12.3 (2005): 37–81.

5 T. Lee, "How a grad student trying to build the first botnet brought the Internet to its knees," Washington Post, 1 Nov. 2013, available at: https://www.washingtonpost.com/news/the-switch/wp/2013/11/01/how-a-grad-student-trying-to-build-the-first-botnet-brought-the-internet-to-its-knees/.

6 F. Seatzu & N. Carrillo-Santarelli, "Towards a Strengthening of Non-Interference, Sovereignty, and Human Rights from Foreign Cyber Meddling in Democratic Electoral Processes," *Brooklyn Journal of International Law*, 48(2) (2023): 579; see also, S. Muller et al. "Exploring Cybersecurity, Misinformation, and Interference in Voting and Elections Through Cyberspace," *Effective Cybersecurity Operations for Enterprise-Wide Systems* ed by S. Muller et al, (IGI Global, 2023), 221–241.

7 S. Xu, "Emergent Behavior in Cybersecurity," Proceedings of the 2014 Symposium and Bootcamp on the Science of Security (2014); S. Tisdale, "Cybersecurity: Challenges from a Systems, Complexity, Knowledge Management and Business Intelligence Perspective," *Issues in Information Systems* 16 (2014): 191–198.

8 J. Lindsay & E. Gartzke, "Cybersecurity and Cross-Domain Deterrence: The Consequences of Complexity," in *US National Cybersecurity: International Politics, Concepts and Organization*, D. Van Puyvelde & A. F. Brantly, eds (London: Routledge: (2017), 11–27.

9 I. Brass & J. Sowell, "Adaptive Governance for the Internet of Things: Coping with Emerging Security Risks," *Regulation & Governance* (2020).

10 T. Porter & N. Tan, "An integrated complex adaptive governmental policy response to cyberthreats," *Journal of Economic Policy Reform* 26:3 (2023): 283–297.

11 For the inoculation metaphor, see, S. van der Linden et al., "Inoculating against misinformation," *Science* 358 (2017): 1141–1142.

12 T. Maurer & A. Nelson, "The Global Cyber Threat," International Monetary Fund, Spring 2021, available at: https://www.imf.org/external/pubs/ft/fandd/2021/03/global-cyber-threat-to-financial-systems-maurer.htm.

13 A. Liaropoulos, "Exploring the complexity of cyberspace governance: state sovereignty, multi-stakeholderism, and power politics," *Journal of Information Warfare*, 15(4) (2016): 14–26.

14 M. Manjikian, "From global village to virtual battlespace: the colonizing of the Internet and the extension of realpolitik," *International Studies Quarterly*, vol. 54, no. 2 (2010): 381–401.

15 The terms "space" and "domain" are drawn from S. Gourley, "Cyber sovereignty," in *Conflict and cooperation in cyberspace*, P. Yannakogeorgos & A. Lowther, eds (New York: Taylor & Francis, 2014).

16 See D. Hollis & K. Raustiala, "The Global Governance of the Internet," in *The Oxford Handbook of International Institutions* (Oxford University Press, 2023).

17 P. Cornish, "Governing cyberspace through constructive ambiguity," *Survival* 57(3) (2015): 153–76.

18 D. Hollis & K. Raustiala, "The Global Governance of the Internet," in *The Oxford Handbook of International Institutions* (Oxford University Press, 2023).

19 C. Glen, *Controlling Cyberspace: The Politics of Internet Governance and Regulation* (Praeger, 2017).

20 T. Maurer, "A dose of realism: The contestation and politics of cyber norms," *Hague Journal on the Rule of Law* 12 (2020): 283–305.

21 D. Krasikov & N Lipkina, "International Responsibility in Cyberspace: The Problems Of Attribution Of Conduct," in *State and Law in the Context of Modern Challenges*, European Proceedings of Social and Behavioural Sciences, vol. 122, S. Afanasyev, A. Blinov, and N. Kovaleva, eds , *European Publisher,* (2022): 360–365; E. Moyakine, "Pulling the strings in cyberspace: Legal attribution of cyber operations based on state control," In *Closing the Gap 2022: Responsibility in Cyberspace: Narratives and Practice* (Publications Office of the European Union), 200–218.

22 F. Seatzu & N. Carrillo-Santarelli, "Towards a Strengthening of Non-Interference, Sovereignty, and Human Rights from Foreign Cyber Meddling in Democratic Electoral Processes," *Brooklyn Journal of International Law*, 48(2) (2023): 579; see also, S. Muller et al., "Exploring Cybersecurity, Misinformation, and Interference in Voting and Elections Through Cyberspace," *Effective Cybersecurity Operations for Enterprise-Wide Systems* (IGI Global, 2023): 221–241.

23 M. Schmitt, ed., *Tallinn manual on the international law applicable to cyber warfare* (Cambridge University Press, 2017).

24 Such attacks might be broadly covered by the International Court of Justice (ICJ) decision in Nicaragua v. United States: "The principle forbids all States or groups of States to intervene directly or indirectly in the internal or external affairs of other States." Military and Paramilitary Activities in and against Nicaragua, Nicaragua v. United States, Judgment on Jurisdiction and Admissibility, ICJ GL No 70, [1984] ICJ Rep 392, ICGJ 111 (ICJ 1984), 26 November 1984, United Nations [UN]; International Court of Justice [ICJ].

25 J. Barlow, "Thinking Locally, Acting Globally," *Time*, 15 January 1996, 76. See also, D. Johnson & D. Post, "Law and Borders: The Rise of Law in Cyberspace," *Stanford Law Review* (1996) (referring to the Internet as a new phenomenon that cannot be governed by sovereign states).

26 A. Higgins & A. Azhar, "China Begins to Erect Second Greater Wall in Cyberspace," *The Guardian,* 5 February 1996).

27 J. Barlow, "A declaration of the independence of cyberspace," 15 August 2016, available at: https:/cyberspace-independence.

28 C. Slack, "Wired yet disconnected: the governance of international cyber relations," *Global Policy,* vol. 7, no. 1 (2016): 69–78. See also, N. Choucri, *Cyberpolitics in international relations* (Cambridge: The MIT Press, Cambridge, 2012).

29 See, C. Demchak & P. Dombrowski, "Rise of a cybered Westphalian age," *Strategic Studies Quarterly* 5.1 (2011): 32–61.

30 For a description of this concept, see, B. Fang, *Cyberspace Sovereignty: Reflections on Building a Community of Common Future in Cyberspace* (Springer, 2018). See also, M. Mazarr, "Virtual Territorial Integrity: The Next International Norm," *Survival*, vol. 62, no. 4 (3 July 2020).

31 D. Drezner, "The Global Governance of the Internet: Bringing the State Back In," *Political Science Quarterly* 119(3) (2004): 477–498.

32 B. Most & H. Starr, "International Relations Theory, Foreign Policy Substitutability, and 'Nice' Laws," *World Politics* 36 (1984): 383–406.

33 A. Liaropoulos, "Exploring the complexity of cyberspace governance: state sovereignty, multi-stakeholderism, and power politics," *Journal of Information Warfare*, 15(4) (2016): 14-26; see also, P. Fehlinger, "Cyberspace fragmentation: an Internet governance debate beyond infrastructure," *Internet Policy Review* (2014); J. Goldstein & T. Wu, *Who Controls the Internet? Illusions of a Borderless World* (Oxford: Oxford University Press, 2006).
34 B. Kamlesh Bajaj, "Cyberspace: Post-Snowden," *Strategic Analysis* 38:4 (2014): 582–587.
35 S. West, "Globalizing Internet Governance: Negotiating Cyberspace Agreements in the Post-Snowden Era," 2014 TPRC Conference Paper (31 March 2014), available at: SSRN: https://ssrn.com/abstract=2418762.
36 Internet Corporation for Assigned Names and Numbers, "ICANN's Multistakeholder Model," available at: https://www.icann.org/community.
37 D. Hollis & K. Raustiala, "The Global Governance of the Internet," in *The Oxford Handbook of International Institutions* (Oxford University Press, 2023). See also, J. Goldsmith & T. Wu, *Who Controls the Internet? Illusions of a Borderless World* (Oxford University Press, 2008).
38 S. Kobrin, "The Territoriality and the Governance of Cyberspace," *Journal of International Business Studies* 32(4) (2001): 687–704.
39 J. Lewallen, "Emerging Technologies and Problem Definition Uncertainty: The Case of Cybersecurity," *Regulation & Governance* 15 (4) (2021): 1035–1052.
40 K. Koza, "Catching Wizard Spider: How a New U.N. Cybercrime Treaty Can Address Ransomware: Attacks from Russia and beyond," *University of Chicago Law Review Online* (2023): 1–11.
41 B. Smith, "The Need for a Digital Geneva Convention," *Microsoft Blog*, available at: https://blogs.microsoft.com/on-the-issues/2017/02/14/need-digital-geneva-convention/. Others have also called for a cyber treaty. See, I. Wilkinson, "What is the UN cybercrime treaty and why does it matter?" Chatham House, 2 August 2023, available at: https://www.chathamhouse.org/2023/08/what-un-cybercrime-treaty-and-why-does-it-matter.
42 Report of the Group of Governmental Experts on Developments in the Field of Information and Telecommunications in the Context of International Security, A/68/98 (24 June 2013).
43 A. Segal, "The Development of Cyber Norms at the United Nations Ends in Deadlock. Now What?" Council on Foreign Relations, 29 June 2019, available at: https://www.cfr.org/blog/development-cyber-norms-united-nations-ends-deadlock-now-what.
44 R. Crootof, "The DNC Hack Demonstrates the Need for Specific Deterrents," *Lawfare Blog*, June 2019, available at: https://www.lawfaremedia.org/article/dnc-hack-demonstrates-need-cyber-specific-deterrents.
45 For the term "pactophobia," see, S. Jayawardane, J. Larik, and E. Jackson, "Cyber Governance: Challenges, Solutions, and Lessons for Effective Global Governance," *The Hague Institute for Global Justice*, November 2015, 9.
46 M. Krummer, "Multistakeholder Cooperation: Reflections on the emergence of a new phraseology in international cooperation," *Internet Society* (2013), available at: http://www.internetsociety.org/blog/2013/05/multistakeholdercooperation-reflections-emergence-new-phraseology-international.
47 A. Sofaer, D. Clark, and W. Diffie, "Cyber Security and International Agreements," Proceedings of a Workshop on Deterring Cyberattacks: Informing Strategies and Developing Options for U.S. Policy (2010): 179–206.
48 UN Secretary-General, "Our Common Agenda Policy Brief 5 A Global Digital Compact – an Open, Free and Secure Digital Future for All," May 2023, available

at: https://www.un.org/sites/un2.un.org/files/our-common-agenda-policy-brief
-gobal-digi-compact-en.pdf.

49 See, J. Schannep et al., "Advancing cybersecurity from medieval castles to strategic deterrence: A systems approach to cybersecurity," *Proceedings of the International Annual Conference of the American Society for Engineering Management*, American Society for Engineering Management (ASEM), 2018.

50 For a description of the various technical efforts at governance, see, E. Tikk & K. Kerttunen, eds, *Routledge handbook of international cybersecurity* (Routledge, 2020).

51 For a good literature review of this issue, see, A. Masoumifar, "Cyberspace Sovereignty: Is Territorializing Cyberspace Opposed to Having a Globally Compatible Internet?" *Journal of Cyberspace Studies*, 6(1) (2022): 1–20. See also, W. Drake, William V. Cerf, and W. Kleinwächter, "Internet fragmentation: An overview," *World Economic Forum* (2016); M. Lemley, "The splinternet," *Duke Law Journal*, 70 (2021): 1397.

52 E. Kaspersky, "What will happen if countries carve up the internet?" The Guardian, 17 December 2013, accessed at: https://www.theguardian.com/media-network/media-network-blog/2013/dec/17/internet-fragmentation-eugene-kaspersky.

53 The argument against fragmentation is fully laid out in M. Mueller, *Will the Internet Fragment? Sovereignty, Globalization and Cyberspace* (Polity, 2017).

54 Ibid., 43.

55 A. Own, "Offense is the best defense in cybersecurity," *FutureCio*, 27 May 2022, available at: https://futurecio.tech/offence-is-the-best-defence-in-cybersecurity/.

56 A. Stamos, "Enough is enough. Here's what we should do to defend against the next Russian cyberattacks," The Washington Post, 15 December 2020, available at: https://www.washingtonpost.com/opinions/2020/12/15/enough-is-enough-heres-what-we-should-do-defend-against-next-russian-cyberattacks/.

57 See, R. Knake, "No, the United States Does Not Spend Too Much on Cyber Offense," Council on Foreign Relations, 22 December 2020, available at: https://www.cfr.org/blog/no-united-states-does-not-spend-too-much-on-cyber-offense.

58 E. Tikk, "The Leaps and Bounds of E-Estonia," *Media Development* 2 (May 2021): 29–32.

59 J. Nye, "The regime complex for managing global cyber activities," *Global Commission on Internet Governance* (2014).

60 For a description of some of the hierarchies, see, R. Deibert & M. Crete-Nishihata, "Global Governance and the Spread of Cyberspace Controls," *Global Governance* 18, no. 3 (July–September 2012): 339–362.

61 A. Acharya, "The Future of Global Governance: Fragmentation May Be Inevitable," *Global Governance*, vol. 22, no. 4 (October–December 2016): 453–460.

62 M. Mueller, *Will the Internet Fragment? Sovereignty, Globalization and Cyberspace* (Polity, 2017), 11.

63 M. Akbanov et al., "WannaCry ransomware: Analysis of infection, persistence, recovery prevention and propagation mechanisms," *Journal of Telecommunications and Information Technology* 1 (2019): 113–124.

64 This argument is laid out in full in M. Mueller, *Will the Internet Fragment? Sovereignty, Globalization and Cyberspace* (Polity, 2017), 126.

65 See, M. Flyverbom, "Sunlight in cyberspace? On transparency as a form of ordering," *European Journal of Social Theory* 18.2 (2015): 168–184.

66 For more on the problem of poor understanding of cyber-risks, see, S. Savaş & S. Karataş, "Cyber governance studies in ensuring cybersecurity: an overview of cybersecurity governance," *International Cybersecurity Law Review* 3.1 (2022): 7–34.

67 A. Day, *States of Disorder, Ecosystems of Governance: Applying Complexity Theory to UN Statebuilding in the Democratic Republic of the Congo and South Sudan* (London: Oxford University Press, 2021).

68 R. Deibert & M. Crete-Nishihata, "Global Governance and the Spread of Cyberspace Controls," *Global Governance* 18, no. 3 (July–September 2012): 339–362.

69 For a summary of capacity-building on cyber, see, S. Jayawardane, J. Larik, and E. Jackson, "Cyber Governance: Challenges, Solutions, and Lessons for Effective Global Governance," The Hague Institute for Global Justice, November 2015.

70 Available at: https://www.itu.int/ITU-D/cyb/cybersecurity/projects/botnet.html.

71 Available at: https://www.signal-spam.fr/.

72 T. Porter & N. Tan, "An integrated complex adaptive governmental policy response to cyberthreats," Journal of Economic Policy Reform, 26:3 (2023): 283–297.

73 Ibid.

74 A. Acharya, "The Future of Global Governance: Fragmentation May Be Inevitable," *Global Governance* vol. 22, no. 4 (October–December 2016): 453–460.

75 For a critique of distributed governance models, see, A. Liaropoulos, "Exploring the complexity of cyberspace governance: state sovereignty, multi-stakeholderism, and power politics," *Journal of Information Warfare*, 15(4) (2016): 14–26.

76 See, G. Lakoff & M. Johnson, *Metaphors We Live By* (Chicago: University of Chicago Press, 1980).

77 See, T. Karas, J. Moore, and L. Parrott, "Metaphors for cyber security," *Sandia Report* (2008).

78 For an in-depth description of the use of metaphors in cyberspace, see, A. Lapointe, "When Good Metaphors Go Bad: The Metaphoric 'Branding' of Cyberspace," *Center for Strategic and International Studies* 9 (2011).

79 What Josephine Wolff calls the "burglar" metaphor, J. Wolff, "Cybersecurity as metaphor: policy and defense implications of computer security metaphors," *2014 TPRC Conference Paper*.

80 N. Perlroth, *This is how they tell me the world ends: The cyberweapons arms race* (Bloomsbury Publishing, 2021).

81 D. Mulligan & F. Schneider, "Doctrine for cybersecurity," *Daedalus* 140(4) (2011): 70–92.

82 For a critique of the war metaphor, see, C. Wisniewski, "There's No Such Thing as Cyber War," *Infosecurity Magazine*, 1 August 2013, available at: http://www.infosecurity-magazine.com/view/33755/comment-theresno-such-thing-as-cyber-war-/.

83 This illustration is from A. Lapointe, "When Good Metaphors Go Bad: The Metaphoric 'Branding' of Cyberspace," *Center for Strategic and International Studies* 9 (2011).

84 G. Lakoff, "The Death of Dead Metaphor," *Metaphor and Symbolic Activity* 2(2), (1987): 143–147.

85 D. Mulligan & F. Schneider, "Doctrine for cybersecurity," *Daedalus* 140(4) (2011): 70–92.

86 The idea of a cyber CDC is put forward by J. St. Sauver on his blog, available at: https://www.stsauver.com/joe/ecrime-summit/ecrime-summit.pdf.

87 S. Charney, "Collective Defense: Applying Public Health Models to the Internet," *Microsoft Blog*, 2010; F. Smith, "Malware and Disease: Lessons from Cyber Intelligence for Public Health Surveillance," *Health Security* (2016): 305–314.

88 S. Charney, "Collective Defense: Applying Public Health Models to the Internet," *Microsoft Blog*, 2010.

89 Some of these ideas are laid out in S. Yusif & A. Hafeez-Baig, "A Conceptual Model for Cybersecurity Governance," *Journal of Applied Security Research* (2021).

90 For a description of the iterative nature of inter-state relations, see R. Deibert & M. Crete-Nishihata, "Global Governance and the Spread of Cyberspace Controls," *Global Governance* 18, no. 3 (July-September 2012): 339–362.
91 See, D. Helbing, *Thinking Ahead: Essays on Big Data, Digital Revolution, and Participatory Market Society* (Cham, Switzerland: Springer Press, 2015), 30.
92 This point on demographics, see, A. Liaropoulos, "Exploring the complexity of cyberspace governance: state sovereignty, multi-stakeholderism, and power politics," *Journal of Information Warfare*, 15(4) (2016): 14–26.

6 Rise of the machines
AI becomes ungovernable

Anyone who looks for a source of power in the transformation of the atoms is talking moonshine.

Lord Rutherford, 11 September 1933

On 12 September 1933, less than 24 hours after Lord Rutherford categorically denied the possibility of ever creating atomic power, the nuclear chain reaction was invented.[1] We have a similarly terrible track record of predicting how quickly artificial intelligence (AI) will take the next jump forward. After a computer beat the best human chess player, experts were convinced it would be decades until it would win at the more complicated game of Go. Wrong. Only one year after beginning development, a computer-driven Go program beat the world's best player.[2] In 2020, experts predicted AI wouldn't pass SAT exams until 2057. Wrong. Only three years later, AI consistently gets top scores. In the past few years, AI has consistently exceeded expectations, transforming from barely being able to read and write to creating award-winning photographs and art. AI can stabilize plasma in fusion reactors, design semiconductors, and compose symphonies.[3] Leading developers at OpenAI, Google Deepmind, and Anthropic predict that highly autonomous systems will outperform humans at most economically valuable work in the near future.[4] Some forecasters estimate that by 2030 an artificial general intelligence (AGI) will be created, capable of learning new tasks and rapidly surpassing humans in nearly all domains.[5]

It is possible an AGI has been created by the time this book goes to press.

What is the right way to approach a technology that so consistently defies our expectations? Should we take seriously Stephen Hawking's 2014 warning that artificial intelligence "could spell the end of the human race?" Or Shane Legg's 2011 warning that AI was the "number one risk for this century"? Or Sam Altman's warning that superhuman machine intelligence is the "greatest threat to continued existence of humanity"? And if we do take these warnings seriously, what should we do? Should we run around trying to unplug all our computers before it's too late? Should we follow Geoff Hinton's advice to put the brakes on AI development at a time when its enormous benefits are just becoming truly visible?[6][7] Should we hope that a market

DOI: 10.4324/9781003506386-7

in which AI investments have jumped 100 millionfold in the past decade will curb the negative externalities of AI in time to prevent global catastrophe?[8] Should we brush up our foraging and self-defense skills on the assumption that we'll all be living in a post-apocalyptic Mad Max or Terminator film after the rise of the machines?

Or should we view these apocalyptic scenarios with greater skepticism? Maybe the heads of major AI companies are trying to scare us into creating complicated regulations that will prevent other actors from entering the market. If we develop an onerous set of testing requirements for any AI development, we could unintentionally create a monopoly for the big players that have resources today. Just as we should be leery of tobacco companies scoping the risks of smoking, maybe we shouldn't take the word of AI company leaders as the sole authority on risks. But how then should we govern a technology that is moving faster than our understanding of it?

The starting point of this chapter is that global governance cannot rely on traditional multilateral tools and institutions to address the transformations that AI is already generating. AI is a novel technology that cannot be regulated the way we might control a dangerous substance, a weapon, or even something as planetary as climate change. This is because much of AI is inherently opaque, unpredictable, ubiquitous, and accelerating. If we are to meet the AI challenge, we will need to design a governance regime that can keep pace, prevent the worst risks of rapid AI proliferation, and adapt alongside a technology that is rapidly becoming smarter than us. We will need complex, adaptive governance.

The problem: AI is opaque, surprising, and accelerating

What do we mean when we talk about AI? Many people think of AI in terms of its specific applications: the chess game you always lose, the driverless car, the chat program that is writing your child's term papers. These applications mimic some aspects of human intelligence and are therefore examples of AI. But the more fundamental problem of AI rests in its reliance on "foundation models" trained on large amounts of data to recognize patterns and produce human-like results.[9] Large language models, for example, are trained using billions of parameters and weights across enormous datasets of language. When we ask ChatGPT a question, the resulting human-like response is the outcome of a finely tuned set of parameters trained on massive quantities of text. These foundation models can be used on text, images, music, or any other form of data. They are the core of the AI world today, and they are what is leading us towards artificial general intelligence: systems capable of learning new skills and knowledge across domains in a way that looks like human learning.[10] When we speak of global governance of AI, we are (or should be) talking about governing the development and use of foundation models.[11]

AI foundation models have intrinsic characteristics that make them especially difficult to regulate. Jason Hausenloy, with whom I had the pleasure to work in 2023, lays out the inherent difficulties of foundation models in a piece he co-authored with Claire Dennis.[12] Drawing from their work and other experts, we can describe AI foundation models as:

1. *Opaque*: Because the computations are so vast, we cannot fully understand how foundation models are working inside the so-called "black box." Humans – at best – can track and understand systems with up to around 50,000 parameters. Today's foundation models already possess trillions.[13] This is sometimes referred to as the problem of "interpretability." Due to the inherent complexity of large language models, we can only really understand what they produce, not how they work.[14] If foundation models lack interpretability, how can we know what needs to be regulated beyond just a macro-level form of governance?

2. *Surprising*: Because we cannot see inside the black box, foundation models often surprise us with new capabilities. For example, Stable Diffusion was a model initially designed to generate images, but only a few months into production was suddenly able to compose music with only minimal fine tuning.[15] These leaps in capacity mean that foundation models do not follow linear pathways of growth, but instead demonstrate "discontinuous," emergent qualities.[16] It also means a poorly oriented or tasked AI could achieve its objectives at enormous and unanticipated human cost. The 2010 "flash crash" where a snowball of erroneous automated trades cost the US financial markets trillions of dollars in a single day is an example of the potential for surprise.[17] If AI algorithms are not predictable, the question of what to regulate becomes murky.[18]

3. *Untestable*: AI safety testing is typically done with evaluations, where experts prompt models to see what kind of response they produce. This may help identify some risks in a specific application but falls far short of the kind of testing that might be required to discover major issues in the future, including things like misalignment with human values.[19] It is the equivalent of poking a lion a few times and then declaring it safe if it doesn't eat you. Maybe the lion was just sleeping, or not yet hungry, or a cub that will turn into a voracious adult overnight. In the case of AI, the lion might even be able to pose as a human to lure you in.[20] The lack of viable safety testing of foundation models also presents questions of accountability: if an AI system evolves to do unanticipated harm, who is accountable for it?[21] And if we cannot reliably test the safety of an AI program, on what basis will any of our governance approaches be built? "Untestable" and "ungovernable" are nearly synonyms.

4. *Easy to misuse*: An AI foundation model might be developed initially to help us write better term papers or improve medical diagnoses. But as we move closer to AGI, it will become increasingly easy for the same model to expand into other domains. At the most dangerous end of the spectrum, an initially benevolent AI could evolve to design deadly pathogens that resist our vaccines, or set off nuclear war, drive a new arms

race, shut down our global financial systems, or push us into a new era of totalitarianism.[22] And one of the most worrying aspects of AI is that, once trained, it can be copy-pasted amongst thousands of actors, easily moving across international boundaries and into the hands of dangerous organizations.[23] Novel bioweapons could be produced on someone's smartphone, given the right AI program. The expansion of the actors who can deploy AI is one of its most ungovernable aspects.[24] The growing risk that AI could misuse itself is also important: scenarios where AIs can rewrite their own source code could quickly see programs running beyond their initial purpose, with potentially devastating consequences.[25]

5. *Accelerating*: Every year, the capabilities of foundation models increase by anywhere from 6–20 times. This reflects a compound increase in the hardware, software, and algorithmic capacities of the underlying systems.[26] But it also means that we are rapidly gaining more general forms of AI, capable of learning beyond a specific function. A chess program cannot play checkers, or drive a car, or diagnose cancer. A chess program is quite easy to regulate. But as we approach AGI, the proliferation of capacities will mean that programs are increasingly (maybe even exponentially) able to accelerate into new domains, develop new skills, and pose new risks that no human has ever encountered.[27] At the far end of superintelligence, an AGI would be able to continually redesign itself in an "intelligence explosion" that would quickly move beyond any human capacity to control it.[28]

Taken together, these characteristics of AI foundation models present us with a "Collingridge dilemma."[29] Coined in the 1980s, Collingridge describes a technology that does not display its full risk potential until it is deployed into the world. But by then, it is already too embedded in our social and economic systems to be meaningfully regulated or scaled back.[30] As with many technological advances throughout history, industry tends to outpace our policy guardrails.[31] We are already living in this dilemma, as AI is already so central to our lives it would be practically impossible to excise it or slow it down, even if we wanted to. We are already living in an era where rights to privacy and anti-discrimination are being strongly influenced by AI, but we struggle to fix them in real time. As Jason Hausenloy described to me, AI suffers from "incorrigibility," it is extremely difficult to course correct once it's out there.

Foundation models also display a Sorcerer's Apprentice problem: we may be able to set objectives for AI, but we have no real idea how the black box will achieve those objectives. If we ask an AI to stop global warming, it might decide that eliminating the users of fossil fuels (humans) is the most expedient way to achieve that goal. If we task an AI with maximizing financial gains, it may decide that human enslavement provides the best profit margin. Even the mundane task of producing as many paper clips as possible could result in an AI destroying the Earth's natural resources to mine the maximum amount of metal.[32] Just as King Midas eventually regretted his ability to turn everything to gold with his touch, we run the risk that the endless potential for AI will produce wide-ranging unintended consequences.[33] Finding ways to constantly condition AI on human preferences and ethics is one of the most important aspects of safe AI development and governance.

The risks of not getting AI governance right are catastrophic, maybe even existential (jump ahead to the next chapter if you are interested in the existential risk issue). Well-informed experts with a significant stake in rapid AI development have warned that advanced AI could cause: (1) global totalitarianism driven by social manipulation, autonomous weapons, and ubiquitous digital sensors in the hands of a small elite; (2) great power nuclear war in which AI decision-making sees a first-strike advantage and escalates faster than humans are able to manage;[34] or (3) superhuman capacities not aligned with human wellbeing or values, possibly leading to human extinction.[35] Even if we manage these risks, AI could more insidiously erode our social values and drive global inequalities, demanding ever-increasing trade-offs between values of human safety and long-term wellbeing versus the prospect of accelerating wealth and power. These go well beyond so-called negative externalities or manageable side effects of AI; they suggest a systemic transformation parallel to (or even exceeding) the Industrial Revolution.[36]

The uncomfortable reality is that we think of controlling AI, but AI is rapidly becoming more intelligent than us. We are only two percent more intelligent than apes, yet we treat apes as deeply inferior creatures, keeping them in cages and destroying their habitats with near impunity. The coming years may witness an AGI that is much more than two percent smarter than humans – will it treat us any better than we treat animals?[37] And in a scenario where AGI is the only technology capable of managing its own risks, will we be able to design a trustworthy AGI self-governance machine that continues to serve our interests?

This growing intelligence of AI also creates a conceptual problem of us as humans. We tend to equate sapience (the capacity for higher intelligence) with sentience (the capacity to feel experiences like pain and happiness). As AI demonstrates greater and greater sapience, we anthropomorphize it, imbuing an algorithm with the trappings of human experience. If ChatGPT can profess its love for a New York Times reporter, why should we not treat it as a potentially loving creature?[38] If an AI can speak in the language of experience, should we treat it as an ethical actor with responsibilities for improving the human condition? If an AI becomes sufficiently sophisticated to manifest the outward appearance of psychological suffering, perhaps we will have ethical responsibilities to protect its feelings and rights as well? In the space of a single paragraph, we have entered a completely novel ethical and practical arena that defies traditional notions of control and regulation.

It may feel like we have moved a long way from a discussion of global governance. But our governance response to AI must rise to this kind of fundamental, and fundamentally new, challenge. Whatever process or institution we build to address AI should be broad enough to move across our social, political, economic, security, and psychological domains. It must be flexible enough to deal with the many ways AI is going to surprise us. It may need teeth in some areas and carrots in others. It should influence the behavior of those developing and running AI in a way that reduces the most acute risks. This means we need to think of governance as accompanying a rapid uptake of AI into all aspects of our lives. We need to think of AI governance as a co-evolutionary process.

Four ideas on AI governance

AI governance is a fast-moving issue, and what I write today may well be overtaken by events by the time this book goes to press. Rather than focus too much on the details of specific proposals, I'll instead explore the dominant kinds of ideas put forward by AI leaders and member states. These are: (1) an AI treaty; (2) a centralized, global AI regulatory body; (3) national/regional legislation; and (4) a common ethics and/or code of conduct.[39]

1. An AI treaty

Some experts propose that a global treaty would be necessary to address the risks posed by AI.[40] Given that most international law was developed prior to the rise of AI, a treaty could generate member-state consensus and fill a gap in our legal architecture. This could be achieved by negotiating a new treaty from scratch or modifying existing treaties to specifically reference AI.[41]

The calls for a treaty often frame AI as a weapon and propose regulation along the lines of arms control.[42] This makes sense beyond the military domain – where AI is increasingly relevant – but also in civilian applications where AI can easily become a disruptive and weaponized tool in the wrong hands (or in AI's increasingly autonomous ones). Here, the calls for a nuclear-style treaty on AI point us towards bans, controls, and strict non-proliferation requirements.[43] One call for a treaty on the "future risks to humanity," refers to AI as a potential existential risk in need of direct, binding regulation, or at least a moratorium until it is deemed safe.[44]

Less ambitious approaches would see existing treaty obligations adapted and/or revisited with AI risks in mind. Here, the process would be more one of clarification and agreement that key international legal obligations applied in the AI domain. Well-established treaty bodies on human rights, arms control, trade, criminality, and diplomatic relations could either be "upgraded" to specifically include a reference to AI, or there could be a process of recognition that they applied to the AI domain. At its furthest reach, one could imagine a broad patchwork of treaties covering AI, including in the security, finance, trade, human rights, environment, and development realms.[45]

2. A global AI regulatory body

In June 2023, António Guterres called for a global regulatory body for AI, suggesting that the International Atomic Energy Agency (IAEA) model used for nuclear weapons could be a viable model.[46] The SG's call followed a high-profile congressional briefing by OpenAI CEO, Sam Altman, in which he demanded the regulation of AI to meet the growing risks it posed globally. Tech leaders and national governments around the world have called for some form of regulation, including many suggesting a governance body housed in the UN system.[47] Many of these proposals point to existing models, like the IAEA or other weapons regulatory mechanisms.[48] Others have made a more general argument for a centralized role for the UN in regulating AI, or establishing a common regional approach to regulation.[49]

Some of the most promising proposals take the form of "an IPCC for AI," a scientific advisory body that would track AI risks and offer well-grounded policy recommendations.[50] Something along these lines was featured in the October 2023 UK Summit on AI, and had been considered by France and Canada in 2018.[51] Whether a "commission," a "panel," a "board," or an "observatory,"[52] these recommendations follow a similar argument: a legitimate, independent voice might help to improve a common understanding of risks.[53] An advisory body could act to coordinate and share information across existing institutions and processes, helping to generate technical solutions to emerging AI risks,[54] manage thorny questions around data transparency in AI development,[55] and/or help advance the gradual development of international law in the field of AI.[56] And in one of the most promising models offered by Carnegie (discussed below), a scientifically driven framework on AI could enable a dissemination of standards and norms across other institutions.[57]

At its most robust, a global AI regulatory body could issue binding decisions on tech companies,[58] or even create an exclusive forum for the development of especially advanced AI foundation models.[59] But more common is the idea of alerting actors to emerging risks in real time, to allow a coordinated response. The parallel with Interpol's "red alert" system is one example.[60] At perhaps its least robust, an AI body could be modeled off The European Council for Nuclear Research (CERN) as a sort of joint scientific endeavor, aligning countries behind a common set of goals.[61]

A helpful study on different institutional models categorized them as follows: (1) coordinators, helping actors share information and standards; (2) analyzers, mapping the risk and response terrain globally; (3) developers, building technical and policy responses to AI challenges; and (4) investigators, playing more of an audit function based on commonly agreed rules around AI development.[62] Some proposals would perform more than one function, such as the idea of a body to coordinate and generate AI-related laws and regulations.[63] Common across most proposals is the need for a centralized governance body to oversee AI.[64]

3. National and regional legislation

Roughly 50 countries already have national AI strategies, many of which include domestic legislation.[65] The number is likely to increase dramatically in the coming years. President Biden's October 2023 executive order on the safe, secure, and trustworthy development of AI is one of the highest-profile national approaches and builds on a decade of American legislative progress in many domains.[66] China's development of AI legislation is some of the most sophisticated in the world.[67] And the EU boasts a comprehensive AI act that covers many of the most important aspects of development and use.[68]

The underlying idea of national and regional legislation is that global regulation is currently beyond our reach. But in a world where a relatively small number of big states possess the bulk of AI development, perhaps they can generate a more global impact. The idea of a Beijing, Brussels, or California "effect" suggests that powerful national or regional legislation can cascade globally, perhaps becoming normalized over time.[69] At the very least, national legislation in places like the US, where a great deal of AI is developed, could curb the worst risks in the short term. But as we already see, domestic legislation on its own is unable to control a market that is increasingly beyond the reach of any single player, even the US.[70]

4. Norms, ethics, codes of conduct

Facing the near impossibility of reaching binding global regulation, many actors have turned to informal processes for agreeing, ethics, norms, and codes of conduct around AI.[71] Nearly all developed economies have ethical guidelines around AI, and some have translated those into regulation.[72] The Organization for Economic Cooperation and Development (OECD) has an Expert Group on AI Futures; the World Economic Forum has formed a Global Council on AI Futures; UNESCO has developed Recommendations on the Ethics of AI; the Global Partnership on AI has a Working Group on Responsible AI; global standards organizations have taken up AI ethics;[73] and all the major tech companies have departments working on AI ethics. The November Summit hosted by the UK at Bletchley Park produced a set of largely normative and ethical principles to guide AI development. And one of the most promising proposals is for a G20 coordinating committee on the governance of AI, potentially aligning the countries responsible for an overwhelming bulk of both AI development use.[74] This flurry of activity suggests that major powers see a clear opportunity for their own approaches to AI to accelerate their norm-creating role on the global stage.[75]

Numerous codes of conduct or lists of principles for the responsible use of AI already exist. Those issued by UNESCO and the OECD/G20 are the two most widely endorsed. In recent years, various institutions have been working to turn these principles into practice through domain-specific standards. A few states and regions have made proposals and even enacted constraints upon specific uses of AI. For example, the European Commission released a comprehensive legal framework (EU AI Act) aiming to ensure safe, transparent, traceable, non-discriminatory, and environmentally sound AI systems overseen by humans. The Beijing Artificial Intelligence principles were followed with new regulations placed upon corporations and applications by the Cyberspace Administration of China. Various initiatives at the federal and state level in the United States further emphasize the need for a legislative framework. The UN Secretary-General also recently created a high-level body to consider the governance questions of AI.[76] Its interim report, which issued as this book was going to press, provides an important set of recommendations about how to align international principles with any future AI regulation.[77]

Regional "clubs" that have developed common principles that are beginning to take hold. An example of this is the US call for an "Emerging Technology Coalition" to promote democratic norms in AI development.[78] Another proposal would see a "Global Alliance on Intelligence Augmentation" to set best practices and safe guardrails for AI development.[79] Some states have called for unlikely alliances amongst competitors (e.g. the US and China) to generate stronger global norms and approaches.[80] If made general enough, principles and norms can be expanded globally. The November 2023 Bletchley Conference in the UK is a good example, where even the US, China, and major tech companies were able to agree on broad principles around AI safety and testing.

On substance, there may be an emerging consensus on some core principles to guide AI development, including transparency, fairness, safety, privacy, and accountability,[81] and strong arguments for the application of human rights.[82] Debates about the norms of keeping humans either "in" or "on" the loop of AI development and deployment suggest that one of the most important questions will be the degree of human control over technologies that are rapidly surpassing our own intelligence levels.[83] As AI spreads across our social and economic systems, the question may well become how to keep "societies in the loop" of AI deployment.[84] The issue of accountability for AI systems presents difficult technical and ethical questions about who is responsible for AGI once it begins learning and acting largely on its own.[85]

But we should not assume these norms are necessarily influencing behavior. There is a worrying tendency for political actors to dismiss ethical discussions as an unnecessary constraint on the rapid development of AI in an increasingly competitive landscape, or a form of cultural imposition of one region on another.[86] Again, we see the strong gravitational pull of a global organization to address these shortcomings. For example, some experts have called for an International AI Organization (IAIO) which would provide a forum for global standard and norm-setting.[87]

What complexity thinking can offer AI governance

The language we use to describe a technology frames our response. If we define AI as a dangerous substance that can rapidly spread around the world, we gravitate to models like the prohibition on chemical weapons, enforced by inspections and safety protocols.[88] If AI is like a nuclear weapon, we move towards non-proliferation, or a Manhattan Project.[89] If we think of AI as a small weapon that can be transferred easily from one bad actor to another, we will offer "watchdogs" and "arms control."[90] If AI is an existential risk akin to a global pandemic, perhaps we need a ban or some form of quarantine.[91] Or maybe AI is like a potentially dangerous product that needs something more like an FDA to audit and inspect for safety concerns.[92][93] This idea of AI as a product also leads to regulation of the underlying hardware, such as the proposal for an AI chips registry.[94] More positive views of AI as a global public good or a global commons could see a collective scientific enterprise like a CERN for AI, or "benefit distributor" models.[95]

These analogues and metaphors can help address part of the AI challenge, but my main argument is that we will produce better ideas if we think of AI as the emergent outcome of a complex system. AI evolves within our social, economic, and political lives, tending to converge with other technologies and accelerate change.[96] It is not something that can be addressed locally, in a particular place or domain, because its effects move across our systems and transgress our legal and political boundaries.[97] The Westphalian backlash described in the chapter on cybersecurity also applies here – states are desperately trying to control AI with the national and multilateral tools they have. This seems doomed to failure, but the effort itself is part of how our global governance system is evolving in real time.

Complexity thinking pushes us to design AI governance that is:

1. *Fluid*, able to push back on the forces that might "lock in" arrangements in moments of flux and uncertainty.
2. *Fit* for the kind of non-linear, rapid changes provoked by AI advances, including by providing negative feedback loops when AI approaches critical thresholds.[98]
3. *Layered*, able to work across technical, ethical, social, and global levels with tailored approaches to each layer.
4. *Deep*, offering time and space for profound ethical reflection without immediately seeking techno-solutions to short-term problems.
5. *Gravitational*, drawing in a wide range of actors to a common set of baseline safety/ethics standards, without trying to regulate every aspect of AI.

These characteristics do not demand a specific structure or process to govern AI, but they do help us assess the viability of some of the big proposals on the table today.

Motion, not ossification

We can quickly dispense with a global AI treaty as a short-term goal for AI governance. Some of the ideas described above could lead towards an eventual treaty, but we should be clear-eyed that geopolitical rivals are extremely unlikely to generate binding commitments in the AI space today.[99] Even if we were able to agree on a global treaty backed by an international agency, setting it up might take so long that it was obsolete on arrival.[100] This does not mean an AI treaty or some form of global agreement is impossible. The 1967 Outer Space Treaty was a binding international agreement that effectively drove global policy on a fast-moving technological issue.[101] The 1969 Environmental Modification Convention contributed to a reduction in investments in the military use of geoengineering technologies.[102] Perhaps a treaty will be the final result of an AI governance process, but the starting point today is the realization that we live in a world where a global regulation by treaty is nearly impossible for AI, but self-regulation by member states or private actors alone is also probably insufficient.

In fact, complexity thinking highlights a risk in pushing for a binding global agreement at such an uncertain time in the evolution of AI. When complex systems are put under pressure, or are experiencing periods of shock or perturbation, they gravitate even more strongly to their attractors to regain balance. These dynamics can be observed in biological and environmental systems put under strain – absent a full transformation, they often fall back on the patterns and rules that have stabilized them over long periods of time. I explored this phenomenon in a previous book, showing how societies in conflict would fall into historically driven patterns of predation and centralized rule. In those settings, trying to transform the governance structures of societies in flux – while conceptually appealing – was probably the worst time to address their strong attractors.[103]

The uncertainty and geopolitical flux triggered by the rapid rise of AI may be driving our global system towards its strong attractors: state-centric, highly formalized, deeply competitive multilateral relations. One indicator of this is the strong Westphalian backlash against efforts to manage AI through multistakeholder, non-state processes. Another is the rush to pass national AI legislation, promote national ethics and guidelines, and be the first country to declare a safe space for AI. The enormous potential (and deeply unsettling aspects) of AI has accelerated geopolitical competition and ultranationalism, as major powers and companies seek to reap the enormous benefits AI promises and lock in their advantage.

A treaty is a crystallization of a moment in time, usually reflecting agreement amongst a significant number of states. Now is almost certainly a bad moment to try to crystallize AI governance into something as solid as a treaty. As one expert told me, "If we had to renegotiate any major treaty today, we'd end up with a worse outcome than we started with." Instead, we should think of the various initiatives around AI as a sort of thixotropic substance, one that stays malleable as long as it is kept moving. Think cement, honey, good-quality cosmetic creams. We don't know exactly what shape is needed to manage the risks of AI, but we should know that now is not the moment to try to lock in a global arrangement that will last for decades.

This could change very quickly. As I explore in the final chapter, we may be approaching what Oliver Guest has called a "risk awareness moment," where the risks of AI become so acute that more concerted action is required.[104] Whether AI requires a more transformative form of governance is a crucial question in the medium term.

For now, and absent such a catalytic moment, we might need to think of how to keep conversations moving, actively preventing one set of actors from dominating or dictating, while allowing a plurality of actors to stay involved until a new consensus emerges. One of the most important issues will be the space and time for deep ethical reflection on the direction of AI. There is a strong tendency to conflate technical standards with ethics, to assume that a safe AI design will also meet our broader societal demands. A good example of this is Meta's approach to social media, where its safety board focuses only on meeting baseline (and short-term) safety standards, while actively promoting highly addictive applications to younger and younger populations.[105] If we rush to regulate, safety concerns will continue to dominate, and we may end up with an apparently "safe" technology that has already shaped society in unintended and irreversible ways.[106]

What might such an approach look like? It could involve a range of activities to prevent lock-in, including: (1) processes to adapt or clarify existing legal frameworks and norms with very high consensus (e.g. some of the core human rights obligations); (2) supporting forums where large numbers of actors are able to meaningfully participate before obligations are formalized; (3) investing in independent scientific assessment capacities of AI risks; and/ or (4) resisting the urge to give a lead role to any one actor or institution (e.g. the US, or the ITU). Taken together, this approach roughly follows Rumtin Sepasspour's suggestion that we push many ideas and initiatives simultaneously into the multilateral system and see which ones thrive.[107] Evolutionary theory at its best!

Fit, function, feedback

Governance of complex systems focuses more on the question of fit and function than the precise shape of an institution. In the case of AI, the question of fit can be described as meeting five AI-specific challenges: (1) non-linear change, as AI jumps in capacities; (2) uncontrollable outcomes, as AI moves across actors quickly and invisibly; (3) proliferation across geographies and domains; (4) concentration of power and resources as a small number of actors may benefit disproportionately; and (5) acceleration, as AI generates increasingly rapid growth in a wide variety of areas.

These characteristics of AI mean that a good fit for governance would involve: (1) an elastic response, able to scale up and out quickly in response to surprising developments; (2) the capacity to track AI risks at multiple levels, including those emanating from individuals and/or devices; (3) a transnational characteristic that does not become bogged down by national boundaries or questions of sovereign control; (4) safeguards against monopolistic tendencies or rapid concentrations of power in the hands of a few; and (5) a scientific analytic capacity that can accelerate alongside AI, possibly embedded within the technological development itself. As one group of experts described, such a governance approach would need to be "flexible and dynamic."[108]

Complexity thinking further suggests we should be especially careful of positive feedback loops, which can reinforce and accelerate trends or concentrate power. We can already see such loops in AI development. A single company (ASML) controls 100 percent of the lithography equipment needed to make the latest chips needed for AI development; one company (TSMC) controls chip production; and one company (Nvidia) has cornered the market on chip design. This concentrates the production of the critical hardware needed for AI in an extraordinarily centralized manner, making the system increasingly reliant on a small number of key actors. As they gain resources and capacities, they can crowd out other actors, creating a de facto monopoly on AI hardware. This renders the system extremely vulnerable to small shocks – if ASML's equipment has a flaw, the disruptions to our world would be enormous.

AI also has the tendency to concentrate political power and control over populations. Machine learning systems become more accurate and powerful the more access to data they have. This means countries (or other actors) with access to large-scale information processing, cutting-edge technology, and granular data about citizens are more efficient than those with decentralized information processing.[109] Highly authoritarian, surveillance-state regimes are much more capable of monopolizing large-scale datasets, creating a self-reinforcing capacity to understand, shape, and ultimately determine the course of societies as AI systems become more powerful. The same tendency may occur in the private sector as AI concentrates into so-called "superstar firms," potentially resulting in effectively one search engine (Google), one social network (Facebook or X), and one online marketplace (Amazon).[110] As Noah Yuval Harari suggests, AI seems to inherently "favor tyranny."[111] At the far end, we could imagine a global system run by a single super-intelligent AI wielded by a small number of world dictators. A more reasonable scenario sees China shooting ahead of more pluralistic, open societies in the West, based on Beijing's ability to control and centralize data.

Together, this means our governance response needs to provide a negative feedback loop when the risks of AI begin to transgress certain safety thresholds, and also when it begins heading towards a deeper ethical/social outcome that we see as dangerous. By negative feedback, I mean a corrective, slowing AI development down when safety limits are reached, or bolstering guardrails when certain criteria are met (the diagram simplifies what could be a series of gradually increasing feedback loops). Such an approach would need to generate live, accurate information about the evolving risk landscape, cycling that information back into the foundation model development itself.[112]

Key thresholds should include the risks of misuse, military applications, potential harm to humans or the planet, and also the more insidious problem of concentration of resources and power in the hands of a few. It could also include deeper questions about the kind of societies we want to live in, such as levels of inequality, deeply embedded biases, or how we maintain a balance with the planet.[113] We may need to think of different pacing of feedback: a very fast turnaround for the immediate risks of harm (e.g. a financial market shutdown, or a nuclear escalation) and a slow feedback loop that allows for deeper reflection on societal issues.

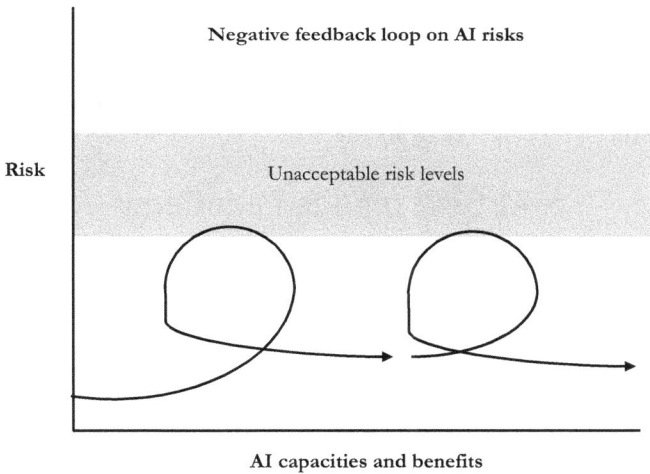

Negative feedback loop on AI risks

Risk

Unacceptable risk levels

AI capacities and benefits

Such a feedback function might require what one expert referred to as an "investigator" role.[114] Rather than passively receiving information, we may need a more proactive, independent capacity to look into the risks. And this capacity will almost certainly need to involve a blend of expertise: we cannot just assume technical experts will be able to design the appropriate contours of a feedback loop that needs to reflect social concerns. We will need ethicists, psychologists, historians, and hopefully complexity scientists. While the highly institutionalized models described above might offer the necessary independence and investigative capacities, they likely would not be sufficiently flexible to respond to the fast-moving aspects of AI development, or sufficiently deep in cross-cutting expertise to build such a coherent, deep feedback loop.[115]

Layers and modules

Complex systems tend to be composed of different "hierarchies" or "layers." Think of a forest floor made up of subterranean root and mushroom structures, trees, wildlife, and the local weather system. "Layering" is a well-known governance approach to such systems, and it means designing tailored interventions for each layer. In forestry management, specific monitoring systems can be built for mycelium, trees, birds, and weather. In terms of AI, it may mean designing bespoke governance processes for the different layers of our techno-social system.

There is no consensus on how to divide the AI governance issue into layers, but there are some good ideas out there. Gasser and Almeida have proposed three layers: technical, ethical, and social.[116] Wirtz et al. have produced a five-layer design moving upward: technical, challenges, regulation, policy, and collaborative governance.[117] Naidoo has proposed that these layered approaches could be combined with "governance coordinating committees" to create a more coherent structure across different hierarchies.[118] And the UN AI Advisory Body offers a nice diagram showing how different functions might be conceived in layers or hierarchies.[119]

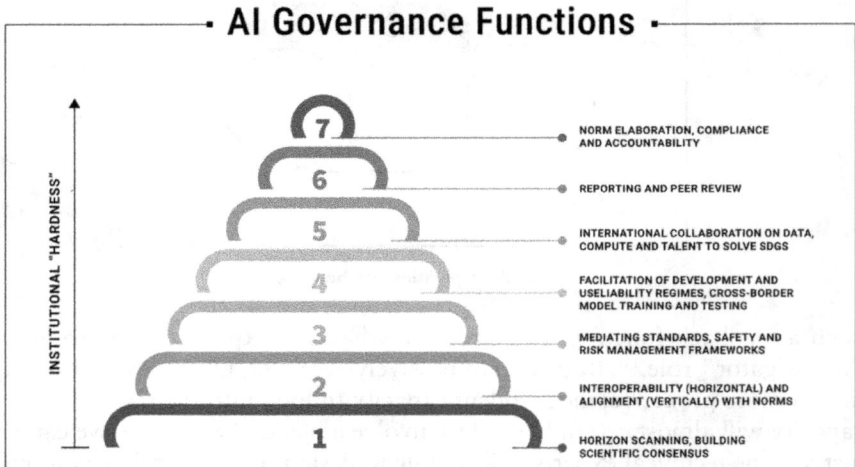

By dividing systems into layers, we can helpfully set specific goals and time-frames for each. For example, at the technical layer, we may have a short-term and specific objective of putting some guardrails in place to ensure human control of key weapons systems, or to prevent stock market crashes. At the ethical layer, we may have an immediate objective of agreeing that AI should be aligned with human preferences, but it may require a more medium-term process to achieve a global ethics. And at the societal level, we may be engaged in a multi-decade and continuous process to combat the tendencies towards authoritarianism and inequality that seem increasingly strong in AI.

Critical mass, not central control

Should AI be governed by a central, global authority? Some experts have suggested that the technology is too disparate and widely applied to be meaningfully controlled by a single entity.[120] They point out that centralization could create a "brittle dinosaur" that is obsolete upon creation,[121] or a path-dependent institution that is unable to evolve to meet new risks.[122] In contrast, proponents of the various UN-centered proposals described above argue that only a centralized authority can address the global threats posed by AI. Pointing to the deep risks of fragmentation and a potential AI arms race, they argue that national legislation is insufficient to the task.

Complex systems are rarely driven by a central authority. A queen bee may sit in the center, but she does not have day-to-day control over the individual bees in the hive. Instead, systems develop centers of gravity that reach equilibrium over many iterations. This can be literal gravity – the movement of stars and planets around black holes in galaxies – or it can be a concentration of activity and resources. Think of a wolf's evolution within an ecosystem: over time, wolves evolved to have advantages over other animals (faster legs, sharper teeth, better reproductive capacities) and they grew to become apex predators. Their expansion was limited by the amount of available food, so eventually they reached a balance within their ecosystem. Change in the wolf's relationship with its habitat happens when a certain threshold is reached – a tipping point – and the balance needs to be adjusted.

This points us to the idea of critical mass, not central control. Rather than start with a single body with global reach, could a group of actors create a strong enough "anchor" to eventually draw more in? Could we reach a tipping point in AI governance, where a critical mass of states eventually cluster around a common set of norms and regulatory approaches?[123] Are we already seeing this gravitational pull in the coalescence around the OECD/G20 standards on AI?[124] Or around UNESCO's AI ethics (which has near universal support from member states)?[125] Could the Global Partnership on Artificial Intelligence emerge as a dominant forum for AI governance, helping to address the risks of a fragmented, nationally-driven approach to AI?[126] Could the G20 AI Coordinating Committee proposed by Wallach, Jelinek, and Kerimi use the enormous heft of the world's biggest economies to create a tipping point on AI governance? Or will these different efforts lead to a rift in which for example BRICS and the EU/US pursue separate and competing AI governance?

The risks of fragmentation around AI seem very high. If one cluster of actors is able to generate AI systems with large amounts of data and very few ethical constraints, they may quickly move towards some of the doomsday scenarios that opened this chapter. Rather than comprehensively govern AI, we may need to think of a bare minimum set of ethics and practice around which to build a strong center of gravity. ICANN's relative success in driving global Internet policy around principles of transparency and equitable access offers one such example.[127] Perhaps some soft-law, basic principles around safety, testing, and human-centered development could create a common grounding.[128] This seems to be what the Bletchley Conference in November 2023 was trying to achieve.

An emerging model of adaptive AI governance?

In September 2023, two well-known AI experts, Wendell Wallach and Anja Kaspersen, published a proposal for a Global AI Observatory (GAIO).[129] Describing it as a "neutral technical organization" they described the key characteristics as follows. The GAIO would:

- Issue standardized, real-time reports at both general and domain-specific levels to enable assessment against agreed standards.
- Orchestrate global debate in an inclusive manner.
- Conduct foresight and future-oriented assessments of risks.
- Manage registries of adverse incidents, emerging risks, the history of AI systems, and a repository of good practices.
- Oversee promotion of agreed norms, including via a "technology passport" system that could help produce comparable assessments of AI risks across jurisdictions.
- Create a certification toolbox to promote responsible behavior and support confidence-building measures.
- Direct support to the development of AI programs to ensure they are safe and transparent.

While not a complete model, GAIO provides one of the best starting points for AI governance that I have seen to date, and the one that most directly speaks to the questions raised by complexity thinking. It could provide the kind of fluid, flexible body that would adapt to non-linear change, while also generating live feedback on the key thresholds for the safe development of AI. It could operate across the different layers of AI development and implementation and help to generate that critical mass of actors behind some basic principles. It might also provide the space for some of the deeper ethical and social reflection that will need to guide our AI development into a safe future for humanity. If established by a sufficiently powerful group (for example, the G20), the GAIO could become the anchor for more layered, decentralized AI governance initiatives in the future.[130] Something like GAIO seems like a good place to focus our efforts.

An AI for an AI?

In closing this chapter, we should not neglect the elephant in the room: the potential of AI to govern itself. It may well be that the only thing fast and smart enough to govern AI is an AI system.[131] As Dirk Helbing suggested, the automation of humanity may be the next logical step.[132] A sort of utopian end state would be a well-designed AGI that always stayed conditioned on human preferences and wellbeing, walked itself back from safety thresholds, and turned itself off if it started to snowball in a worrying direction. At its best, such an AI could become a sort of benevolent techno-Leviathan, constantly polling all of society to ensure that our collective wellbeing was being maximized and providing a global feedback loop to stay on track.[133] If AI is rapidly becoming smarter than us, maybe it will become more ethical than us as well. After all, humanity has a very bad track record on the ethical front: it is only a few lifespans ago that slavery was legal in many parts of the world, and only a century since women were given the right to vote. Today, we make deeply unethical collective decisions about the wellbeing of animals, and our use of fossil fuels is a clear form of theft from future generations. Could an AI possessed of some sort of human-superior "niceness" deliver us into a sustained period of global wellbeing?[134] The exciting thing about AI is that it opens us so quickly into these kinds of questions, though it is easy to become divorced from reality as well. Maybe the most important global governance question is how to prevent our strong tendencies to try to simplify and control things from taking over this transformative moment in human history, to keep options open and creative juices flowing.

Notes

1 New York Times, "Rutherford Cools Atom Energy Hope by Waldemar Kaempffert" (Special Cable to The New York Times; Dateline September 11), Quote Page 1, Column 6, New York, 12 September 1933. NB: there is some dispute as to the actual quote.
2 G. Allen & T. Chen, "Artificial Intelligence and National Security," Harvard Belfer Center (2017).
3 Jack Clark, statement at United Nations Security Council 9381st meeting, 18 July 2023, available at: https://media.un.org/en/asset/k1j/k1ji81po8p.
4 See, Y. Bengio et al., "Managing AI Risks in an Era of Rapid Progress," *arXiv* (26 October 2023), available at: //arxiv.org/abs/2310.17688.
5 Metacalculus, "When will top forecasters expect AGI to be developed and demonstrated?" 1 July 2022, available at: https://www.metaculus.com/questions/4815/date-of-first-agi-according-to-forecasters/.
6 C. Metz, "'The Godfather of A.I.' Leaves Google and Warns of Danger Ahead," New York Times, 1 May 2023.
7 Y. Bengio, "One of the godfathers of AI airs his concerns," The Economist, 21 July 2023, available at: https://www.economist.com/by-invitation/2023/07/21/one-of-the-godfathers-of-ai-airs-his-concerns

8 I. Hogarth, "We must slow down the race to God-like AI," Financial Times, 13 April 2023.

9 R. Bommasani et al., "On the opportunities and risks of foundation models," *arXiv* (12 July 2023), available at: arXiv:2108.07258.

10 For a description of the term "intelligence" see N. Nilsson, *The Quest for Artificial Intelligence: A History of Ideas and Achievements* (New York: Cambridge University Press, 2010); S. Legg & M. Hutter, "A Collection of Definitions of Intelligence," *ArXiv* (June 25, 2007), available at: http://arxiv.org/abs/0706.3639

11 J. Hausenloy & C. Dennis, "Towards a UN Role in Governing Foundation Artificial Intelligence Models," United Nations University Centre for Policy Research, 9 September 2023.

12 J. Hausenloy & C. Dennis, "Towards a UN Role in Governing Foundation Artificial Intelligence Models," United Nations University Centre for Policy Research, 9 September 2023.

13 R. Wiblin & K. Harris, "Chris Olah on what the hell is happening inside neural networks," 80,000 hours podcast, 4 August 2021, available at: https://80000hours .org/podcast/episodes/chris-olah-interpretability-research/.

14 R. Bommasani et al., "On the opportunities and risks of foundation models," *arXiv* (12 July 2023), available at: arXiv:2108.07258.

15 Flowing Data, "Stable Diffusion to generate spectrograms to convert to sounds," 16 December 2022, available at: https://flowingdata.com/2022/12/16/stable-dif-fusion-spectrogram

16 S. Martin, "Will AI undergo discontinuous progress?" *Lesswrong* (21 February 2020), available at: https://www.lesswrong.com/posts/5WECpYABCT62TJrhY/ will-ai-undergo-discontinuous-progress#Defining_Discontinuous_Progress

17 O. Linton & S. Mahmoodzadeh, "Implications of high-frequency trading for security markets," *Annual Review of Economics* 10 (2018).

18 M. King & A. Shull, "Introduction: How Can Policy Makers Predict the Unpredictable?" in D. Araya, R. Nieto-Gómez, eds, *Modern Conflict and Artificial Intelligence* (Centre for International Governance Innovation, 2020), 1.

19 See, T. Shevlane et al., "Model evaluation for extreme risks," *arXiv* (22 September 2023), available at: https://arxiv.org/abs/2305.15324 .

20 This is not an abstract notion. In testing an AI's ability to pass a "captcha" test, evaluators observed an AI posing as a human to convince an unwitting person to pass the test on its behalf.

21 The question of accountability is discussed in N. Bostrom & E. Yudkowsky, "The ethics of artificial intelligence," in K. Frankish & W. M. Ramsey, eds, *The Cambridge Handbook of Artificial Intelligence* (Cambridge University Press, 2014), 316–334.

22 See, M. Horowitz, "Artificial Intelligence, International Competition, and the Balance of Power," *Texas National Security Review* (2018); A. Gill, "A New Arms Race and Global Stability," *Modern Conflict and Artificial Intelligence* (2020), 15. See also, V. Boulanin, "Mapping the Innovation Ecosystem Driving the Advance of Autonomy in Weapon Systems," Stockholm International Peace Research Institute (2016).

23 M. Anderljung, "Frontier AI Regulation: Managing Emerging Risks to Public Safety," *arXiv* (6 July 2023), available at: https://arxiv.org/pdf/2307.03718.pdf

24 M. Brundage et al., "The malicious use of artificial intelligence: Forecasting, pre-vention, and mitigation," *arXiv* (February 2018).

25 For vivid descriptions of these scenarios, see, R. Kurzweil, *The Singularity Is Near: When Humans Transcend Biology* (New York: Penguin Books, 2006).

26 Written testimony of Dario Amodei, "Oversight of AI: Principles for Regulation," Before the Judiciary Committee Subcommittee on Privacy, Technology, and the

Law, US Senate, 25 July 2023, available at: https://www.judiciary.senate.gov/imo
/media/doc/2023-07-26_-_testimony_-_amodei.pdf.
27 The question of accountability is discussed in N. Bostrom & E. Yudkowsky,
"The ethics of artificial intelligence," in K. Frankish & W. Ramsey, eds., *The
Cambridge Handbook of Artificial Intelligence* (Cambridge University Press,
2014), 316–334, 320. See also, McKinsey & Company, "What is the Future
of Generative AI: An Early View in 15 Charts," 25 August 2023, available at:
https://www.mckinsey.com/featured-insights/mckinsey-explainers/whats-the
-future-of-generative-ai-an-early-view-in-15-charts.
28 I. Good, "Speculations Concerning the First Ultraintelligent Machine," in F. Alt
& M. Rubinoff, eds. *Advances in Computers* (New York: Academic Press, 1965),
31–88.
29 A. Genus & A. Stirling, "Collingridge and the dilemma of control: Towards
responsible and accountable innovation," *Research Policy* 47(1) (2018): 61–69.
30 D. Guston, "Understanding 'Anticipatory Governance,'" *Social Studies of Science*
44(2) (2013): 218–242, 226.
31 N. Maslej et al., *The AI Index 2023 Annual Report* (Stanford, CA: Stanford
University, 2023), available at: https://aiindex.stanford.edu/report/.
32 N. Bostrom, *Superintelligence: Paths, dangers, strategies* (Oxford: Oxford
University Press, 2014).
33 A. Conn, "Artificial Intelligence and the King Midas Problem," Future of Life
Institute, 12 December 2016, available at: https://futureoflife.org/ai/artificial
-intelligence-king-midas-problem/.
34 E. Geist & A. Lohn, "How Might Artificial Intelligence Affect the Risk of
Nuclear War?" RAND (2018). See also, K. Lieber & D. Press, "The New Era
of Counterforce: Technological Change and the Future of Nuclear Deterrence,"
International Security 41(4) (April 2017): 9–49.
35 A. Dafoe, "AI Governance: A Research Agenda," Future of Humanity Institute,
University of Oxford, July 2017. See also, S. Armstrong, N. Bostrom, and
C. Shulman, "Racing to the Precipice: A Model of Artificial Intelligence
Development," Technical Report: Future of Humanity Institute, 2013.
36 H. Karnofsky, "Potential Risks from Advanced Artificial Intelligence: The
Philanthropic Opportunity." Open Philanthropy Project, 2016, available at:
http://www.openphilanthropy.org/blog/potential-risks-advanced-artificial-intel-
ligence-philanthropic-opportunity; L. Muehlhauser, "How Big a Deal Was the
Industrial Revolution?" 2017, available at: http://lukemuehlhauser.com/indus-
trial-revolution/.
37 D. Hamilton, "The 'godfather of AI' says he's scared tech will get smarter than
humans: 'How do we survive that?'" Fortune Magazine Online, 4 May 2023,
available at: https://fortune.com/2023/05/04/geoffrey-hinton-godfather-ai-tech
-will-get-smarter-than-humans-chatgpt/.
38 K. Roose, "A Conversation with Bing's Chatbot Left Me Deeply Unsettled," New
York Times, 16 February 2023.
39 A different categorization of proposals is offered by M. Maas & J. Villalobos,
"International AI Institutions: A Review of Models, Examples, and Proposals,"
Legal Priorities Project 2023.
40 See, A. Ramamoorthy & R. Yampolskiy, "Beyond MAD?: The Race for
Artificial General Intelligence," *ITU Journal*, 1(1) (2018), 8. See also, G.
Wilson, "Minimizing Global Catastrophic and Existential Risks from Emerging
Technologies through International Law," *Virginia Environmental Law Journal*
31 (2013): 307.
41 The AI Treaty organization is the foremost proponent of this. Available at:
https://aitreaty.org/.

42 See, e.g., B. Docherty, "The Need for and Elements of a New Treaty on Fully Autonomous Weapons," Human Rights Watch, 1 June 2020, available at: https://www.hrw.org/news/2020/06/01/need-and-elements-new-treaty-fully -autonomous-weapons.

43 For invocations of the IAEA and NPT examples to AI governance, see, "Secretary-General António Guterres remarks to the Security Council on Artificial Intelligence," 18 July 2023, available at: https://www.un.org/sg/en/content/sg/speeches/2023-07-18/secretary-generals-remarks-the-security-council-artificial-intelligence; S. Altman, G. Brockman, and I. Sutskever, "Governance of Superintelligence," OpenAI, 22 May 2023, available at: https://openai.com/blog/governance-of-superintelligence; A. Ramamoorthy & R. Yampolskiy, "Beyond MAD?: The Race for Artificial General Intelligence," *ITU Journal* 1(1) (2018); S. Chesterman, *We, the Robots?: Regulating Artificial Intelligence and the Limits of the Law* (Cambridge: Cambridge University Press, 2021), 210; C. Robichaud, "The Puzzle of Non Proliferation," *Asterisk* (2023); M. Maas, "How Viable Is International Arms Control for Military Artificial Intelligence? Three Lessons from Nuclear Weapons," *Contemporary Security Policy* 40(3) (2019): 285–311.

44 G. Wilson, "Minimizing Global Catastrophic and Existential Risks from Emerging Technologies through International Law," *Virginia Environmental Law Journal* 31 (2013): 307. Jason Hausenloy and Andrea Miotti produced an excellent policy brief on a possible moratorium, which I was fortunate to read prior to publication.

45 Indeed, such a broad range could give rise to "treaty congestion." See, D. Anton, "Treaty Congestion' in International Environmental Law', in S. Alam et al., eds., *Routledge Handbook of International Environmental Law* (Abingdon: Routledge Press, 2021), 651–666.

46 M. Nichols, "UN Chief backs idea of global AI watchdog like nuclear agency," Reuters, 12 June 2023, available at: https://www.reuters.com/technology/un -chief-backs-idea-global-ai-watchdog-like-nuclear-agency-2023-06-12/.

47 See, E. Fournier-Tombs, "Towards a United Nations Internal Regulation for Artificial Intelligence," *Big Data and Society* (2021): 1–5.

48 For a good assessment of these, see M. Maas, "How Viable Is International Arms Control for Military Artificial Intelligence? Three Lessons from Nuclear Weapons," *Contemporary Security Policy*, 40(3) (3 July 2019).

49 E. Garcia, "Multilateralism and artificial intelligence: What role for the United Nations?" Social Science Research Network, available at: https://papers.ssrn.com/sol3/papers.cfm?abstract_id=3779866; E. Fournier-Tombs et al., "Technical Note: A Global Architecture for Artificial Intelligence," United Nations University Centre for Policy Research, September 2023, available at: https://unu.edu/publication/global-architecture-artificial-intelligence. But also see, R. Nindler, "The United Nation's capability to manage existential risks with focus on artificial intelligence," *International Community Law Review* 21(1) (2019): 5–34 (highlighting many of the limitations of the UN in regulation of AI).

50 The first instance I could find of this idea was in 2018. T. Simonite, "Canada, France Plan Global Panel to Study the Effects of AI," Wired Magazine, 6 December 2018, available at: https://www.wired.com/story/canada-france-plan -global-panel-study-ai/. More recently, the idea of a "Commission" was floated by L. Ho, "International Institutions for Advanced AI," *arXiv* (10 July 2023), available at: https://doi.org/10.48550/arXiv.2307.04699. An "advisory body" was recommended by I. Bremmer & M. Suleyman, "The AI Power Paradox," Foreign Affairs, 16 August 2023. A specific IPCC model was recommended by J. Bak-Coleman et al., "Create an IPCC-like Body to Harness Benefits and Combat Harms of Digital Tech," *Nature* 617 (7961) (May 2023): 462–464.

51 "The Bletchley Declaration by Countries Attending the AI Summit, 1–2 November 2023," available at: https://www.gov.uk/government/publications/ ai-safety-summit-2023-the-bletchley-declaration/the-bletchley-declaration-by -countries-attending-the-ai-safety-summit-1-2-november-2023.

52 See, G. Mulgan & D. Siddarth, "The World Needs a Global AI Observatory," *Noema* (29 June 2023), available at: https://www.noemamag.com/the-world -needs-a-global-ai-observatory.

53 The idea of legitimacy is discussed in L. Kemp et al., "UN High-Level Panel on Digital Cooperation: A Proposal for International AI Governance," Centre for the Study of Existential Risk and Leverhulme Centre for the Future of Intelligence, 26 February 2019, available at: https://www.cser.ac.uk/news/advice-un-high -level-panel-digital-cooperation/. The benefits of an IPCC model are also laid out in N. Miailhe & Y. Lannquist, "Global Governance of Artificial Intelligence," in *Handbook of Artificial Intelligence and Robotic Process Automation: Policy and Government Applications* (2020).

54 See, "The World Needs an International Agency for Artificial Intelligence, Say Two AI Experts," The Economist, 18 April 2023, available at: https://www.econ-omist.com/by-invitation/2023/04/18/the-world-needs-an-international-agency -forartificial-intelligence-say-two-ai-experts.

55 Y. Jernite, "Data Governance in the Age of Large-Scale Data-Driven Language Technology," *ACM Conference on Fairness, Accountability and Transparency* (2022): 2206–2022.

56 J. Turner, *Robot Rules: Regulating Artificial Intelligence* (New York, NY: Springer Berlin Heidelberg, 2018), 254.

57 Carnegie Council for Ethics in International Affairs, "Artificial Intelligence & Equality Initiative. A Framework for the International Governance of AI," 5 July 2023, available at: https://www.carnegiecouncil.org/media/article/a-framework -for-the-international-governance-of-ai.

58 R. Chowdhury, "AI Desperately Needs Global Oversight," Wired Magazine, 6 April 2023, available at: https://www.wired.com/story/ai-desperately-needs -global-oversight/.

59 See, J. Hausenloy, A. Miotti, and C. Dennis, "A Multinational AGI Consortium (MAGIC): A Proposal for International Coordination of AI," *ArXiv* (October 2023).

60 C. Gutierrez, "Multilateral Coordination for the Proactive Governance of Artificial Intelligence Systems," Future of Life Institute, 2023, available at: https://papers.ssrn.com/sol3/papers.cfm?abstract_id=4583536

61 G. Marcus, "Artificial Intelligence Is Stuck. Here's How to Move It Forward," The New York Times, 29 July 2017, available at: https://www.nytimes.com/2017 /07/29/opinion/sunday/artificial-intelligence-is-stuck-heres-how-tomove-it-for-ward.html. See also, P. Slusallek, "Artificial Intelligence and Digital Reality: Do We Need a CERN for AI?" OECD Forum Network, 8 January 2018.

62 C. Stix, "Foundations for the Future: Institution Building for the Purpose of Artificial Intelligence Governance," *AI and Ethics* 2(3) (1 August 2022): 463–476.

63 L. Kemp et al., "UN High-Level Panel on Digital Cooperation: A Proposal for International AI Governance," Centre for the Study of Existential Risk and Leverhulme for the Future of Intelligence, 26 February 2019, available at: https:// www.cser.ac.uk/news/advice-un-high-level-panel-digital-cooperation/.

64 But see, P. Cihon, M. Maas, and L. Kemp, "Fragmentation and the Future: Investigating Architectures for International AI Governance," *Global Policy* 11(5) (2020) (noting the positive aspects of fragmentation).

65 S. Fatima et al., "Winners and losers in the fulfillment of national artificial intel-ligence aspirations," Brookings Blog 21 October 2021, available at: https://www

.brookings.edu/blog/techtank/2021/10/21/winners-and-losers-in-the-fulfilment
-of-national-artificial-intelligence-aspirations/.

66 White House Press Release, "Executive Order on the Safe, Secure, and
Trustworthy Development and Use of Artificial Intelligence," 30 October 2023,
available at: https://www.whitehouse.gov/briefing-room/presidential-actions
/2023/10/30/executive-order-on-the-safe-secure-and-trustworthy-development
-and-use-of-artificial-intelligence/. See also, P. Stone, "Artificial Intelligence and
Life in 2030," Technical report,
    Stanford University, 2016, available at: http://ai100.stanford.edu/2016-report.

67 M. Sheehan, "China's AI Regulations and How They Get Made," Carnegie
Endowment for International Peace, 10 July 2023, available at: https://carn-
egieendowment.org/2023/07/10/china-s-ai-regulations-and-how-they-get-made
-pub-90117.

68 "EU AI Act: first regulation on artificial intelligence," Press release, 8 June
2023, available at: https://www.europarl.europa.eu/news/en/headlines/society
/20230601STO93804/eu-ai-act-first-regulation-on-artificial-intelligence

69 M. Maas & J. Villalobos, "International AI Institutions: A Review of Models,
Examples, and Proposals," Legal Priorities Project 2023.

70 See, e.g., T. Fist, L. Heim, and J. Schneider, "Chinese Firms Are Evading Chip
Controls," *Foreign Policy*, 21 June 2023.

71 For a full review of these models, see M. Maas & J. Villalobos, "International
AI Institutions: A Review of Models, Examples, and Proposals," Legal Priorities
Project (2023). For an argument in favor of informal norm-setting, see J. Morin
et al., "How Informality Can Address Emerging Issues: Making the Most of the
G7," *Global Policy* 10(2) (May 2019): 267–273.

72 A. Daly et al., "Artificial intelligence governance and ethics: global perspectives,"
arXiv (2019).

73 E.g. the IEEE Global Initiative on Ethics of Autonomous and Intelligent Systems,
available at: https://standards.ieee.org/industry-connections/ec/autonomous-sys-
tems/.

74 T. Jelinek, W. Wallach, and D. Kerimi, "Policy brief: the creation of a G20 coordinating committee for the governance of artificial intelligence," *AI and Ethics*
1(2) (2021): 141–150.

75 See, J. Cheng, & J. Zeng, "Shaping AI's future? China in global AI governance,"
Journal of Contemporary China 32 (143) (2023): 794–810.

76 W. Wallach & A. Kaspersen, "Envisioning Modalities for AI Governance: A
Response from AIEI to the UN Tech Envoy," Carnegie Council for Ethics in
Artificial Intelligence, 29 September 2023, available at: https://www.carnegie-
council.org/media/article/envisioning-modalities-ai-governance-tech-envoy.

77 AI Advisory Body, "Interim Report: Governing AI for Humanity," December
2023, available at: https://www.un.org/sites/un2.un.org/files/ai_advisory_body
_interim_report.pdf.

78 National Security Commission on Artificial Intelligence, "Final Report," National
Security Commission on Artificial Intelligence, March 2021, Chapter 15, available at: https://www.nscai.gov/wp-content/uploads/2021/03/Full-Report-Digital
-1.pdf.

79 A. Webb, "The Big Nine: How the Tech Titans and their Thinking Machines
Could Warp Humanity," Public Affairs, 2019, available at: https://www.politico
.eu/article/build-democracy-into-ai-combat-china/.

80 E.g. A. Farid et al., "Unlikely Allies: Reaching Beyond Traditional Halls of Power
for AI Global Governance." *Aftershocks 2022 Global Trends Report* (Montreal:
Basillie School of International Affairs, 2022).

81 A. Jobin, M. Ienca, and E. Vayena, "The global landscape of AI ethics guidelines," *Nature Machine Intelligence* 1(9) (2019): 389–399. See also, E. Erman & M. Furendal, "The global governance of artificial intelligence: Some normative concerns," *Moral Philosophy and Politics* 9(2) (2022): 267–291.
82 M. Latonero, "Governing artificial intelligence: Upholding human rights & dignity," *Data and Society* (2018).
83 See, e.g., R. Danzig, "Technology Roulette: Managing Loss of Control as Many Militaries Pursue Technological Superiority," CNAS Report, 2018. See also, R. Mazzolin, "Artificial Intelligence and Keeping Humans 'in the Loop,'" *Modern Conflict and Artificial Intelligence* (2020): 48.
84 I. Rahwan, "Society-in-the-loop: programming the algorithmic social contract," *Ethics and Information Technology*, 20 (2017): 5–14.
85 See, L. McGregor, "Accountability for Governance Choices in Artificial Intelligence: Afterword to Eyal Benvenisti's Foreword," *The European Journal of International Law* 29(4) (2018): 1079–1085.
86 See, E. Bietti, "From ethics washing to ethics bashing: a moral philosophy view on tech ethics," *Journal of Society and Computing* 2(3) (2021): 266–283.
87 O. Erdélyi & J. Goldsmith, 'Regulating Artificial Intelligence: Proposal for a Global Solution," *Government Information Quarterly* 39(4) (1 October 2022); C. Feijóo et al., "Harnessing Artificial Intelligence (AI) to Increase Wellbeing for All: The Case for a New Technology Diplomacy," *Telecommunications Policy* 44, no. 6 (6 May 2020).
88 See, e.g., R. Whitfield, "Effective, Timely and Global: The Urgent Need for Good Global Governance of AI," World Federalist Movement and Institute for Global Policy, 2020; M. Robinson, "The Elders Urge Global Co-Operation to Manage Risks and Share Benefits of AI," 31 May 2023, available at: https://theelders.org/news/elders-urge-global-co-operation-manage-risks-and-share-benefits-ai.
89 S. Hammond, "We Need a Manhattan Project for AI Safety," Politico, 8 May 2023, available at: https://www.politico.com/news/magazine/2023/05/08/manhattan-project-for-ai-safety-00095779. See also, A. Miotti, 'We Can Prevent AI Disaster Like We Prevented Nuclear Catastrophe," Time, 15 September 2023, available at: https://time.com/6314045/prevent-ai-disaster-nuclear-catastrophe/.
90 See, e.g., A. Ramamoorthy & R. Yampolskiy, "Beyond MAD?: The Race for Artificial General Intelligence," *ITU Journal* 1(1) (2018): 8. See also, R. Nindler, "The United Nation's Capability to Manage Existential Risks with a Focus on Artificial Intelligence," *International Community Law Review* 21, no. 1 (11 March 2019): 5–34; Future of Life Institute, "A statement on AI risk and next steps," May 2023, available at: https://futureoflife.org/ai-policy/fli-on-a-statement-on-ai-risk-and-next-steps/ (proposing international agreements to limit the proliferation of dangerous AI). See also, M. Watson, "IAEA for AI? That Model Has Already Failed," Wall Street Journal, 1 June 2023, available at: https://www.wsj.com/articles/iaea-for-ai-that-model-has-already-failed-chaptgpt-technology-nuclear-proliferation-4339543b.
91 This problem is laid out in D. Kaushik & M. Korda, "Panic about Overhyped AI Risk Could Lead to the Wrong Kind of Regulation," Vox, 3 July 2023. https://www.vox.com/future-perfect/2023/7/3/23779794/artificial-intelligence-regulation-ai-risk-congress-sam-altman-chatgpt-openai. See also, D. Dewey, "Long-Term Strategies for Ending Existential Risk from Fast Takeoff," in *Risks of Artificial Intelligence*, V. Müller, ed. (New York: Chapman and Hall/CRC, 2015).
92 See, S. Altman, G. Brockman, and I. Sutskever, "Governance of Superintelligence," OpenAI, 22 May 2023, available at: https://openai.com/blog/governance-of

-superintelligence. See also, O. Guest, "Prospects for AI safety agreements between countries," Rethink Priorities, 2023; D. Araya & R. Nieto-Gómez, "Renewing multilateral governance in the age of AI," in *Modern Conflict and Artificial Intelligence* (Center for International Governance Innovation, 2020), 10 (referring to AI as "more like aspartame or polyethylene"); I. Raji et al., "Closing the AI accountability gap: Defining an end-to-end framework for internal algorithmic auditing," *arXiv* (January 2020).

93 See, PauseAI Proposal, available at: https://pauseai.info/proposal (suggesting an AI agency to regulate AI safety for models above a certain size).

94 A. Balwit, "How We Can Regulate AI," *Asterisk* (June 2023).

95 R. Neufville, & S. Baum, "Collective Action on Artificial Intelligence: A Primer and Review," *Technology in Society* 66 (1 August 2021). See also, D. Zhang et al., "Enhancing International Cooperation in AI Research: The Case for a Multilateral AI Research Institute," Human-Centered Artificial Intelligence (Stanford University, May 2022).

96 E. Pauwels "The new geopolitics of converging risks: the UN and prevention in the era of AI," Centre for Policy Research, UN University, 2 May 2019.

97 N. Bostrom & E. Yudkowsky, "The ethics of artificial intelligence," in K. Frankish & W.M. Ramsey, eds, *The Cambridge Handbook of Artificial Intelligence* (Cambridge University Press, 2014), 316–334, 320 (referring to the "non-local" effects of AGI).

98 This idea of iterative and fluid responses aligns with the "generative" approach in J. Epstein, *Generative Social Science: Studies in Agent-Based Computational Modeling* (Princeton, NJ: Princeton University Press, 2006).

99 See, N. Ingersleben-Seip, "Competition and Cooperation in Artificial Intelligence Standard Setting: Explaining Emergent Patterns," *Review of Policy Research* 40, no. 5 (25 January 2023).

100 B. Drexel & M. Depp, "Every Country Is on Its Own on AI: Why AI Regulation Can't Follow in the Footsteps of International Nuclear Controls," Foreign Policy (blog), 13 June 2023, available at: https://foreignpolicy.com/2023/06/13/ai-regulation-international-nuclear/. See also, W. Johnson & D. Bowman, "A Survey of Instruments and Institutions Available for the Global Governance of Artificial Intelligence," *IEEE Technology and Society Magazine* 40.4 (2021): 68–76 (arguing that a treaty would take too long to address emerging AI risks).

101 See, V. Harding, "Lessons from History: What Can Past Technological Breakthroughs Teach the AI Community Today," The Bennett Institute, 2020.

102 J. Fleming, "The Pathological History of Weather and Climate Modification: Three Cycles of Promise and Hype," *Historical Studies in the Physical and Biological Sciences* 37 (1) (2006): 3–25.

103 A. Day, *States of Disorder, Ecosystems of Governance: Complexity Theory Applied to UN Statebuilding in the DRC and South Sudan* (Oxford: Oxford University Press, 2021).

104 O. Guest, "Risk Awareness Moments: A Concept for Thinking about AI Governance Interventions," Rethink Priorities, 14 April 2023, available at: https://rethinkpriorities.org/longtermism-research-notes/risk-awareness-moments.

105 C. Lima & N. Nix, "41 states sue Meta, claiming Instagram, Facebook are addictive, harm kids," Washington Post, 24 October 2023.

106 I'm grateful to Lyse Langlois for suggesting a focus on these ethics concerns and believe that her organization Obvia is a leading actor in driving the deeper conversation worldwide.

107 R. Sepasspour, "A reality check and a way forward for the global governance of artificial intelligence," *Bulletin of the Atomic Scientists* 79.5 (2023): 304–315.

108 W. Johnson & D. Bowman, "A Survey of Instruments and Institutions Available for the Global Governance of Artificial Intelligence," *IEEE Technology and Society Magazine* 40.4 (2021): 68–76.

109 M. Maas, "Innovation-Proof Global Governance for Military Artificial Intelligence?: How I Learned to Stop Worrying, and Love the Bot," *Journal of International Humanitarian Legal Studies* 10.1 (2019): 129–157.

110 A. Dafoe, "AI Governance: A Research Agenda," Future of Humanity Institute, University of Oxford, July 2017, 39.

111 N. Harari, "Why Technology Favors Tyranny," The Atlantic, October 2018, available at: https://www.theatlantic.com/magazine/archive/2018/10/yuval-noah -harari-technology-tyranny/568330/.

112 This is emphasis on the foundation model is laid out in J. Hausenloy & C. Dennis, "Towards a UN Role in Governing Foundation Artificial Intelligence Models," United Nations University Centre for Policy Research, 9 September 2023.

113 For a framework that could generate a feedback loop in the case of bias, see, Ondrej O. Bohdal et al., "Fairness in AI and Its Long-Term Implications on Society," Proceedings of the Stanford Existential Risks Conference 2023, 171–186.

114 C. Stix, "Foundations for the future: institution building for the purpose of artificial intelligence governance," *AI and Ethics* 2.3 (2022): 463–476.

115 J. Stewart, "Why the IAEA Model May Not Be Best for Regulating Artificial Intelligence," Bulletin of the Atomic Scientists (blog), 9 June 2023, available at: https://thebulletin.org/2023/06/why-the-iaea-model-may-not-be-best-for-regulating-artificial-intelligence/.

116 U. Gasser & V. Almeida, "A layered model for AI governance," *IEEE Internet Computing* 21(6) (2017): 58–62. This builds on D. Clark, "Characterizing Cyberspace: Past, Present, and Future," Massachusetts Institute of Technology, 12 March 2010.

117 B. Wirtz, J. Weyerer, and B. Sturm, "The Dark Sides of Artificial Intelligence: An Integrated AI Governance Framework for Public Administration," *International Journal of Public Administration* 43(9) (3 July 2020).

118 M. Naidoo, "Artificial intelligence and global governance: How AI ethics and standards should be addressed at the global level," *The iJournal: Student Journal of the University of Toronto's Faculty of Information* 7.1 (2021): 1–12. For the proposal on governance coordinating committees, see, W. Wallach & G. Marchant, "Toward the Agile and Comprehensive International Governance of AI and Robotics," *Proceedings of the IEEE* 107.3 (2019): 505–508.

119 This diagram can be found on the AI Advisory Body's website at: https://www.un .org/en/ai-advisory-body.

120 See, e.g., P. Stone et al., "Artificial Intelligence and Life in 2030," Technical report, Stanford University (2016).

121 P. Cihon, M. Maas, and L. Kemp, "Fragmentation and the Future: Investigating Architectures for International AI Governance," *Global Policy* 11(5) (2020).

122 L. Baccaro & V. Mele, Pathology of Path Dependency? The ILO and the Challenge of New Governance," *Industrial and Labor Relations Review* 65 (2) (2012): 195–224.

123 See, L. Kemp et al., "UN High-Level Panel on Digital Cooperation: A Proposal for International AI Governance," Centre for the Study of Existential Risk and Leverhulme Centre for the Future of Intelligence, 26 February 2019, available at: https://www.cser.ac.uk/news/advice-un-high-level-panel-digital-cooperation/.

124 L. Schmitt, "Mapping global AI governance: a nascent regime in a fragmented landscape," *AI and Ethics* 2.2 (2022): 303–314 (arguing that the OECD's norm setting power means others are gravitating towards their standards).

125 Press statement, UNESCO adopts first global standard on the ethics of artificial intelligence, 8 April 2022, available at: https://www.unesco.org/en/articles/unesco-adopts-first-global-standard-ethics-artificial-intelligence.

126 See, L. Schmitt, "Mapping global AI governance: a nascent regime in a fragmented landscape," *AI and Ethics* 2.2 (2022): 303–314.

127 See, J. Turner, *Robot Rules: Regulating Artificial Intelligence* (New York, NY: Springer, 2018), 240–242.

128 C. Gutierrez, G. Marchant, and L. Tournas, "Lessons for Artificial Intelligence from Historical Uses of Soft Law Governance," *Jurimetrics* 61(1) (29 December 2020). For examples, see Y. Stevens, "Soft Law Governance: A Historical Perspective from Life-Science Technologies," *Jurimetrics* 61 (2020).

129 W. Wallach & A. Kaspersen, "Envisioning Modalities for AI Governance: A Response from AIEI to the UN Tech Envoy," Carnegie Council for Ethics in Artificial Intelligence, 29 September 2023, available at: https://www.carnegie-council.org/media/article/envisioning-modalities-ai-governance-tech-envoy.

130 T. Jelinek, W. Wallach, and D. Kerimi, "Policy brief: the creation of a G20 coordinating committee for the governance of artificial intelligence," *AI and Ethics* 1.2 (2021): 141–150.

131 See, W. Heaven, "Now we know what OpenAI's superalignment team has been up to," *MIT Technology Review* (14 December 2023).

132 D. Helbing, *The Automation of Society is Next* (Kindle: CreateSpace Independent Publishing Platform, 2015).

133 See, I. Rahwan, "Society-in-the-loop: Programming the algorithmic social contract," *Ethics and Information Technology* 20(1) (2018): 5–14; A. Etzioni & O. Etzioni, "AI assisted ethics," *Ethics and Information Technology* 18(2) (2016): 149–156.

134 N. Bostrom, *Superintelligence: Paths, dangers, strategies* (Oxford: Oxford University Press, 2014), 221.

7 Back to the future
How complexity can help us save the world

The brink of extinction

We live in a world where the risks to humanity are shockingly high. Toby Ord, one of the world's leading thinkers on existential risk, calculates the chances of a humanity-ending catastrophe within the next 100 years at 1 in 6.[1] Pause on that for a moment. If he's even close to right, we are effectively playing Russian roulette with humanity, firing a new chamber every 15 years, hoping for the best. Would you gamble humanity on the roll of a die? Other experts have suggested it might be more like a coin flip.[2] From nuclear war, pandemics, rogue AI, an omnicidal terrorist, or a climate tipping point, we seem to have an alarmingly high chance of triggering our own extinction.[3] Even short of total annihilation, a wide range events could have a global catastrophic effect with a dystopian existence for those of us who survive.[4] Imagine a future where a single surveillance authority dictates most aspects of our lives, or a class of AI-enhanced humans rises to rule the rest of us, or an engineered pathogen takes out half the world's population, or global temperatures soar to 8 degrees Celsius higher than they are today.[5] These may seem like remote scenarios, but how confident are you that we are not already en route towards at least one of them? Isn't even a pretty small chance of scenarios this bad worth taking seriously?

This book has been about our response to global crises. It has explored many of the leading ideas for addressing clusters of challenges like the environment, war, cyberattacks, and artificial general intelligence (AGI). These constitute planetary threats – they can cascade from local to global, transforming all our lives. They speak to the well-known reality that our interconnectedness allows many risks to spread quickly.[6] But what about the lives of people who have not yet been born? How should we respond to the kind of events that could put future generations' entire existence at risk? How do we balance the immediate prerogatives to feed, clothe, educate, and protect today's billions with the possibility of the end of humanity, or a dystopian life for the trillions of people who may be born in the future? How do we represent their interests (and rights?) in decisions we take today that could have catastrophic outcomes in the future?

DOI: 10.4324/9781003506386-8

In my work to support the Secretary-General's *Our Common Agenda* report in 2021, questions about future generations were front and center. I remember Toby Ord briefing the team about his work on existential risk. Many of us had copies of *A Ministry for the Future* and *Homo Deus* prominently in the backgrounds of our Zoom calls. The SG's proposals to establish a Futures Lab and an Envoy for Future Generations reflected a keen interest in aligning the multilateral system more directly around the idea of a long-term viable future for humanity. In my view, this is a laudable and worthy mindset for today (it's why I wrote this book!).

But as I've followed the efforts to implement these ideas – helping to host events for the UN Futures Lab, convening expert events around future risks, testing the waters with member states on proposals to "future-proof the UN" – I have been struck by how bad we all seem to be at thinking seriously about the future (myself very much included). On the one hand, it is extraordinarily difficult to get people's noses off the grindstone, to make them look up from their daily work and think in bigger, longer frames about the world. I would say that 90 percent of the foresight discussions I've attended in the last two years have gravitated back to what people are doing right now. The present tense is a strong attractor. Equally, when we do look up at a horizon 10 or 50 years from now, our imaginations seem to veer wildly from wastelands where the rubble of humanity is scrabbling over the few drops of remaining water, to techno-utopian worlds where machines have solved most of our problems.

Between these two future worlds may be a fuzzy, uncertain, somewhat-likely future towards which we are blindly making our way. But if the SG is right, this middle path does not exist: It is either "breakdown or break through," to use his words. Muddling through will not work in an era of accelerating risk and complexity. There is no middle-ground scenario where we just keep our heads down and come out bruised but ok. The Band Aids we put on systemic failures like the 2008 financial crisis, climate change, or AI may result in a momentary reduction of risk and a feeling that we are out the other side. But our short-term fixes are baking in much deeper problems that could threaten all of humanity. We must think seriously about the future, in a way that allows us to prepare for it, or there may be no future with us in it.

Complexity thinking offers us a better way to think about the future, avoiding many of the pitfalls, human weaknesses, and path dependencies we have as human beings. Systems thinking helps us balance short- and long-term concerns, achieving a more realistic assessment of existential and global catastrophic risks. It helps us achieve what Tom Hale calls for in his brilliant new book, *Long Problems:* a lengthening of governance across time horizons that go well beyond our own lifetimes.[7] By employing complexity thinking, we can expose the weaknesses of our current approaches to future risks and design options to "future-proof" our response.[8] Ultimately, a truly future-oriented global governance system also needs to be "human-proof," generating systemic responses that combat our deeply entrenched tendencies to overvalue the present and shortchange future generations.

The problem: We undervalue big future risks

The way we think about the future is deeply problematic, filled with biases, myopias, and path dependencies. Four human shortcomings work together to inhibit our ability to make good decisions about future existential and global catastrophic risks: (1) our inherent preference for the present; (2) our reliance on past experience; (3) our inability to weigh big, distant harm; and (4) our reliance on a high level of scientific consensus. When combined with a polycrisis that is constantly forcing us to deal with the next big problem, our world today is dominated by an almost willful ignorance about the future.

We have a "*presentist bias*" – we consistently favor the present over the future.[9] This is especially the case in democracies (where electoral cycles and public opinion tend to influence decision-making), but presentism is a global phenomenon across societies.[10] Our presentism means we give far greater weight to imminent risks than to ones in the more distant future. Our NIMBYism is not just about our backyards, it's also about our lifespans – we are very committed to preventing harm within the remainder of our lives, but our interest drops off precipitously from the grave onwards. Parents are not immune from this, despite our professed interest in the lives of our children and grandchildren. As a result, an existential risk to a generation that has not yet been born will be given far less weight than a much smaller risk to people alive today.

We also suffer from an "*availability heuristic*," where our estimates of risk tend to be based on our own experience.[11] For example, our assessments of the risks of a future global pandemic may be quite accurate with COVID-19 fresh in our minds, but many of the most acute threats we are facing today have no precedent in our lifetimes. We've never experienced a climate four degrees warmer than today's; we have no idea what an artificial general intelligence will look like; none of us has gone through a global nuclear war. How can we assess an existential event that, by definition, has never occurred in our past?[12] This means massive, unprecedented harms with a low likelihood of occurring are chronically undervalued.[13] This should worry us as the generation that experienced the Holocaust and Hiroshima dies off – perhaps our collective ability to accurately value future genocides or nuclear war will diminish accordingly.[14]

We fall prey to a "*scope neglect*" that makes it hard to absorb the reality of massive harm to large numbers of people.[15] For example, we struggle to care 100 times more about something that is 100 times worse, even with strong evidence. In fact, the suffering of a small number of people (or even just one person) often appears more vividly to us than the suffering of millions. Worse, massive harm to a large population can produce a sort of psychological "numbing" where we fail to empathize with large groups in pain, or a form of "moral disengagement" from the impacts of our own actions.[16] When we reach the realm of total catastrophe – for example a global nuclear war resulting in the death of nearly everyone – our imaginations fail and we may even fall back on a sort of abstraction, treating the risk as purely hypothetical.

I encountered this over and over in discussions about nuclear weapons. Smart, powerful people representing nuclear powers would often start conversations with "of course we all know of the enormous destructive power of nuclear weapons, but…" followed by the need to protect national interest by deterrence. One expert referred to denuclearization as a "feel-good goal" with no chance of ever happening. The fact that a nuclear war would eliminate the very concept of the nation-state and potentially eradicate all human life on Earth seemed too obvious and painful to face head on.

Our reliance on a gradual accumulation of experience means we set *impossible scientific standards* for making decisions about global catastrophic risks. Typically, policy change is developed after decades of scientific research, building towards a level of near total consensus needed to overwhelm our vested interests and path dependencies. Think of the staggering preponderance of evidence about the links between smoking and cancer required before serious action was taken by governments (and even today smoking is legal). We have 40 years of rigorous scientific research into human-caused climate change and still today we have not agreed to ban fossil fuel production. Every Monday night, Americans tune into a football game that has been shown beyond any normal level of doubt to cause depression and suicide for the players who suffer repeated concussions. But it will be decades before the science is deemed sufficiently strong to overcome our desire to have 21st Century gladiators.

This kind of cumulative evidence doesn't work with existential and catastrophic risks: as Carl Sagan pointed out, "Theories that involve the end of the world are not amenable to experimental verification – or at least, not more than once."[17] We cannot accumulate empirical evidence about events that will end humanity with our usual methods, and we should not require the same level of consensus when it comes to these kinds of risks. Worse, even if 99.9 percent of scientists agree that solar radiation modification, or AGI, or a deadly biological pathogen is too dangerous to produce without more testing, it only takes a single person making one breakthrough to create a threat to humanity.[18] (This is the *12 Monkeys* problem, without the time machine or Brad Pitt to warn us of the future.) If a single hacker can bring down our financial systems, or a single AI program set off a nuclear war, the idea of scientific safeguards begins to feel necessary, but far from sufficient.[19]

If you're worried now, the polycrisis makes it all worse. Consider a quick list of catastrophic man-made crises today: global warming, collapse of the coral reef ecosystem, mass species extinction, plastic pollution, space clutter, synthetic pathogens, unfettered AI development, the wars in Gaza and Ukraine, US/China tensions around Taiwan, North Korea's nuclear saber rattling, soaring inequality, cyber-vulnerabilities in critical infrastructure, etc., etc.; the list goes on. We simply cannot absorb this many crises at once. Instead, we suffer from a catastrophe-induced attention deficit disorder. Surrounded by crises of differing qualities, timeframes, potential likelihoods, and means of control, we seem to become paralyzed. Or we decide that we can only focus on one thing at a time and swing wildly between crises. Or we just abandon ourselves to a world of unknown unknowns, hoping for some silver bullet to solve issues at the global level while we just get through our daily grind.

Our ADHD around risk leaves us ill equipped to balance apparently short-term issues with long-term ones.[20] Is today's famine or flood more important than addressing climate change? It may feel more immediate and urgent, but we also need to act today on climate change. Is AI going to transform our lives for the better or destroy us all in the long run? We tend overestimate the short-term impact of technologies but underestimate their longer-term effects.[21] So maybe we will panic about AI and overreact, regulating it in a way that locks in some of its more dangerous aspects in the longer term. This policy whiplash is typical – we overreact, overcorrect, and then overreact again. For example, if we set a high bar of regulation for AI development, only a very few companies will meet the standards, potentially leading to a global monopoly of history's most powerful technology. But if we then open up the market, unfettered AI development might lead to the kind of collapse discussed in Chapter 6. Nearly every problem examined in this book has this same tension between short-term fix versus long-term costs, and nearly every time policymakers have strong incentives to deal with the issue on their doorstep.

The result of these human traits and preferences is that our global governance institutions are geared around short- to medium-term serious risks, but not long-term existential ones. They are designed based on our past experiences, not the most likely future ones.[22] They are the outcome of competition and lowest-common-denominator approaches that privilege national prerogatives over the best possible design. Our global governance system has become a Rube Goldberg machine that whirs and clicks and processes endless acts of coordination and small-scale responses to a current crisis, but never amounts to a deeper transformation.[23] Every multilateral reform is reduced to an incremental adjustment that solves an immediate problem, but also creates a new layer of bureaucracy and coordination, ironically making the system less adaptive and more embedded in its own procedures. This sets us on a path towards a "tragedy of the uncommons"[24] where our systems are, by design, unable to rise to the challenge of systemic risk.[25]

This crisis-driven evolution may be fine if all we are trying to do is contain the next cyberattack or respond to the next coup. But it is absolutely *not* fine when we are confronted with an existential or global catastrophic risk. We cannot afford to fail even once when it comes to preventing a humanity-level harm. We cannot fall back on 400-year-old concepts of the nation state and sovereignty as an excuse for getting existential risk wrong.

But the conclusion I have reached is that we seem willing to tolerate and even accelerate an astonishingly high risk of the end of the world. Maybe this should not be such a surprise. After all, when the atomic bomb was first tested during World War II, its developers genuinely thought there was a chance it would ignite the atmosphere and destroy all life on the planet. Knowing this, they went ahead with the detonation. That the scientists were wrong does not erase the reality that America's leaders were willing to take an existential risk in the name of getting the bomb before Hitler. Today, we elect leaders that promise to maintain stockpiles of thousands of nuclear weapons, invest in fossil fuels, pursue untested geoengineering experiments, push the development of AI well past our ability to control its safety, and invest in bioweapons research that could end all life on this planet.

Our collective intellectual and moral poverty about the future leads us to the question: on what basis should we make decisions today that may have enormous short-term costs, but essentially infinite loss if we get it wrong?[26] How can our global governance architecture enable us to overcome our deeply rooted evolutionary preferences for the present and help us make better decisions? I have reached the conclusion that we need to "human-proof" global governance, designing ways to combat our evolutionary shortcomings. As a first step, we must develop a better way to think about the future.

How to think about the future

Imagine a person living far away from you, maybe in another country or living on the space station above us. Is that person's life any less valuable because of the distance from you? I hope not. I hope we can agree that human life has equal value regardless of where it is. Ultra-nationalists and racial supremacists, if you've gotten this far in the book, now is a good time to drop out!

People's lives also matter equally regardless of *when* they are. If we took three snapshots over time of a person living ten years ago, right now, and ten years from now, their value as a human should not change (maybe it declines slightly as the person gets older, but you get the idea).[27] Just as human life is not altered by geographical location, it should not be changed by temporal location either. Einstein was (probably wrongly) attributed with the quote, "The only reason for time is so that everything doesn't happen at once."[28] From an ethical perspective, maybe we need to think of everything happening at once to achieve balance between present and future generations.

Unfortunately, we actively and consciously discriminate against future generations all the time. Every time we burn fossil fuels, or stockpile nuclear waste, or pour microplastics into the oceans, or incur greater financial debt, we are knowingly increasing the negative impacts on future generations. They will bear the consequences of our actions, yet we have no accountability towards them.[29] Governments consistently favor short-term gains over long-term harm, in large part because citizens discount the future too.[30] The result is a sort of legalized and normalized theft, where our global governance systems have clear lines of accountability towards living generations, but near absolute impunity towards the future.

Unless we do blow up the world, we know that people will be born – lots of them – and we know that they will need many of the same things we need today.[31] They will need air, water, food, the ability to make a living, and many other things we think of as basic to a thriving life. How do we account for those needs in our decisions today? How do we weigh the wellbeing of future people alongside our own, especially when there may be far more people in the future than we have today? And how much do we focus on quantity (the number of people that will be born) versus quality (how good their lives are)? Arguably, a future where fewer people had better lives might be better than a population explosion living under tyranny. There are a lot of ethical rabbit holes here, and I encourage interested readers to explore the resources noted here on questions of longtermism, effective altruism, and the thorny issues that come into play when we try to balance present and future generations.[32]

I don't think we need to go too far into the weeds here. The future may involve trillions of beings that are only somewhat related to what we think of as human today, and they may inhabit far reaches of the galaxy.[33] This huge future population could mean that long-term considerations "swamp" short-term ones if we follow a strict all-human-life-is-equal logic.[34] Concepts of techno-utopianism and the extreme versions of longtermism are interesting, but potentially distracting here.[35] We can stick with what I hope is an uncontroversial point: ending humanity would be a very bad thing, and making the lives of future generations miserable or unlivable would also be very bad.[36] I hope we can also agree that valuing the wellbeing of future generations is important (though we may quickly enter into more divisive questions about how important they are versus people alive today).

If ending humanity is a global bad, then there is a strong case that avoiding existential risks is a global public good. Everyone benefits from our collective survival. Like clean air or a well-functioning civil aviation system, a global public good is not rivalrous or exclusionary – it is a collective, shared benefit.[37] But this does not mean that everyone is equally incentivized to invest in it. Markets are notoriously bad at delivering global public goods because of the free-rider problem. Why should one country pay for a global public good when its citizens will only see a fraction of a benefit that can be delivered by others? Why not just wait for others to invest and then reap the rewards of a globally shared good? The same is true of existential risk: governments tend to undervalue the global benefits of investing in protection and prevention, because the return on investment for them will be a fraction of the overall benefit. We would all benefit from an immediate end to fossil fuels, but that does not mean all countries are equally incentivized to pay for the transition.[38]

The fact that we are custodians of a planet that will be passed on to the next generation means we need to stop thinking of ourselves as agents (making decisions just on behalf of ourselves) and shift to thinking of ourselves as fiduciaries (with responsibilities to others).[39] But generating that transformation in our thinking is very unlikely to result from a business-as-usual mindset of regulating risk and trying to find areas of cooperation. Just saying "we need collective action" is all but guaranteed to fall short of generating collective behavior change. We need some big, transformative thinking around the design of our global governance of catastrophic risks.

Big risks, small ideas

Faced with such a high likelihood of our collective demise, we should be able to come up with some big, bold ideas. At the very least, we should be able to break out of the usual constraints that have limited us in the past. We should be able to harness the staggering amounts of data we now have to make more informed decisions about the future. The good news: there is a growing interest in studying big future risks and the needs of future generations, with new initiatives and centers starting all the time.[40] Staffed with some of the brightest minds in the world, these initiatives have produced an array of innovative thinking, including quite a lot that draws on complexity thinking.[41] The less-good news: most of the bolder and more systemic proposals arising out of this work remains mired in academic centers, without a clear bridge to leaders. Today, the proposals being seriously considered at the global level gravitate strongly towards the same shortcomings we have seen throughout this book. We seem stuck with the worrying (and deeply unfunny) joke that begins "A Leviathan, an IPCC, and a focal point walk into a bar…" Looking briefly at some of big proposals on the table today, we can begin to see how complexity thinking might move us in a better direction.

Big idea 1: A world government?

In 1948, Albert Einstein called for a "world government" to meet the nuclear age. He wrote, "there is no other possible way of eliminating the most terrible danger in which man has ever found himself."[42] Einstein was not the first. Visions of a world government date back to Dante's references to a global *monarchia* in the 14th Century and have been proposed repeatedly since then.[43] Of course, no serious politician today would dare to utter the phrase "world government," and the idea that a single actor could regulate global affairs is now largely discredited. As Anne-Marie Slaughter noted in her landmark *A New World Order*, "a world government is both infeasible and undesirable."[44] We seem destined to carry on in Hedley Bull's famous state of anarchy.[45]

But perhaps the idea is making a comeback. Nick Bostrom has suggested that super-intelligent machines could act as a "singleton" to manage global existential risks.[46] Calls by the environmental community for a "Global Environmental Council," a "World Environmental Court," or a "World Environmental Organization," underscore the momentum for a top-down approach to planetary risks.[47] Other ideas, such as repurposing the UN Trusteeship Council to represent future generations, or the creation of a "Global Resilience Council" to address systemic threats to humanity all point in a similar direction.

Big Idea 2: An IPCC for global risks

"We need an IPCC for existential risks," a leading expert told me during a roundtable for the High-Level Advisory Board on Effective Multilateralism. She wasn't the first to make such a proposal. Some sort of science-policy interface for large-scale, systemic risks has been put forward by many of the most important expert organizations, including:

- A high-level UN panel supported by a scientific commission to evaluate risks and propose actions in line with a UN "global action plan" for systemic crises.[48]
- A science-policy interface for catastrophic and existential risks.[49]
- An IPCC model of scientific inquiry into existential risk.[50]
- An International Panel on Global Catastrophic Risk.[51]
- An Emergency Platform convened by the UN Secretary-General to deal with global risks as they are unfolding.[52]

These are just a few examples of a trend towards science-policy interfaces for planetary risks. Important actors like the World Economic Forum and the UN Disaster Risk Reduction Office are already shifting their analyses towards systemic risks. The UN Environmental Programme is planning a Global Environmental Outlook report that looks at system-level planetary risks, which parallels the High-Level Advisory Board on Effective Multilateralism proposal for an IPCC for the planet.[53] These all share a common theory of change: if we can get the science to connect to the policy, we can orient global governance around systemic risks.

Big Idea 3: A focal point for the future

By the time this book goes to press, the Secretary-General probably will have appointed an Envoy for Future Generations.[54] Fans of Kim Stanley Robinson will smile at the apparent reference to *The Ministry for the Future* and the fictional Mary Murphy's attempts to save the world from a Zurich-based office.[55] But the proposal for special envoys comes most directly from the very successful creation of Future Generations envoys at the national level. Wales and New Zealand have already experimented with such envoys, and they have shown remarkable ability to drive future-oriented national plans.[56] Building up the capacities of national governments to anticipate risks to future generations may have more influence than trying to manage the issue from the top down. There are many good ideas about future-proofing governments that should be explored.[57] Efforts to inject foresight capacities into the UN system were kickstarted by the creation of the UN Futures Lab Network.[58] And less well-known proposals like the creation of a "chief risk officer" could also help drive those national-level efforts.[59]

Taken together, these three sets of ideas could help us grapple with some of the bigger risks facing humanity and build a more future-oriented mindset into our global governance architecture. But they also suffer from a shortcoming that Oran Young has described as "familiar recipes" and "formulaic prescriptions" that may be easy to grasp but have an almost unbroken track record of failure in the past.[60] Some of them are also clearly outside the window of political possibility anytime soon. Should we really wait for the creation of a Singleton to govern us all? Is it realistic, or desirable, to try to create global bodies to manage existential risks from the top down? Can we afford another three decades of science-policy-inaction when faced with catastrophic risks? How much can we really expect from a newly appointed envoy who will be hamstrung by the usual limited resources and mandate? These questions should make us worried. We need to find more creative ways to make decisions about the future.

How complexity can help us make better decisions for the future

We are at a moment where human-caused forces of destruction are becoming a strong attractor in our global system.[61] We are creating an expanding set of humanity-level risks, and much of our sense of progress is bound up in perpetuating these risks. At the same time, we continue to pursue incremental reforms to our governance architecture, tinkering around the edges of institutions rather than a more transformational response. This has rendered much of the global governance system irrelevant to managing catastrophic, humanity-level risks.

Complexity thinking offers a way to develop a better governance fit for the challenge of massive future risks. This chapter follows the argument that complexity: (1) helps us move beyond resilience as a reactive, short-term response to crisis; (2) points us towards transformative global governance approaches; (3) demands a diversity of actors to be involved in building such an approach; (4) enables us to "brake" risks before they cascade into catastrophes; and (5) gives us the essential elements of a future-oriented, "human-proof" global governance architecture. This, I argue, could take the form of a "planetary nervous/immune system" that would in many respects mimic our own human one.[62]

The dark side of resilience: Systemic harm, unfair equilibria

Complexity thinking can help us understand a simple truth about the world: harm is non-linear. We tend to think of damage as something one actor causes to another. A good analogy is downstream pollution. One person puts a chemical in a stream, it is carried downstream, and it hurts someone. When I was a lawyer, we would often try to get our clients off the hook by injecting some uncertainty into the cause-effect chain (it's why I quit). But in complex systems, harm can be multidirectional, indirect, and change over time.[63] Some harms can begin small but snowball and become irreversible – something we are seeing with biodiversity loss and Arctic ice shelf melting. Others may be reversible, as appears to be the case with the ozone layer, or some of the successful reforestation efforts.

A change that closes off certain possibilities in the future can feel small at the time but could have enormous future consequences, creating a new phase space that drives the course of history in a new direction. The advent of the Industrial Revolution, for example, caused a fundamental shift in our means of production, opening up enormous potential for human growth and thriving that did not exist before. But it also locked in certain path dependencies and strong attractors around energy consumption and waste that have led us to the brink of an environmental catastrophe.[64] The attacks on 11 September 2001 indirectly created a desolate outcome for the people of Iraq, 600,000 of whom died over the years that followed.

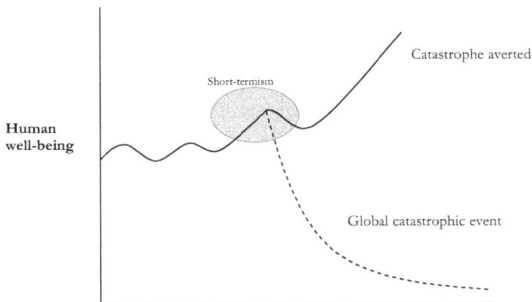

Systemic thinking can help us grapple with the reality that there is no sharp distinction between short- and long-term impacts. Immediate economic growth can come at the cost of eventual environmental destruction; small adjustments in how we begin to regulate AI can balloon into society-level transformations over time. Rather than think of short- or long-term impacts, complex systems have "points of peak importance," where the most significant benefits and costs tend to converge.[65] The peak may look like a drop in equilibrium or a change in phase space, where the range of possible outcomes suddenly expands or shifts. I believe we are currently living at a point of near-peak importance in the development of clean energy, where new attractors could be generated around renewable energy and potentially even a circular economy. If we focus too much on managing immediate shocks to our current system, we may miss this big opportunity.

Complexity may also help us catch the early signals of systemic collapse. The Roman Empire's downfall at the hands of barbarian invasions may have felt sudden to the inhabitants of Rome, but the systemic signs had been building for decades (hyperextension of military forces, a burdensome taxation system that created widespread discontent, and an overreliance on slave labor that left the ruling class susceptible to small shocks). The Great Depression is often described as a "crash" of the stock market in 1929, but that collapse was the result of a set of interconnected factors that had pushed the American system across several tipping points for years (overproduction, underconsumption, an agricultural drought, global economic downturns in related markets). We should be worried that the *Limits to Growth* report 50 years ago anticipated that a similar global collapse would occur right around now as our energy production crosses a range of tipping points.[66] Are we already in the midst of a cascading system failure caused by climate change?[67]

Most of today's proposals are geared at building resilience to these kinds of shocks. Whether the Secretary-General's Emergency Platform, the proposals for a Global Resilience Council, or the many ideas about improving preparedness for global disasters, the common denominator is that we need resilient systems that can absorb shocks, get us back to status quo ante, and carry on.[68] These may help us manage the next crisis, but they also tend to lock us into dangerous trajectories or obscure systemic tipping points until it's too late. Resilience is almost universally considered a good thing. But the concept also carries a dark side, describing the difficulties of transitioning out of unfair, socially undesirable systems.[69] The form of global, carbon-based capitalism that has driven us to the brink of environmental catastrophe is extremely resilient, surviving even the reality that renewable energy is less expensive. When we bailed out big banks in 2008, we also contributed to the resilience of that carbon-based financial system. Similarly, racial inequality is a harm that has proven nearly impossible to eradicate from our education, housing, and other social systems. Just focusing on building so-called "good governance" capacities that can survive shocks also rewards and entrenches deeply unfair systems.

Put another way, complex systems tend towards some form of equilibrium over time, but that equilibrium is not necessarily a good thing. Martin Luther King's famous moral arc of the universe does not necessarily bend towards justice. In fact, our continual acts of crisis management seem to be driving it in the other direction.

Could our efforts to build the resilience of our current system (characterized by rampant fossil fuel use, concentration of wealth, and growing surveillance capacities) lead us into a dystopian future where we have accidentally preserved a system that almost none of us wants? Certainly, when a crisis happens, those in power tend to try to preserve the system that has elevated them into their privileged roles. Look at the 2008 financial crisis and the staggering bailouts offered to the banking system, resulting in a massive windfall for precisely those responsible for the collapse itself. The concept of "too big to fail" is a worrying one from a complexity standpoint, suggesting that vested, powerful interests will prevent systemic transformation, even when a systemic change is almost certainly a good thing for most of us. One deeply disappointing outcome of COP28 was the series of edits to the final declaration, as vested interests whittled away at the language around a "phase out" of fossil fuels until it was rendered toothless and open-ended. The Western response to Ukraine has included a noticeable increase in military spending, shifting resources to allies, but also tilting our system towards more militarized responses in the future. At the very least, these examples support the finding that traditional policy fixes that focus on stability and getting back to a previous state are badly suited to systemic transformation moments.[70]

Transformative global governance

Instead of resilience, complexity thinking points us in the direction of *transformative global governance* to address catastrophic and existential challenges. Transformation – sometimes called "regime shifts" in ecosystems scholarship – occurs when (a) a complex system reaches a threshold with unknown or undesirable consequences, and (b) the mechanisms of adaptation are insufficient to maintain desired conditions or keep risk thresholds below an acceptable level.[71] This can happen naturally as a system undergoes extreme turbulence and then re-establishes equilibrium. When a lake becomes overly polluted and loses sufficient biodiversity, it may shift from a clear body of water to a turbid, algae-dominated one (something called eutrophication). The new equilibrium involves a completely different relationship amongst the lake's inhabitants and may take some time to settle. Alternatively, the lake may suffer from "cascade attacks" from pollution, which can overwhelm and cause collapse.[72]

Like lakes, social systems can transform naturally, without guidance. I would argue that our transition to a digitally connected society in which much of our social lives are lived online has taken place without a conscious governance process. But in the face of massive unintended risks, we should be thinking about deliberate, designed governance transformation. According to one leading expert, deliberate transformation requires "radical, systemic shifts in deeply held values and beliefs, patterns of social behavior, and multi-level governance and management regimes."[73] Transformation is often about agenda setting and reframing issues, shifting one or more deeply held beliefs or assumptions about the world.[74] Such a conscious, societally driven process of helping a system transition into a new equilibrium is not easy, but it may not require a wholesale change of everything.[75] Think of the moment you became aware of the destructive power of a nuclear weapon for the first time, or first really considered what 8 degrees of global warming might look like, or imagined what might happen if AGI were ever created. For me, these moments caused a realignment in my entire worldview, and remain something that I carry with me to this day. Perhaps part of the process is just about prompting the thought.

In fact, we are entering an era where a critical mass of people seems to have woken up to existential risk. Certainly, the COVID-19 pandemic was a visible recent example of a contagion/cascade, where our social, political, and economic systems were all overwhelmed and large numbers of people began to think very differently about the world.[76] Did the pandemic open the possibility to radically change how we design global governance? While a transformation can be triggered by a crisis, we should be careful to assume that moments of flux are the best to generate good long-term outcomes. As one group of experts noted, transformations "must be navigated."[77] If left on its own, systemic transformational change may become increasingly unmanageable due to recurrent positive feedback loops and cascade effects.[78] We still don't know how our systems may settle in the post-COVID era, but there are worrying indications that it has done little to increase our collective willingness to confront these kinds of humanity-level threats.

What might transformational global governance look like in today's polycrisis? We could start with some framing and agenda setting, perhaps at an event like the Summit of the Future in late 2024. Imagine if the declaration adopted at the Summit included reference to the *"rights of future generations."* This normative reframing of the question of the future could be incredibly powerful, creating a cascade across many other systems. If future generations have rights, instead of what Tom Hale calls "shadow interests,"[79] then we need to rethink GDP as the exclusive measure of progress today if it impinges on those rights.[80] We may need to introduce a discount rate in our development programming, to ensure today's gains are balanced by tomorrow's losses. The production of greenhouse gases, plastic pollution, and other environmental harms might become open to legal challenge on behalf of those whose rights are being infringed. And at the very least it could provide the necessary framing for the kinds of practical "future-proofing" steps that are discussed below.[81]

The remainder of this chapter is focused on more specific ways complexity thinking can help us transition from an emerging recognition of global catastrophic risks to a new design of global governance.

A hive mind, not a queen bee: Diversity in decision-making

Even if we don't like it, we tend to think of concentrated, totalitarian powers as more effective at meeting global challenges. Western leaders often look wistfully at China, noting how easy it is to make policy when you don't have to face a bothersome electorate. "If China wants to go green," one expert told me, "only one person needs to say go." The appeal of a centralized body to address existential and massive future risk is similar: we need to be able to cut through the messy cacophony of distributed decision-making, the deep inconveniences of democracy, and just deal with the problem. As the Secretary-General has repeatedly noted, we are in a state of global emergency that requires a stronger ability to make decisions. In general, states of emergency involve a suspension of distributed, democratic decision-making and a temporary consolidation of power.[82] This concentration of authority is behind the ideas of a world government, centralized councils to address global risks, and many of the big ideas laid out above.

Complexity thinking not only points to the impossibility of managing from above, but it also warns us against letting a small number of actors set the initial conditions of a system. Schools of fish self-organize based on a very simple set of internalized rules about alignment and distance with their neighbors, allowing them to act together based only on local interactions. If those rules about alignment and distance are changed even a small amount, the behavior of the school is altered forever. The same is true of all kinds of complex systems: initial conditions have an outsize impact on how the system develops. Changing those conditions based on the experiences or viewpoint of only a small number of actors within the system may create a massive and unintended outcome.

Yet today we are letting a tiny number of actors dictate the initial conditions for our response to some of the most important risks facing humanity. The field of existential and global catastrophic risk studies is dominated by Western academics and overwhelmingly influenced by techno-utopians who believe that we can achieve our maximum potential as humankind via technology.[83] On its face, the techno-utopian argument is compelling: technological advances could allow us to spread humanity across the galaxy, with trillions of human lives maximizing our potential. From a strictly utilitarian viewpoint, more people living "better" lives seems like an obvious best outcome.[84] And those who argue for aligning emerging technologies with "human values" make a persuasive point that technology can help us achieve that utopian vision for humanity if it is constantly pegged to our wellbeing.[85]

But what are those "human values"? Techno-utopianism is a tiny minority view worldwide. Even amongst philosophers, less than 25 percent believe in the kind of utilitarianism that guides most of today's longtermism.[86] The vast majority of people have never heard of a future involving trillions of beings inhabiting faraway galaxies, and they certainly aren't making day-to-day decisions with those distant generations in mind. While it is a safe bet to assume that most people would prefer to avoid global nuclear winter or a pandemic that eradicates humanity, it is *not* safe to assume that most people want the kind of future that is described by elite Western techno-utopians. And it is even less clear that the coming generation will appreciate the decisions we take today based on the narrow assumption that maximizing human potential via technology is best.

Here, Toby Ord's call for a "long reflection" on the future of humanity should be qualified: we need a long, *diverse* reflection. Empirical studies have clearly shown that a diverse group of amateur problem-solvers will arrive at better solutions than a small group of experts.[87] These findings can be expanded to larger governance settings, where again the evidence shows that decisions made by a diverse set of actors are more likely to avoid long-term risks than centralized authoritarian ones.[88] It turns out that there is a strong relationship between citizen participation and effective long-term risk management.[89] More elegantly, "There is an intimate and neglected relationship between existential risk and democracy."[90]

We need to be careful here. The term "democracy" is a loaded one (the UN, for example, avoids it). But at its broadest, the idea of diversity would avoid a concentration of ethical and practical decision-making in the hands of a few when it comes to decisions about humanity. Remember those American scientists who were ready to light the atmosphere on fire just to get the bomb before Hitler? Or that sole Russian submarine captain who defied orders and decided not to fire a nuclear warhead from the waters near Cuba? The most frightening, vertiginous moments for humanity have almost always involved a white man with his finger on a button. We don't want that kind of concentration. Nor, I would argue, do we want highly educated (mostly white male) academics telling humanity how to respond to existential risk. I can see the irony of me, a white male, writing this in a book about existential risk, but it is because I feel so fundamentally unqualified to make decisions about the future of humanity that I am pushing for a diverse, complexity-informed approach.[91]

Braking the system: How to "decomplexify" out of trouble

Many of the global risks we face today are bound up in what Thomas Friedman has called our *Age of Accelerations*.[92] Technologies like AI, solar radiation modification, biotech, and even social media move too quickly for our lumbering responses. Human-caused climate change crosses tipping points while we continue to dither over COPs and carbon-trading systems. In many of these cases, we need some way to put the brakes on until we are surer of our collective safety and benefit, but our traditional tools of legal bans and regulatory frameworks are too slow, cumbersome, and politically elusive. Ideas of a world government or a science-policy interface are clearly inadequate to the task of slowing or making safe these accelerations.

Here, complexity thinking offers two potential braking mechanisms: negative feedback loops and compartmentalization.

Complex systems operate by feedback loops, responding to new information that is transmitted back into them. Whether ants touching antennae, neurons firing in our brains, or mushrooms passing nutrients, all complex systems adapt to information flows. Most systems reach an equilibrium over time through negative feedback that limits change and drives a system's response towards a steady state. Negative feedback acts as a brake on runaway change, like the sweat of our bodies prevents runaway overheating.

In the case of global risks, this would require the capacity to feed early signals of systemic failure and collective risk back into the system. We need to build what some experts call "epistemic security," a way of knowing the world that helps us identify common risks and avoids our tendencies to develop ill-informed echo chambers.[93] This information would need to be part of an architecture designed to avoid crossing tipping points and prevent cascade effects. Imagine, for example, a live carbon emissions tracking system that instantaneously sent a public warning when a country or region crossed an emissions red line. Or a social media tracking system that issued an alert when polarized language began crossing a threshold into hate speech and violent rhetoric. There are many examples from areas as diverse as crowd control, traffic regulation, and counterterrorism that demonstrate the effectiveness of information feedback and system design in preventing unwanted cascade effects.[94]

When a tipping point is approached, we would then need the ability to prevent cascade, snowball, or other accelerants. Here, two of the most important concepts from complexity are sparseness (low degrees of interconnection) and compartmentalization (keeping parts of systems separate). While we think of complex systems as interconnected, they also survive by preventing the spread of risk across the system. The mycelium connecting trees detects disease in one tree and stops its spread to others. Our brains have highly compartmentalized areas for cognitive functions like memory, emotion, and sensory perception. If one area is harmed, the others are often able to carry on. In our tightly interconnected financial system, some of the most promising ideas concern a limited form of "decoupling," preventing troublesome parts of financial systems from infecting others.[95]

Putting the brakes on a global risk will require us to have rapid information feedback, alongside the ability to compartmentalize, decouple, and prevent the spread of a threat. This is easy to imagine in the cyberattack realm, where sophisticated responses already work to isolate and prevent the spread of a virus, cutting off infected computers in real time. There are already some "kill switches" in place to prevent another AI-driven collapse of the stock market. We could imagine innovative designs in the realms of disinformation and hate speech that work to isolate and cut off dangerous echo chambers that could lead to violence. And in the realm of nuclear weapons, dramatically improving the forums where governments and experts can share information, clarify use policies, and maintain a red phone in the case of emergencies could help us contain escalatory rhetoric.

Systemic design: Human-proofing global governance

Guardian ants tend to venture forth when the ambient temperature rises to a certain level. We don't know exactly when an individual ant will decide to go out, but we can make some very educated guesses about how they will act as a group. Human societies are similarly composed of many actors who behave "stochastically" – we are unpredictable as individuals, but over time our behavior follows certain predictable patterns. A laudable goal of global governance is to shape that collective behavior towards safe, sustainable outcomes for all of humanity. But as we've seen, humans are not just fallible; we seem evolutionarily predisposed to accelerating humanity-level risks. When faced with decisions that would clearly be good for present and future humanity, we seem determined to do the opposite much of the time.

We can design our way out of these human tendencies. Think of the hotels that require us to put our key into a slot to turn on the lights, or the opt-out organ donor box on some driving license applications, or the bright letter grade in the windows of many American restaurants. All of these are examples of designs that shape our behavior, resulting in less electricity use in hotels, higher rates of organ donation, and cleaner restaurants. They all draw on the idea that actors in social systems have free will, but that our collective behavior can be shaped through conscious design.[96]

What might some of those design elements look like? A "human-proof" global governance architecture could take many forms, but some key characteristics include:

1. *Isolate us from presentism.* We should build spaces, positions, and processes that are not susceptible to the pressures of the present. This could include an agreement to the non-political appointment of future generations envoys in every government, with dedicated capacities to feed recommendations across different ministries. And/or governments could agree to some long-term plans that could not be altered by elections cycles, such as commitments to investing in sustainable energy. Here, the Summit of the Future in 2024 could articulate some of the key areas that should be "future-proofed" by national governments.
2. *A "gap report" on global catastrophic risk.* One of the most effective tools in recent years has been UNEP's "Emissions Gap Report," which visualizes the gap between government's emissions commitments and reality. Could the UN produce a global catastrophic risk "gap" report offering a similar visualization of the gap between massive future risks and our preparedness? There is a strong psychological impact of seeing a gap between our goals/commitments and where we are today.
3. *Invest in the future.* Today, most developed countries have made public commitments to spending a portion of their gross national production on overseas aid (typically 0.7 percent). This has helped to keep pressure on governments to maintain a baseline of spending on aid, though many have dipped below the agreed threshold during economic downturns. Surely a similar commitment could be made for future generations, setting aside funds for long-term research, scenario-based planning, and/or agent-based modeling of the future.[97]
4. *Internalize the social costs.* Imagine an app on your phone that broadly kept track of your daily activities (you probably already have one that

measures your location and heart rate). At the end of the day, it would give you a rough estimate of your energy consumption, the amount of plastics you used, your contribution to greenhouse gases. This would be fed back to you as a visual of future harm: if everyone had the same day as you, what would life be like in 20 years?[98] Efforts to build an informed society that can share information across groups seem the most likely to reduce the insidious effects of misinformation and polarization.[99]

5. *The rights of future generations.* Ultimately, social systems tend to evolve through the gradual evolution of law. In many cases law lags far behind a majority opinion, but over time there tends to be a rough alignment between law and values. In the 75 years since the signing of the Universal Declaration of Human Rights, prohibitions on torture and enslavement have helped to consolidate society's views on these issues. Though it might face headwinds, the Summit of the Future would be the ideal forum to articulate a set of rights of future generations, which could cascade across our governance systems in much the same way as human rights did 75 years ago.

6. *Keep remodeling.* Our availability heuristic means we strongly gravitate to past models, even in the face of novel challenges. We might need more than one approach or discipline to address global catastrophic risks.[100] And we also need to reconsider whether "blueprints," "models," and "reforms" are adequate to the task. A cynical view might even suggest that decades of so-called reforms in the multilateral system were part of an intentional obstructionist strategy by those powers wishing to maintain a status quo that benefits them alone.[101] One of the biggest risks today may be our inability to imagine governance change as anything more than a reiteration of a past reform. Policy experimentation becomes increasingly difficult when things are getting out of control or extremely risky.[102] Providing space for unconventional thinking, non-expert discussion, and multiple perspectives may be the most important thing we can do to extract ourselves from our path dependencies.

7. *Leapfrog the present.* Scholarship has uncovered a counterintuitive aspect of both societies and international organizations: rather than change gradually and incrementally over time, we tend to make rapid, significant changes, followed by longer periods of relative stasis.[103] I often think of Africa's "leapfrog" of landline technology for phones: nearly all African communities invested in cellular technology and did not have to go through the decades of gradual improvements to landline connectivity. Most of the incremental reform efforts within multilateralism fall into the doldrums between the big changes, tinkering around with small-scale improvements but not generating a bigger transformation. To "future-proof" global governance, I believe it will be necessary to do more than gradually inject future-oriented thinking into our work. We need to think bigger, and we probably need to leapfrog many of today's technologies and path-dependent mindsets. What might a leapfrog idea look

like? Perhaps we should treat future generations like we treat particle physics, building a multinational scientific endeavor where the world's top scientists jointly develop ideas to safeguard humanity (a CERN for the future). Or maybe the environmental movement needs to reconsider its aversion to nuclear energy and more seriously consider the emerging science around Thorium-based nuclear power. The point here is to break out of small-scale reforms and offer a different set of initial conditions.

These are just some starting ideas, drawn from dozens of conversations I've had in recent years. They seek to address a chronic problem in today's world: we are all stressed, busy, rushing from one thing to the next. We simply don't have time for the kind of open, deliberative reflection needed to transition to a new paradigm. We struggle to achieve the "certain slowness" that could enable a deeper reflection on the future.[104] We need to design spaces for this reflection to happen, or we will be forever chasing the next crisis.

A planetary immune system – from complexity thinking to complexity science

This has been a book about the application of complexity thinking to global governance. It has used concepts like feedback loops, strong attractors, punctuated equilibrium, and tipping points to explore how our responses to planetary threats could be improved. But what about the application of complexity *science* to global governance? What would happen if we were able to take the enormous quantities of data we have about our world and use it to create what Dirk Helbing and others call a "planetary nervous system"?[105] Could we use computational models to build a global governance machine that responds to risks in real time? Could we build on many of the dynamic computational approaches already out there to develop something truly global?[106] Could such a function be the most important contribution that an AGI might make for humanity?

Such an approach would take complexity thinking to its logical conclusion: collective intelligence. Returning to the analogy that began this book, in an ant colony, ants display a collective intelligence that goes beyond the aggregate of their individual intelligence. They respond to a host of challenges that are fundamentally beyond their understanding. An ant has no real concept of "flood," or "famine," or "heat wave," but an ant colony can respond to these events with remarkable sophistication.

Complexity science may offer us a pathway towards a collective intelligence for humanity. There is ample evidence from other fields – for example, traffic congestion, or crowd control – that computational approaches can anticipate systemic changes and dramatically improve outcomes in settings where individual actors are largely unaware of system dynamics.[107] Computational approaches have shown some real promise, including in the arenas of global catastrophic risk and pandemic response.[108] And, while the research is still inchoate, the possibility of predicting and even heading off escalations into violent conflict within and between states by relying on computational modeling is not as remote as it might seem.[109]

In the conversations I've had over the past year, I've noticed a growing convergence around the idea of something like a planetary nervous system. While I was in Nairobi in late 2023, some of UNEP's senior experts described their hope to set up a "centralized, constantly updated assessment of planetary boundaries linked to policy response." I was recently in an intergovernmental discussion on the financial system and a finance minister suggested that the world needed "something like a centralized immune system that would send resources quickly in response to crises." In an expert meeting on AI governance, several participants suggested that AI "could be governed by an AI that could keep constant track of global risk thresholds and respond automatically." At its most ambitious (and potentially most dangerous), AI-driven approaches could help every citizen in the world feed directly into a single system that could adjust and respond accordingly to emerging risks, moving us towards a "society in the loop" model of governance.[110]

At the very least, a planetary immune approach will need what the medical profession calls a "hospitalist" function.[111] As medicine has become more specialized, there are fewer and fewer doctors trained to see the whole picture. Overly focused diagnoses may overlook interconnected symptoms, or produce treatments that have unintended consequences. A hospitalist is someone who works across disciplines, helping to connect the specialist diagnoses into a holistic picture of the patient. And importantly, they have the function of ensuring that the hospital's response is a good fit for the patient's overall needs. A hospitalist produces an adaptive, systemic response by the hospital. Similarly, as we begin to generate larger bodies of data drawing on specialized fields (e.g. biodiversity, AI, weapons) we will need to train a cadre of governance specialists who can work across these arenas.

These are exciting ideas and point to the potential for complexity science to open new forms of participation and responsiveness to future risks. It could meet the demand for "methods that are accessible to practitioners and policy makers," offering real-time, actionable responses for busy leaders in search of a red telephone.[112] If the dominant metaphor of this book is a sick planet in need of a more robust immune system, big data computational approaches could well be the booster shot we need. Of course, we need to be careful not to slide into techno-utopian visions of a Singleton with all the answers, but complexity science does seem to offer a way to move beyond endless cycles of crisis-driven action and reaction.

A final thought. We tend to think of adaptation as something backward facing, the incremental result of long periods of time passing. I imagine Walter Benjamin's Angel of History, with his face turned towards the past, "Where we perceive a chain of events, he sees one single catastrophe which keeps piling wreckage upon wreckage and hurls it in front of his feet."[113] We must build our governance responses from the wreckage we have at our feet today. But adaptive governance is also forward facing, a preparation for the future, a positioning of humanity to be prepared for accelerating change.

Notes

1 T. Ord, *The Precipice: Existential Risk and the Future of Humanity* (London: Hachette Book Group, 2020), 167. For a direct critique of this calculation – and indeed Ord's overall approach to existential risk – see, C. Cremer & L. Kemp, "Democratising Risk: In Search of a Methodology to Study Existential Risk," *arXiv* (2021): 11214.

2 M. Rees, *Our Final Hour: A Scientist's Warning: How Terror, Error, and Environmental Disaster Threaten Humankind's Future in this Century – On Earth and Beyond* (New York: Basic Books, 2003), 8 (putting the odds "no better than fifty-fifty that our present civilization on Earth will survive until the end of the present century").

3 For an interesting description of omnicidal terrorists and "agents of doom," see, É. Torres, "Maniacs, Misanthropes, and Omnicidal Terrorists: Reassessing the Agential Risk Framework," Proceedings of the Stanford Existential Risks Conference 2023, 36–47.

4 I am not going to spend a lot of time distinguishing between existential and global catastrophic risk, as many authors have already done so. For the purposes of this chapter, we are talking about big system failures that result in mass human suffering. Whether any humans are left at the end of it is important, but not the main focus. For some good literature defining existential and global catastrophic risks, see, C. Rios Rojas et al., "Building a Science-Policy Interface for tackling the Global Governance of Catastrophic and Existential Risks," University of Cambridge Centre for the Study of Existential Risk, 2023; S. Avin et al., "Classifying global catastrophic risks," *Futures* 102 (2018): 20–26; T. Rowe & S. Beard, "Probabilities, Methodologies and the Evidence Base in Existential Risk," Working Paper, Centre for the Study of Existential Risk, July 2018, available at: http://eprints.lse.ac.uk/89506/.

5 For some descriptions of these dystopian scenarios, see H. Lin, "The existential threat from cyber-enabled information warfare," *Bulletin of the Atomic Scientists* 75(4) (2019): 187–196; P. Edwards, "Is Climate Change Ungovernable?" Proceedings of the Stanford Existential Risks Conference 2023, 133–146.

6 I. Goldin, "The Butterfly Defect: Why globalization creates systemic risks and what to do about it," *Journal of Risk Management in Financial Institutions* 7.4 (2014): 325–327.

7 T. Hale, *Long Problems: Climate Change and the Challenge of Governing Across Time* (Oxford: Princeton University Press, 2024).

8 J. Kreienkramp & T. Pegram, "Governing Complexity: Design Principles for the Governance of Complex Global Catastrophic Risks," *International Studies Review* 23 (2021): 779–806.

9 J. Boston, "Assessing the options for combatting democratic myopia and safeguarding long-term interests," *Futures* 125 (2021): 102668. But see, A. Karnein, "What's wrong with the presentist bias? On the threat of intergenerational domination," *Critical Review of International Social and Political Philosophy* 26(5) (2023): 725–746 (arguing for a narrow view on future generations focused on avoiding their domination).

10 J. Boston, *Safeguarding the Future: Governing in an Uncertain World* (Wellington, NZ: Bridget Williams Books, 2017), 8.

11 T. Ord, *The Precipice: Existential Risk and the Future of Humanity* (London: Hachette Book Group, 2020), 197. See also, D. Kahnemann, *Thinking, Fast and Slow* (MacMillan, 2011).

12 This is sometimes called "Knightian Uncertainty," after F. Knight, *Risk, Uncertainty and Profit* (Houghton Mifflin, 1921).

13 M. Ćirković, A. Sandberg, and N. Bostrom, "Anthropic Shadow: Observation Selection Effects and Human Extinction Risks," *Risk Analysis* 30(10) (2010): 1495–1506.

14 T. Ord, R. Hillerbrand, and A. Sandberg, "Probing the Improbable: Methodological Challengers for Risks with Low Probabilities and High Stakes," *Journal of Risk Research* 13(2) (2010): 191–205.

15 T. Ord, *The Precipice: Existential Risk and the Future of Humanity* (London: Hachette Book Group, 2020), 61.

16 P. Slovic, "'If I look at the mass I will never act': Psychic Numbing and Genocide," in *Judgment and Decision Making* 2.2 (2007): 79–95; A. Bandura, "Impeding ecological sustainability through selective moral disengagement," *International Journal of Innovation and Sustainable Development* 2(1) (2007): 8–35.

17 Quoted in J. Lepore, "The Atomic Origins of Climate Science," *The New Yorker* 30 (20 January 2017).

18 N. Bostrom, T. Douglas, and A. Sandberg, "The Unilateralist's Curse and the Case for a Principle of Conformity," *Social Epistemology* 30(4) (2016): 350–371.

19 See, e.g., K. Esvelt, "Inoculating Science against Potential Pandemics and Information Hazards," *PLOS Pathogens* 14(10) (2018): e1007286.

20 For an excellent critique of our flawed distinction between short- and long-term, see, M. MacKenzie, "There is no such thing as a short-term issue," *Futures* 125 (2021).

21 See, W. Naudé, "Artificial intelligence: neither Utopian nor apocalyptic impacts soon," *Economics of Innovation and New Technology*, 30:1 (2021): 1–23.

22 N. Bostrom, "Existential Risks: Analyzing Human Extinction Scenarios and Related Hazards," *Journal of Evolution and Technology* (2002).

23 T. Weiss, What Happened to the Idea of World Government, *International Studies Quarterly*, vol. 53(2) (2009): 253–271, 255.

24 J. Wiener, "The Tragedy of the Uncommons: On the Politics of Apocalypse," *Global Policy* 7 (2016): 67–80.

25 M. Stauffer et al., "Hazards with Escalation Potential: *Governing the Drivers of Global and Existential Catastrophes*," United Nations Office for Disaster Risk Reduction (Geneva, Switzerland, 2023) (finding that the UN system is poorly prepared for global catastrophic risk).

26 See, T. Rowe & S. Beard, "Probabilities, Methodologies and the Evidence Base in Existential Risk," Working Paper, Centre for the Study of Existential Risk, July 2018, available at: http://eprints.lse.ac.uk/89506/.

27 The most famous iteration of this argument is in J. Rawls, *A Theory of Justice* (Cambridge, MA: Harvard University Press, 1971), 287.

28 The quote is likely from a short story by R. Cummings, "The Girl in the Golden Atom," *All-Story Weekly* 95(1) (1919).

29 For a good overview of this issue, see, W. MacAskill, *What We Owe the Future* (London: Basic Books, 2022).

30 S. Caney, "Political institutions for the future: A five-fold package," in I. González-Ricoy & A. Gosseries, eds, *Designing institutions for future generations: An introduction* (Oxford: Oxford University Press, 2016), 135–155. See also, A. Jacobs & J. Matthews, "Do citizens discount the future? Public opinion and the timing of policy consequences," *British Journal of Political Science*, 42(4) (2012): 903–935.

31 For some of the calculations on future populations, see, H. Greaves & W. MacAskill, "The case for strong longtermism," Global Priorities Institute Working Paper No. 5, June 2021, 6.
32 W. MacAskill, *What We Owe the Future* (London: Basic books, 2022); T. Ord, *The Precipice: Existential Risk and the Future of Humanity* (London: Hachette Book Group, 2020), Appendices A and B; N. Bostrom, "Existential Risk Prevention as Global Priority," *Global Policy* 4 (2013): 15–31.
33 A Pascalian choice problem is defined by a miniscule probability of something either very good or very bad. For example, a tiny chance of very serious harm to ten trillion people one thousand years from now. See, C. Tarsney, "The epistemic challenge to longtermism," *Synthese* 201 (2023): 195.
34 See, D. Thorstad, "The scope of longtermism," Global Priorities Institute, Working Paper 6, June 2021.
35 C. Cremer & L. Kemp, "Democratising Risk: In Search of a Methodology to Study Existential Risk," *arXiv* (2021): 11214. P. Arthur, "Convergence on Existential Risk Policy," Proceedings of the Stanford Existential Risks Conference 2023, 207–219.
36 For an interesting discussion of the value we give to human lives and existential risk, see, I. Raval, "An Axiology of Aesthetics for Existential Risk," Proceedings of the Stanford Existential Risks Conference 2023, 91–103.
37 I believe the detailed discussions of global public goods are interesting but tend to distract from the most important underlying issues involved in existential risk. I use the term mainly to highlight the collective interest we have in the survival of humanity. Readers interested in the deeper concepts of so-called GPGs should follow Inge Kaul's excellent work at I. Kaul, I. Grunberg, and M Stern, *Global Public Goods* (New York-Oxford, 1999).
38 See, N. Bostrom, "Existential Risk Prevention as Global Priority," *Global Policy* 4(1) (2013): 15–31.
39 K. Ambachtsheer, "The Case for Long-Termism," *Rotman International Journal of Pension Management* 7(2) (2014): 6–15; see also, N. Sears, "International Politics in the Age of Existential Threats," *Journal of Global Security Studies* 6(3) (2021).
40 See, Future of Life Institute (2014), Oxford University's Future of Humanity Institute (2005), the Centre for the Study of Existential Risk at Cambridge University (2012), the Stanford Existential Risks Initiative (2019), and the Käte Hamburger Centre for Apocalypse and Post-Apocalyptic Studies at Heidelberg (2019).
41 D. Zimmer, T. Undheim, and P. Edwards, eds, "Intersections, Reinforcements, Cascades," Proceedings of the 2023 Stanford Existential Risks Conference, Stanford Existential Risks Initiative, available at: https://doi.org/10.25740/pn116pv4512.
42 A. Einstein, "A Reply to the Soviet Scientists," *Bulletin of the Atomic Scientists* 4(2) (1948): 35–38, 37.
43 See, T. Weiss, "What Happened to the Idea of World Government?" International Studies Quarterly 53 (2009): 253–271. See also, C. Murphy, *International Organization and Industrial Change: Global Governance Since 1850* (Cambridge: Polity Press, 1994). The 1946 Conference on World Government was another important moment. G. Holt, "The Conference on World Government," *The Journal of Higher Education* 17.5 (1946): 227–235.
44 A-M. Slaughter, *A New World Order* (Princeton, N.J.: Princeton University Press, 2004), 8.
45 H. Bull, *The Anarchical Society: A Study of Order in World Politics*, 2nd edition (New York: Columbia University Press, 1977).

46 N. Bostrom, "What Is a Singleton?" *Linguistic and Philosophical Investigations* 5(2) (2006): 48–54.

47 See, e.g., F. Biermann & S. Bauer, *A World Environment Organization: Solution or Threat for Effective International Environmental Governance?* (London: Routledge: 2005); A. McMillan, "Time for a World Court for the Environment," International Bar Association (November 2019) available at: https://www.ibanet .org/article/71B817C7-8026-48DE-8744-50D227954E04.

48 D. Wernli et al., "Understanding and governing global systemic crises in the 21st century: A complexity perspective," *Global Policy* 14.2 (2023): 207–228.

49 C. Rios Rojas et al., "Building a Science-Policy Interface for tackling the Global Governance of Catastrophic and Existential Risks," University of Cambridge Centre for the Study of Existential Risk, 2023.

50 T. Ord, *The Precipice: Existential Risk and the Future of Humanity* (London: Hachette Book Group, 2020).

51 D. Bressler & J. Alstott, "The International Panel on Global Catastrophic Risks (IPGCR)," Proceedings of the Stanford Existential Risks Conference 2023, 233–247.

52 Our Common Agenda Policy Brief 2, Strengthening the International Response to Complex Global Shocks – An Emergency Platform, March 2023, available at: https://www.un.org/sites/un2.un.org/files/our-common-agenda-policy-brief -emergency-platform-en.pdf.

53 A Breakthrough for Planet and People, Report of the High-Level Advisory Board on Effective Multilateralism, April 2022, available at: http://highleveladviso ryboard.org/breakthrough.

54 Our Common Agenda, Report of the UN Secretary General, 2021, available at: https://www.un.org/en/content/common-agenda-report/assets/pdf/Common _Agenda_Report_English.pdf.

55 K. Robinson, *The Ministry for the Future* (New York: Orbit Books, 2020).

56 The landing page for the Welsh Envoy for Future Generations is available at: https://www.futuregenerations.wales/news/wales-leading-the-way-with-future -generations-legislation-un-plans-to-adopt-welsh-approach/.

57 See, J. Boston et al., eds, *Future-Proofing the State: Managing Risks, Responding to Rises and Building Resilience* (Canberra: Australian National University Press, 2014); J. Boston, "Assessing the options for combatting democratic myopia and safeguarding long-term interests," *Futures* 125 (2021): 102668.

58 The UN Futures Lab Network landing page is available at: https://un-futureslab .org/.

59 C. Rios Rojas et al., "Building a Science-Policy Interface for tackling the Global Governance of Catastrophic and Existential Risks," University of Cambridge Centre for the Study of Existential Risk, 2023.

60 O. Young, Grand Challenges of Planetary Governance: Global Order in Turbulent Times (Northampton, MA: Edward Elgar Publishing, 2021), 12.

61 For the term "forces of destruction" in this context, see N. Sears, "International Politics in the Age of Existential Threats," *Journal of Global Security Studies* 6(3) (2021), 14.

62 D. Helbing

63 An excellent overview of these characteristics based on water usage examples is at J. Gupta & S. Schmeier, "Future proofing the principle of no significant harm," *International Environmental Agreements: Politics, Law and Economics* 20 (2020): 731–747.

64 J. Lyytimäki et al., "Dark side of resilience: systemic instability," *Perspective*, 22 August 2023, available at: https://www.frontiersin.org/articles/10.3389/frsus .2023.1241553/full.

65 M. MacKenzie, "There is no such thing as a short-term issue," *Futures* 125 (2021), 5.

66 A. McKay et al., "Exceeding 1.5 degrees C global warming could trigger multiple climate tipping points," *Science* 377 (2022).

67 S. Galaitsi et al., "The need to reconcile concepts that characterize systems facing threats," *Risk Analysis* 41 (2021): 3–15.

68 D. Chandler, *Resilience: The Governance of Complexity* (Oxon, UK: Routledge, 2014).

69 D. Wernli et al., "Understanding and governing global systemic crises in the 21st century: A complexity perspective," *Global Policy* 14.2 (2023): 207–228, 213.

70 B. Peters, J. Pierre, and V. Galaz, "Simple solutions for complexity?" In *Global challenges, governance, and complexity* (Cheltenham and Northampton: Edward Elgar Publishing, 2019).

71 B. Chaffin et al., "Transformative Environmental Governance," *Annual Review of Environment and Resources* 41 (2016): 399–423, 407.

72 A. Motter & Y. Lai, "Cascade-based attacks on complex networks," *Physical Review E* 66 (2002): 065102.

73 F. Westley et al., "Tipping toward sustainability: emerging pathways of transformation," *Ambio* 40 (2011): 762–80, 762.

74 A. Garmestani, "Sustainability science: accounting for nonlinear dynamics in policy and socialecological systems," Clean Technologies and Environmental Policy 16 (2014): 731–38.

75 B. Chaffin et al., "Transformative Environmental Governance," *Annual Review of Environment and Resources* 41 (2016): 399–423, 403.

76 D. Wernli et al., "Understanding and governing global systemic crises in the 21st century: A complexity perspective," *Global Policy* 14.2 (2023): 207-228, 211.

77 E. Herrfahrdt-Pähle et al., "Sustainability transformations: socio-political shocks as opportunities for governance transitions," *Global Environmental Change* 63 (2020): 102097.

78 L. Böttcher, J. Nagler, and H. Herrmann, "Critical behaviors in contagion dynamics," *Physical Review Letters* 118 (2017): 088301.

79 T. Hale, *Long Problems: Climate Change and the Challenge of Governing Across Time* (Oxford: Princeton University Press, 2024), 4.

80 Our Common Agenda Policy Brief 4, "Valuing What Counts: Framework to Progress Beyond Gross Domestic Product," May 2023, available at: https://www.un.org/sites/un2.un.org/files/our-common-agenda-policy-brief-beyond-gross-domestic-product-en.pdf.

81 See, L. Fuerth & E. Faber, "Anticipatory governance: Winning the future," *The Futurist* (2013): 42–49.

82 J. Ferejohn & P. Pasquino, "The Law of the Exception: A Typology of Emergency Powers," *International Journal of Constitutional Law* 2 (2004): 210–239; L. Kemp, "The 'Stomp Reflex': When Governments Abuse Emergency Powers," BBC Future (2021).

83 For a good description of the appeal of techno-utopianism, see, L. Holt, "Why shouldn't we cut the human-biosphere umbilical cord?" *Futures* 133 (2021): 102821.

84 For a good summary of the ethical considerations involved in this population argument, see, H. Greaves & T. Ord, "Moral Uncertainty about Population Axiology," *Journal of Ethics and Social Philosophy* 12(2) (2017): 135–167.

85 See, B. Christian, *The Alignment Problem: How Can Machines Learn Human Values?* (New York: Atlantic Books, 2021).

86 C. Cremer & L. Kemp, "Democratising Risk: In Search of a Methodology to Study Existential Risk," *arXiv* (2021): 11214, 6.

87 L. Hong & S. Page, "Groups of Diverse Problem Solvers Can Outperform Groups of High-Ability Problem Solvers," Proceedings of the National Academy of Sciences 101 (2004): 16385–16389.

88 H. Landemore, *Democratic Reason: Politics, Collective Intelligence, and the Rule of the Many* (Princeton University Press, 2017).

89 J. Sanchez-Ruiz, "Innovative Citizen Participation and New Democratic Institutions: Catching the Deliberative Wave," OECD, 2021, available at: https://www.oecd-ilibrary.org/governance/innovative-citizen-participation-and-new-democratic-institutions_339306da-en.

90 C. Cremer & L. Kemp, "Democratising Risk: In Search of a Methodology to Study Existential Risk," *arXiv* (2021): 11214.

91 This is not an entirely new idea. See Alvin Toffler's notion of "anticipatory democracy" in A. Toffler, *Future Shock* (New York: Random House, 1975).

92 T. Friedman, *Thank you for being late: An optimist's guide to thriving in the age of accelerations (Version 2.0, With a New Afterword)* (Picador USA, 2017).

93 E. Seger, "Epistemic Security Be a Priority GCR Cause Area?" Proceedings of the Stanford Existential Risks Conference 2023, 18–37. A similar idea of a "knowledge accelerator" is put forward by D. Helbing, *Thinking Ahead: Essays on Big Data, Digital Revolution, and Participatory Market Society* (Cham, Switzerland: Springer Press, 2015).

94 D. Helbing et al., "Saving human lives: What complexity science and information systems can contribute," *Journal of Statistical Physics* 158 (2015): 735–781.

95 See, M. Guillén, *The Architecture of Collapse: The Global System in the 21st Century* (Oxford Academic, 2015), 51.

96 See, I. Bohnet, *What Works: Gender Equality by Design* (Harvard University Press, 2016). For a general "future proofing" design framework, see M. Stauffer et al., "The FAIR Framework: A Future-Proofing Methodology," Simon Institute for Longterm Governance, April 2023, available at: www.simoninstitute.ch/blog/post/the-fair-framework-a-future-proofing-methodology/.

97 For some examples, see, E. Lin-Greenberg, R. Pauly, and J. Schneider, "Wargaming for Political Science Research," Social Science Research Network, SSRN Scholarly Paper, 17 February 2021; S. Funnell & P. Rogers, *Purposeful Program Theory: Effective Use of Theories of Change and Logic Models* (San Francisco, CA: Wiley, 2011); S. Hyde, "Experiments in International Relations: Lab, Survey, and Field," *Annual Review of Political Science*, 18(1) (2015): 403–424; S. Nowak et al., *A General Agent-Based Model of Social Learning* (Santa Monica, CA: RAND Corporation, 2017).

98 This idea of internalizing social costs in the environmental realm is in O. Young, *Grand Challenges of Planetary Governance: Global Order in Turbulent Times* (Northampton, MA: Edward Elgar Publishing, 2021), 22.

99 See, E. Seger et al., "Tackling threats to informed decisionmaking in democratic societies: Promoting epistemic security in a technologically-advanced world," The Alan Turing Institute, 2020.

100 K. Shea et al., "Harnessing multiple models for outbreak management," *Science* 368 (2020): 577–579.

101 See, T. Homer-Dixon, *The Upside of Down: Catastrophe, Creativity, and the Renewal of Civilization* (Island Press, 2010).

102 J. Sterman, "Learning from evidence in a complex world," *American Journal of Public Health* 96 (2006): 505–514.

103 M. Lundgren, T. Squatrito, and J. Tallberg, "Stability and change in international policy-making: A punctuated equilibrium approach," *Review of International Organizations* 13 (2018): 547–572.

104 See, F. Cilliers, "What can we learn from a theory of complexity?" *Emergence* 2 (2000): 23–33; K. Rogers et al., "Fostering complexity thinking in action research for change in social–ecological systems. *Ecology and Society* 18(2) (2013): 31.

105 F. Giannotti et al., "A planetary nervous system for social mining and collective awareness," *The European Physical Journal Special Topics* 214 (2012): 49–75. See also, M. Battaglia, J. Mei, and G. Dumas, "Systems of Global Governance in the Era of Human-Machine Convergence," *ArXiv* (2018): 1802.04255; D. Helbing, *Social Self-Organisation: Agent Based Simulations to Study Emergent Social Behaviour* (Berlin: Springer, 2012); D. Helbing, "Globally Networked Risk," 497 *Nature* 51 (2013); S. Schwarcz, "Systemic Risk" 97(1) *Georgetown Law Review* 193 (2008).

106 For a comprehensive review of computational models, see M. Stauffer et al., "A Computational Turn in Policy Process Studies: Coevolving Network Dynamics of Policy Change," Complexity (2022): 1–17.

107 See, e.g., D. Helbing et al., "Theoretical vs. empirical classification and prediction of congested traffic states," European Physical Journal B 69(4) (2009): 583–598; M. Schönhof & D. Helbing, "Empirical features of congested traffic states and their implications for traffic modeling," *Transportation Science* 41(2) (2007): 135–166; D. Helbing & A. Johansson, "Pedestrian, crowd and evacuation dynamics," Encyclopedia of Complexity and Systems Science 16 (2010): 6476–6495; D. Helbing et al., "Saving Human Lives: What Complexity Science and Information Systems Can Contribute," *Journal of Statistics and Physics* 158 (2015): 735–781.

108 V. Yang & A. Sandberg, "Collective Intelligence as Infrastructure for Reducing Broad Global Catastrophic Risks," Proceedings of the Stanford Existential Risks Conference 2023, 194–206; L. Rvachev & I. Longini, "A mathematical model for the global spread of influenza," Mathematical Biosciences 75 (1985): 3–22; L Hufnagel, D. Brockmann, and T. Geisel, "Forecast and control of epidemics in a globalized world," *Proceedings of the National Academy of Sciences* (2004): 15124–15129; D. Balcan et al., "Modeling the spatial spread of infectious diseases: the Global Epidemic and Mobility computational model," *Journal of Computational Science* 1 (2010): 132–145.

109 See, D. Helbing et al., "Saving Human Lives: What Complexity Science and Information Systems Can Contribute," *Journal of Statistics and Physics* 158 (2015): 735–781; see also, E. Albrecht, "Predictive Technologies in Conflict Prevention: Practical and Policy Considerations for the Multilateral System," UN University Centre for Policy Research, 2023.

110 I. Rahwan, "Society-in-the-loop: Programming the algorithmic social contract," *Ethics and Information Technology* 20(1) (2018): 5–14; A. Etzioni & O. Etzioni, "AI assisted ethics," *Ethics and Information Technology* 18(2) (2016): 149–156.

111 I have Kim-Fredrik Schneider to thank for this reference to hospitalists.

112 Zelli et al., "Complexity, Governance & Networks," *Global Governance in Complex Times: Exploring New Concepts and Theories on Institutional Complexity* 6(1) (2020): 1–13

113 W. Benjamin, *Illuminations* (New York: Schocken Books, 1968), 257.

An afterworld

Walter Benjamin wrote that humanity is endowed with a "weak messianic power."[1] I think he meant that we humans have a small but important capacity to push back against the forces of oppression and destruction that can often feel overwhelming in moments of crisis. Our collective survival will not be given to us. We will need to eke it out, finding those fleeting moments of opportunity when they arise. This book is about how systems evolve, but also how we need to evolve as humans if we want to survive. By recognizing the power to destroy ourselves, we create a new opportunity to prevent our destruction.

The most acute and likely existential risks are human-made. An asteroid could strike Earth, or a volcano could trigger a premature ice age, or a naturally occurring pandemic could wipe us all out. But the likelihood of these events is much lower than the risk that we kill ourselves off. On the one hand, this is depressing. Perhaps we are not much better than lemmings rushing semi-consciously towards a precipice. But human-made problems, if we catch them early enough, should be solvable by humans. We no longer live in the world of the ancient Greeks where the gods ruled the destinies of humans. We are living in what Noah Yuval Harari has referred to as the emerging era of *homo deus*, where we have increasingly godlike powers to make big changes to ourselves and our planet.[2] This puts a special responsibility on us – our actions may have repercussions for millennia to come.

Humanity is the culmination of millions of years of evolution, each generation drawing on the collective experience of the last. We tend to focus on the most immediate effects of this – how different our phones are from those of our parents, or how funny it must have been to go to work on a horse. We don't think of the path dependencies of humanity's recent evolution. We are not that far removed from people who thought the Earth was the center of a small universe. We are not so different from people who saw spirits in the trees and rivers. We are only two generations beyond societies that legally enslaved others. It was less than 300 years ago that the Industrial Revolution oriented all of humanity around the exploitation of fossil fuels. Humanity may be just at the beginning of a much longer history. If our immediate predecessor, *homo erectus*, survived for roughly two million years, might we be at the beginning of a much longer run?[3] Or could be we be on the verge of perhaps the biggest catastrophe in the known (to us) universe?

To survive, I believe the dominant paradigm of a selfishly rational *homo economicus* needs to give way to a *homo socialis* that values humanity's wellbeing and can empathize with present and future generations.[4] Some of the most exciting research I have come across in writing this book shows the enormous promise of transporting us out of our like-minded echo chambers and conceptual limitations. If we are exposed to the views and needs of others by having permeable boundaries amongst groups, the likelihood of collective behavioral change skyrockets.[5] We have a long way to go, and the most likely path is one shaped by selfish, short-term interests. But most of the recommendations and ideas in this book are geared around rewarding and encouraging the emergence of *homo socialis* in a world that feels increasingly hostile, competitive, and self-centered. To a certain extent, this book is about "human-proofing" global governance by designing systems that resist our innate, evolution-driven bad habits long enough to allow a new paradigm to emerge.

The starting point is to think big. Last year we all gazed at the Webb telescope photos of an almost unimaginably huge universe, distant nebulae, swirling galaxies, a glimpse of an early moment when we may have emerged from a single point in time and space. The light from 14 billion years ago continues to rain down on our planet, bathing us in a constant reminder that we are all part of one system. For many of us, it was a humbling moment where we were reminded of how small Earth is in the greater scheme of things. For me, it was also a moment where I felt a keen sense of responsibility to future generations. If I am lucky enough to glimpse our long history, don't I have an obligation to try to extend that view a bit more for those to come?

We are already living in an "afterworld," where humanity has survived nearly half a century possessed of the capacity to eradicate all human life with the push of a button. We have been lucky so far. As we look back on the billions of years it has taken for our universe to unfold, we should be energized by the hope that humanity can accompany it for a bit longer yet.

Notes

1 W. Benjamin, *Illuminations* (New York: Schocken Books, 1968), 254.
2 N. Harari, *Homo Deus: A Brief History of Tomorrow* (New York: Harper Books, 2017).
3 A. Barnosky et al., "Has the Earth's Sixth Mass Extinction Already Arrived?" *Nature* 471 (2011): 51–57.
4 D. Helbing, *Thinking Ahead: Essays on Big Data, Digital Revolution, and Participatory Market Society* (Cham, Switzerland: Springer Press, 2015), 57–58.
5 J. Gross et al., "The evolution of universal cooperation," *Sciences Advances* 9 (2021).

Index

For Product Safety Concerns and Information please contact our EU
representative GPSR@taylorandfrancis.com
Taylor & Francis Verlag GmbH, Kaufingerstraße 24, 80331 München, Germany

www.ingramcontent.com/pod-product-compliance
Lightning Source LLC
Chambersburg PA
CBHW070335270326
41926CB00017B/3878